TOURING
South and South West England

visit **Britain**
publishing

Published by VisitBritain Publishing
Thames Tower, Blacks Road, London W6 9EL

First published 2006

Maps reproduced by kind permission of Ordnance Survey on behalf of HMSO.
© Crown copyright 2006. All rights reserved. Ordnance Survey Licence number 100040235.

ISBN 0 7095 8280 3
Product code: TOURG01

A CIP catalogue record for this book is available from the British Library.

Produced for VisitBritain Publishing by Departure Lounge Limited
Contributing authors: Etain O'Carroll, Nick Rider, Andrew Stone, Nick Traynor
Cartography: Cosmographics (pages 8–9); Draughtsman Maps;
Reprographics by Blaze Creative
Printed and bound in the UK by Butler and Tanner

Jacket: Coastal road, Cornwall

Title page: Stourhead Garden, Wiltshire; **pages 6–7**: Seven Sisters Chalk Cliffs, East Sussex; **pages 10–11**: West Coast, Devon; **pages 44–45**: Pulteney Bridge and the River Avon, Bath; **pages 82–83**: Church near Wooten, Surrey; **pages 104–105**: Wakehurst Place Gardens, Kent

TOURING
South and South West England

TWENTY SPECIALLY CREATED DRIVING ITINERARIES

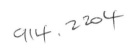

Published by VisitBritain

Contents

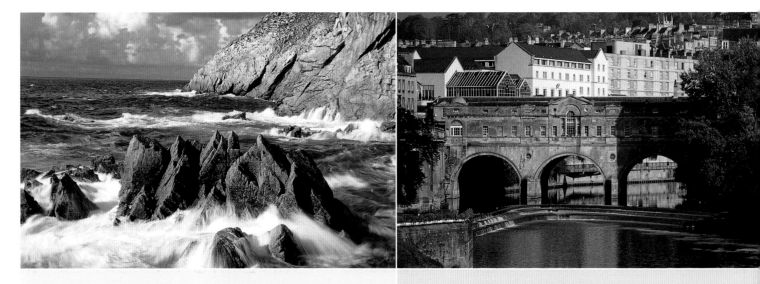

Cornwall and Devon

Somerset, Dorset and Wiltshire

Hampshire and Surrey

East and West Sussex and Kent

South and South West England

From the Georgian elegance of Bath to the Jurassic Coast, our tours of the South West will sweep you across rolling hills, through brooding moorland to stunning coastal scenery and pretty fishing villages in search of legend and folklore - and delicious cream teas. While in the South, so long a protector of England as well as a gateway to it, we will lead you down meandering country lanes, ascending the beautiful downs and through ancient forests to discover the tucked-away villages and splendid castles and country houses of this richly historic region.

Specialist travel writers have crafted the 20 guided driving tours in this book to cover circular routes of two to four days, which include famous and lesser-known sights alike. The itineraries can be joined at any point along the way or easily linked to shape a longer journey, and where appropriate, each itinerary also suggests ways to extend your trip with scenic walks, tours on heritage railways and boat trips.

A PROMISE OF QUALITY

We have not included specific details in this guide of places to stay on your short break in England, but you will find a wide choice of places to stay across the region. Choosing somewhere displaying the Enjoy England Quality Rose ensures you know what to expect and can book with confidence.

The following tourist board websites will provide you with detailed information on where you can stay and eat in the areas covered by this guide, as well as other useful travel advice.

www.enjoyengland.com
www.visitbritain.com
www.visitsoutheastengland.com
www.visitsouthwest.co.uk

The Tours

The book comprises four colour-coded chapters divided by county, each of which contains between four and six tours. Each tour follows the route plotted on the map, giving short descriptions of places of interest along the way. Feature boxes highlight additional information such as literary links and walks. A final box suggests places off the tour route that, with a little more time, are worth a detour. Remember, in larger towns and cities and at popular attractions, it's a good idea to use park-and-ride schemes where they are provided.

Bristol Channel

CARDIFF

BRISTO

pages 38-43
Lundy
Ilfracombe
Barnstaple
Great Torrington

pages 46-51
Lynton   Minehead
Dunster
Exmoor

page:
Wells

SOMERSET

pages 52-55
Yeov
Crewkerne
Lyme Regis   Bridport

DEVON

pages 26-31
Okehampton
EXETER
Dartmoor
Bovey Tracey
Tavistock

Lyme Bay

pages 20-25
Camelford
Padstow
CORNWALL
Bodmin

pages 32-37
Torquay
Totnes
PLYMOUTH
Salcombe   *Start Point*

pages 12-19
Truro
St Ives
Penzance   Falmouth
Land's End

Isles of Scilly

Lizard Point

THE TOURS

Introduction
Each tour has a short introduction that gives a flavour of the area covered by the tour route.

Tour map
Each route is plotted on the tour map in blue. Blue numbered bullets correspond to the number of each entry and the name is labelled in blue. Places mentioned in the 'with more time' box are also labelled in blue – and where located off the map, are arrowed off.

Approximate length of tour in distance and duration.

Selected Tourist Information Centres in the area.

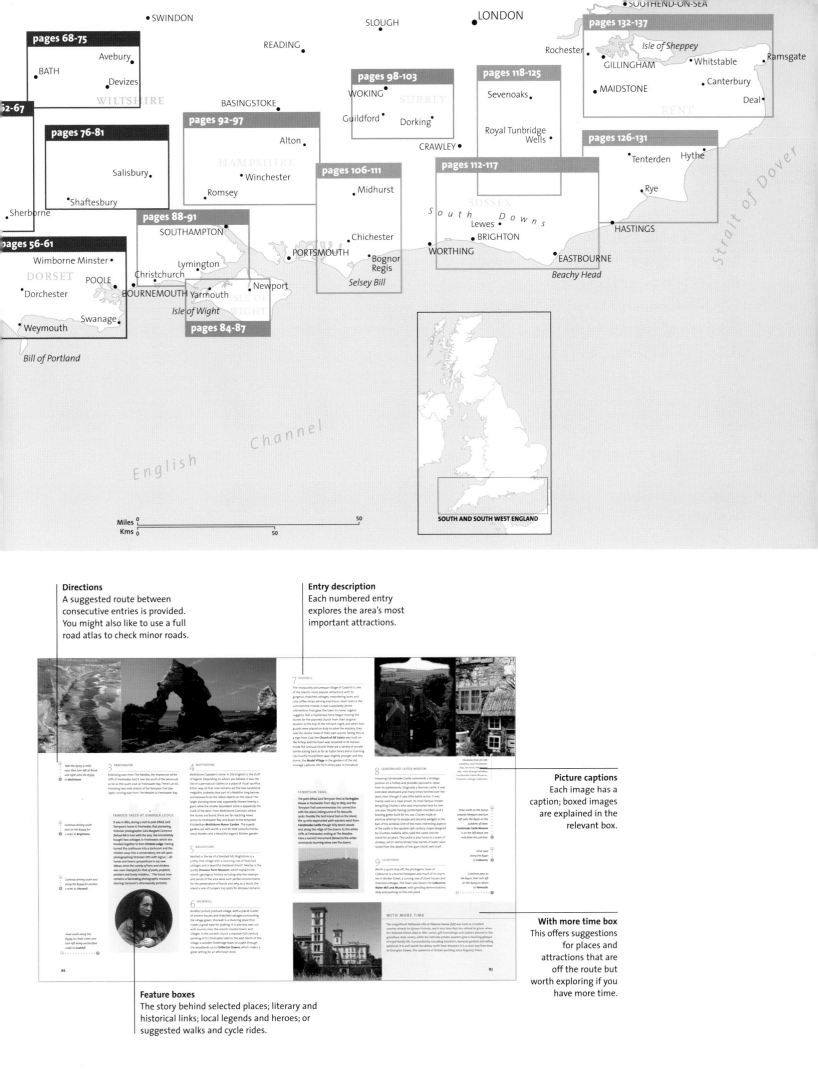

SWINDON

LONDON

SLOUGH

READING

pages 132-137

Isle of Sheppey

Rochester

Ramsgate

GILLINGHAM

Whitstable

pages 68-75

Avebury

BATH

Devizes

Canterbury

MAIDSTONE

Deal

WILTSHIRE

BASINGSTOKE

pages 98-103

WOKING

SURREY

pages 118-125

Sevenoaks

KENT

62-67

pages 92-97

Alton

Guildford

Dorking

Royal Tunbridge
Wells

pages 76-81

Salisbury

HAMPSHIRE

Winchester

CRAWLEY

pages 126-131

Tenterden

Hythe

Shaftesbury

Romsey

pages 106-111

Midhurst

pages 112-117

Rye

Sherborne

South   Downs

SUSSEX

Lewes

HASTINGS

ages 56-61

pages 88-91

SOUTHAMPTON

Chichester

BRIGHTON

Wimborne Minster

Lymington

WORTHING

EASTBOURNE

DORSET

POOLE

Christchurch

PORTSMOUTH

Bognor
Regis

Beachy Head

Dorchester

BOURNEMOUTH

Yarmouth

Newport

Selsey Bill

Swanage

ISLE OF
WIGHT

Weymouth

Isle of Wight

pages 84-87

Bill of Portland

English Channel

Strait of Dover

Miles 0   50

Kms   0   50

SOUTH AND SOUTH WEST ENGLAND

Directions
A suggested route between consecutive entries is provided. You might also like to use a full road atlas to check minor roads.

Entry description
Each numbered entry explores the area's most important attractions.

Picture captions
Each image has a caption; boxed images are explained in the relevant box.

With more time box
This offers suggestions for places and attractions that are off the route but worth exploring if you have more time.

Feature boxes
The story behind selected places; literary and historical links; local legends and heroes; or suggested walks and cycle rides.

9

Cornwall and Devon

Along the rugged Cornish coast

The spectacular Atlantic Ocean crashes relentlessly onto the dramatic coastline of north Cornwall, a land steeped in folklore and alive with tales of smugglers and giants. Here gaunt tin mine engine houses – testimony to a once flourishing mining industry – tower above golden sandy beaches that are a magnet for thrill-seeking surfers. Along the gentler south coast are shady creeks, unspoilt bays and timeless fishing villages where colour-washed cottages tumble to the harbours below. The intense quality of the light in this part of the country has made the area a magnet for painters and artists since the early 19th century.

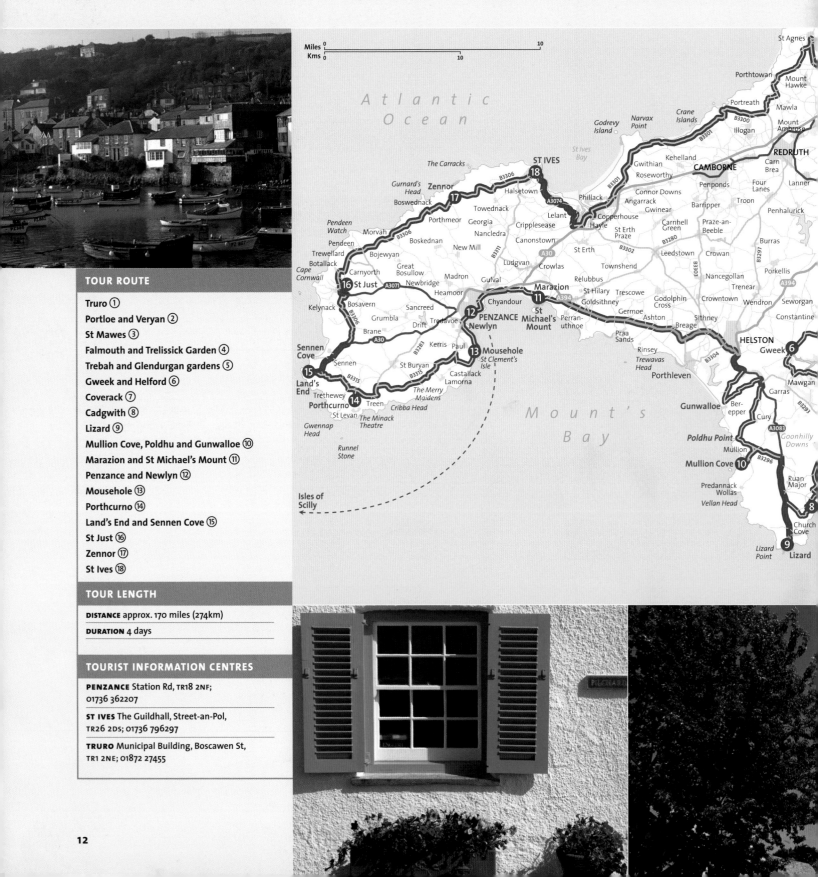

TOUR ROUTE

Truro ①
Portloe and Veryan ②
St Mawes ③
Falmouth and Trelissick Garden ④
Trebah and Glendurgan gardens ⑤
Gweek and Helford ⑥
Coverack ⑦
Cadgwith ⑧
Lizard ⑨
Mullion Cove, Poldhu and Gunwalloe ⑩
Marazion and St Michael's Mount ⑪
Penzance and Newlyn ⑫
Mousehole ⑬
Porthcurno ⑭
Land's End and Sennen Cove ⑮
St Just ⑯
Zennor ⑰
St Ives ⑱

TOUR LENGTH

DISTANCE approx. 170 miles (274km)
DURATION 4 days

TOURIST INFORMATION CENTRES

PENZANCE Station Rd, TR18 2NF;
01736 362207

ST IVES The Guildhall, Street-an-Pol,
TR26 2DS; 01736 796297

TRURO Municipal Building, Boscawen St,
TR1 2NE; 01872 27455

Clockwise from far left:
Mousehole; St Michael's
Mount; Truro Cathedral;
cottage, St Mawes

1 TRURO

The wealth of grand Georgian mansions in Truro are testimony to this small city's former role as a significant port and mining centre. Particularly fine architectural examples can be found on Lemon Street and Walsingham Place. Dominating the town centre is **Truro Cathedral**, built in the Gothic revival style on the site of the church of St Mary the Virgin and completed in 1910. Part of the original church is incorporated in the new building, where the spacious vaulted interior features some impressive stained glass, among the finest in the country. Look out for the heavily carved reredos behind the altar and splendid font of polished porphyry. Other treasures include a copy of a letter from Charles I thanking the Cornish for their loyalty during the Civil War. From the cathedral, amble around the cobbled streets and picturesque alleyways or 'opes' – with amusing names like Squeezeguts Alley – that have survived from Truro's heyday as a port. Then pay a visit to the excellent **Royal Cornwall Museum**, which explores Cornwall's history and features works from the Newlyn School of artists *(see p16)*. Afterwards you can stroll along the Riverside Walk and watch the passenger boats cruising down the river, or make the most of Truro's excellent shopping centre, two covered markets and the range of specialist shops on Lemon Quay.

Head east on the A39/A390.
At Tresillian turn right onto
unclassified roads through
Ruan Lanihorne, crossing
over the A3078 to ***Portloe***
and then ***Veryan***. ❷

2 PORTLOE AND VERYAN

Dramatically set in a break in the cliffs, with white-washed cottages clustering round a tiny harbour, **Portloe** is one of Cornwall's most unspoilt and photo-genic fishing hamlets. The village hotel, set right at the water's edge, is an ideal spot for a contemplative drink.

Just a short distance inland from Portloe lies the village of **Veryan**, famous for its five circular thatched cottages topped by crosses. The unusual 19th-century houses were designed to ward off the devil, who, it was thought, would be unable to hide if there were no corners.

Continue west on
unclassified roads to the
A3078 and turn left to
St Mawes.
→ • • • • • • • • • ❸

⊕ *Catch the car ferry across the estuary from St Mawes to **Falmouth**. Return by ferry to your car and exit St Mawes on the A3078. Turn left onto the B3289 and cross the River Fal on the King Harry Ferry to*
④ ***Trelissick Garden**.*

⊕ *Continue west on the B3289, turning left onto unclassified roads through Penpol to the A39 and then left again. On reaching Mabe Burnthouse, take unclassified roads south to **Trebah** and*
⑤ ***Glendurgan gardens**.*

*Drive west on unclassified roads via Porth Navas to **Gweek**. Continue round the head of the River Helford to Mawgan then east to **Helford**.*

→ • • • • • • • • • • ⑥

3 ST MAWES

Dazzling white yachts bob in the harbour of this fashionable sailing mecca, which boasts fine estuary views and a network of inland waterways. The pretty waterfront leads west to the well-preserved clover-leaf **St Mawes Castle**, built by Henry VIII (together with its twin, Pendennis, across the water) to guard the entrance into Carrick Roads Estuary. From here there is a lovely two-mile walk north along the water's edge to **St Just in Roseland**. The ancient church here, set in lush, tropical gardens, was described by poet John Betjeman as 'the most beautiful (churchyard) on earth'.

4 FALMOUTH AND TRELISSICK GARDEN

Regular ferries run across the estuary from St Mawes to the old seafaring town of **Falmouth**. This is a place of great vistas, and it's well worth climbing the 110 steps known as Jacob's Ladder for a bird's eye view of the harbour, as well as exploring **Pendennis Castle**, set on a headland with sweeping panoramas.

The town's excellent **National Maritime Museum Cornwall**, housed in swanky new waterfront premises, boasts a huge collection of boats of all sizes, as well as lots of interactive exhibits, audio-visual displays and a 29-m tall tower (95ft) affording fantastic views over the harbour and estuary. Return to St Mawes and continue by road to the peaceful **Trelissick Garden**, 210ha (525 acres) of stunning parkland and woods, famed for its hydrangeas and camellias.

5 TREBAH AND GLENDURGAN GARDENS

The peaceful wooded River Helford and its numerous secretive creeks are blessed with a mild climate that allows sub-tropical gardens to flourish. It provides the setting for the wild and enchanting **Trebah Garden**, nestled in a steep ravine where a stream cascades through rhododendrons, tree ferns and huge, menacing gunnera to the River Helford below. Just as magical is **Glendurgan Garden**, with its restored laurel maze and winding paths leading down through exotic plant species to the miniscule fishing village of Durgan, where boats cluster on the tiny beach.

6 GWEEK AND HELFORD

At the head of the River Helford is the small port of **Gweek** with its delightful clutter of boatyards and the **National Seal Sanctuary**, where injured seals and sea lions are nursed to health before being released back into the wild. Further east is **Helford** with its pretty whitewashed cottages and a thatched pub. From here, follow the signposted footpath to Frenchman's Creek: this mysterious winding inlet was the inspiration for – and title of – Daphne du Maurier's romantic tale of piracy and smuggling.

7 COVERACK

The tiny harbour at pretty Coverack, once the haunt of smugglers and pirates, provides one of the few safe havens on this unforgiving shore. The photographs in the bar of the Paris Hotel (named after an American liner wrecked offshore) show just how devastating a storm off this stretch of coast can be.

8 CADGWITH

Drivers need their wits about them when navigating the steep lanes down into this picturesque little fishing village, crammed haphazardly with old thatched cottages. Cadgwith is the perfect spot to indulge in an afternoon tea before taking a short walk along the coast to the Devil's Frying Pan, a collapsed blowhole – its name takes on real meaning when the sea is rough.

Clockwise from far left:
St Mawes Castle; Lizard
Peninsula; Trebah Garden

A CHANGE OF PACE

For a more leisurely pace, abandon the car and take to the **South West Coast Path**, which provides some of the most exhilarating and scenic coastal walking in Britain, particularly around Lizard Point *(below)* and Land's End (check www.southwestcoastpath.com for recommended walks). Alternatively, swap four wheels for two on the flat plateau of the **Lizard Peninsula**, which is ideal for lazy cycling, especially in spring when wild daffodils, bluebells and primroses carpet the roadside banks.

9 LIZARD

Lizard does a brisk trade in souvenirs made from local serpentine, which, when cut and polished, was much admired by Queen Victoria. Stroll down to the dramatic cliffs of **Lizard Point**, the most southerly point in mainland Britain, and take in the awe-inspiring views from the top of the lighthouse, whose powerful beam is visible 26 miles away. On a sunny day, it's worth making the short journey to nearby **Kynance Cove**, a renowned beauty spot with golden sands and glistening rock pools.

↓ Travel south on unclassified roads via St Anthony and St Keverne to the B3294 and turn left to **Coverack**. ⑦

↓ Take the unclassified road to the B3293 and turn left. After about 2 miles turn left onto the unclassified road south to **Cadgwith**. ⑧

↓ Leave Cadgwith on unclassified roads to join the A3083 and turn left to **Lizard**. ⑨

Travel north on the A3083, and turn left on the B3296 via Mullion to **Mullion Cove**. Return to Mullion and turn left to **Poldhu**. From here follow unclassified roads north and turn left on the A3083. Shortly after turn left on the unclassified road to **Gunwalloe**. → ⑩

10 MULLION COVE, POLDHU AND GUNWALLOE

To the west of the bustling inland village of Mullion are a succession of little coves, strung out like pearls along the coast. The pretty weather-worn harbour of **Mullion Cove** is a National Trust gem; to its north the sandy bay of **Poldhu** has a simple cliff-top monument marking the spot where Marconi transmitted the first wireless message across the Atlantic in 1901; and further north still, tiny **Gunwalloe** is blessed with a 15th-century church set among the sand dunes.

Drive north east to the A3083 and turn left. At Helston take the A394 west and after about 8 miles 11 turn left to *Marazion*.

11 MARAZION AND ST MICHAEL'S MOUNT

First granted a charter in 1257, Marazion is one of Cornwall's oldest chartered towns and was the most important settlement around Mount's Bay until the late Middle Ages. The busy main street is lined with shops and galleries, while the golden sandy beach is a magnet for windsurfers. Behind the beach, the RSPB's **Marazion Marsh Nature Reserve** is a popular spot with birdwatchers.

At low tide a cobbled causeway leads from Marazion to the magical rocky islet of **St Michael's Mount**, crowned dramatically by its medieval castle and priory built on the site of a Benedictine monastery. At high tide the islet is accessible only by ferry. From the landing stage, a steep path leads up to the impressive castle. Highlights of a visit include the Chevy Chase Room, formerly the monks' refectory, and the Garrison Room from where the Spanish Armada was famously sighted in 1588.

Drive west on the unclassified road to join the A30, then turn left into *Penzance*. From here, travel along the Esplanade to *Newlyn*.

12 PENZANCE AND NEWLYN

Penzance gained notoriety in 1595 when Spanish galleons appeared in the bay, and the town was sacked and burned. Today, most of the town's interesting buildings lie along winding Chapel Street, which leads down from the granite Market House (built in 1836), to the quay. Among those of particular note are the flamboyant 19th-century **Egyptian House** (No. 6–7), built in 1835 as a museum, and **No. 25**, home to Maria Branwell – mother to the famous authors, Charlotte, Emily and Anne Brontë – until 1812. Other sights of interest include the statue of Penzance-born Sir Humphrey Davy – the inventor of the eponymous miners' safety lamp – which sits at the top of the main Market Jew Street, and **Penlee House Gallery and Museum**, which exhibits works from the highly regarded Newlyn School of painting.

Newlyn is a lively little port that lies along the promenade about one mile south west of town. It gained fame when Stanhope Forbes came here to paint in 1884. Attracted by the exceptional quality of the light in the area, Forbes was soon joined by other painters and the Newlyn School was born. The town is still popular with artists, many of whom show their works in the **Newlyn Art Gallery**.

Take the unclassified coast road south from Newlyn to *Mousehole*.
13

Clockwise from far left: beach, Porthcurno; Minack Theatre, Porthcurno; Land's End; harbour, Penzance

13 MOUSEHOLE

It is wise to park on the outskirts of Mousehole and enter the village on foot, as the roads are narrow and parking is limited. This all adds to the undeniable charm of this lovely little fishing village, which clusters around its almost circular harbour. Nearby, Keighwin House is the only house to survive the 1595 Spanish raid. Mousehole is also famous as the home of Dolly Pentreath, the last person to speak the ancient Cornish language, which died with her some 200 years ago. Her memorial lies in the churchyard at **Paul**, a half-mile walk away.

14 PORTHCURNO

En route to Porthcurno, stop off just outside Lamorna, to see the stone circle of the **Merry Maidens**, reputedly all that remains of 19 local lasses turned to stone for dancing on the Sabbath. The two large stones of The Pipers nearby are thought to be the musicians who suffered the same fate. A few miles further west is the gorgeous beach of **Porthcurno** with its crystal-clear waters. It was here that the first transatlantic underground cable was laid, linking Britain to the rest of the world, and the story is told at the **Porthcurno Telegraph Museum**. Steep steps lead from the beach up to the **Minack Theatre**, a stunning open-air amphitheatre carved into the cliff. An evening performance here – with the moon shining and the waves lapping below – is pure magic. Even if you can't see a performance, it's worth visiting for the sweeping views over Porthcurno Bay and the visitor's centre telling the remarkable story of its founder, Rowena Cade.

15 LAND'S END AND SENNEN COVE

Tantalising sea views stretch from **Land's End** past wind-beaten outcrops and the Longships Lighthouse to the Wolf Rock Lighthouse, the beam of which is visible nine miles out to sea. England's westernmost tip has always been a tourist magnet, and there are visitor attractions aplenty here if that's what you're after. Along the coast, lies the pretty village of **Sennen Cove** where you can have an evening drink at the old inn before taking a barefoot stroll along the sandy beach as the sun sinks over the sea.

A FISHY TALE

During the Christmas festive season, lights are hung all around the village of Mousehole and even out to sea. One is in the shape of a 'Stargazey Pie', a local speciality made with whole fish and cooked each year on the 23rd of December. The tradition commemorates the dreadful winter night some 200 years ago when local fisherman Tom Bawcock braved terrible storms to bring home fish to feed the starving villagers.

*Head south out of Mousehole and west to the B3315 and turn left. Stop off in the layby for the Merry Maidens then continue for about 4 miles and turn left for **Porthcurno**.* 14

*Return to the B3315 and turn left to **Land's End**. From here, travel north east on the A30 for about 2 miles and turn left for **Sennen Cove**.* 15

*Rejoin the A30 and turn left. After about 1 mile, turn left on the B3306 and left again on the A3071 to **St Just**.* 16

16 ST JUST

Take the B3306
following the coast north
east to **Zennor**.

Stark silhouettes of the entrances to abandoned tin mines dot the rugged landscape around St Just. One of the most spectacularly sited is **Botallack**, with its disused engine houses perched precariously on the cliffs. At **Geevor Tin Mine**, the harsh realities of a miner's existence are brought to life by a visit to its 18th-century 'adits' or tunnels, often only 1.5m high (5ft). Up until its closure in 1990 this was Cornwall's largest mine, extending far out under the sea.

17 ZENNOR

Zennor's low grey houses huddle together on a stretch of wild and windswept coast scattered with archaeological remains and steeped in tales of folklore. One such tale involves a stone behind the church where it is said the benevolent Giant of Zennor would sit. He one day patted a man on the head, inadvertently cracking his skull, and the giant then died of a broken heart. The **Wayside Folk Museum** houses a rich collection of relics from this isolated little hamlet and is well worth a visit. Zennor's claim to fame is its connections to D H Lawrence, who lived here with his German wife during World War I, while writing *Women in Love*. He was driven away on suspicion of signalling to German U-Boats.

Continue on the B3306
east to **St Ives**.

Clockwise from far left:
beach, St Ives; Tate Modern,
St Ives; Barbara Hepworth
Museum, St Ives; Botallack
tin mine, St Just

THE ST IVES SCHOOL

Following J M W Turner's first visit in 1811, the coming of the railways brought a wave of artists to St Ives. Whistler and Sickert were followed by the likes of Sir Alfred Munnings, Barbara Hepworth, Christopher Wood and Ben Nicholson. They converted the town's old pilchard cellars and sail lofts into studios and established the St Ives School, which flourished in the 1950s. It was Nicholson and Wood who discovered Alfred Wallis, probably Britain's best-known naïve artist, whose primitive maritime scenes were often rendered on scraps of driftwood. Nicholson, together with Russian Naum Gabo, also greatly influenced the work of St Ives-born Peter Lanyon, whose abstract work is inspired by the local landscape.

More recent artists with links to the town include Patrick Heron and Sir Terry Frost as well as Bryan Pearce, currently one of Britain's fore-most naïve painters. The **St Ives Society of Artists**, founded in 1927, displays some excellent examples of local work in the Old Mariner's Church in Norway Square. Just outside St Ives, Higher Stennack is home to **Leach Pottery** (re-opening spring 2007) where Bernard Leach's Japanese-inspired ceramics are displayed alongside works of his contemporaries, including his associate Shoji Hamada.

18 ST IVES

The sheer beauty of this lovely fishing town – with its sandy beaches and steep alleyways clustered around the harbour – together with the incredibly intense light here has captivated artists since the early 1800s. Works of 20th-century St Ives painters including Ben Nicholson, Alfred Wallis and Peter Lanyon are among the modern art on display at the exceptional **Tate St Ives**. Spectacularly set above Porthmeor Beach, the sparkling white, modern building is an architectural delight in its own right. It houses changing displays from the Tate's national collection, as well as pottery by Bernard Leach and sculptures by Barbara Hepworth.

Nearby on Barnoon Hill is the **Barbara Hepworth Museum and Sculpture Garden**, where an impressive collection of the sculptor's works and all manner of memorabilia are on display in the studio where she lived until her tragic death in 1975. Her sculptures are also artistically exhibited in the adjoining garden.

As if this wasn't enough, St Ives also offers a plethora of private galleries and studios as well as some superb sandy beaches and bracing headland walks.

Take the A3074 south and turn left on the B3301 to Portreath. Continue on unclassified roads through Porthtowan to St Agnes, then turn right on the B3277/A390 to return to **Truro**.

← • • • • • • • • • • • • ❶

WITH MORE TIME

It is well worth the expense of taking the 20-minute helicopter flight from Penzance across to the **Isles of Scilly**, where the pace of life is slow and gentle. The largest island, St Mary's, is only three miles wide and two miles long with ten miles of beautiful coastline. The next largest, Tresco, boasts fabulous beaches and is home to the sub-tropical Abbey Garden *(left)* and Valhalla Collection with its relics from shipwrecks. You can also fly to the islands from Land's End airport or hop on a ferry from Penzance, which takes just over two and a half hours.

The wilds of Bodmin Moor

The smallest of the West Country moors, spanning just ten miles in diameter, Bodmin Moor is a bleak and desolate wilderness scattered with rocky outcrops, eroded by years of wind and rain, and peppered with the remains of ancient civilisations. Further north, the dramatic Cornish coastline is characterised by windswept headlands, sweeping sea views, quintessential fishing harbours, picturesque resorts and historic houses, which have remained unchanged for centuries. Steeped in folklore and intriguing legends of King Arthur, the area's strong connection to Britain's ancient past adds to its infinite appeal.

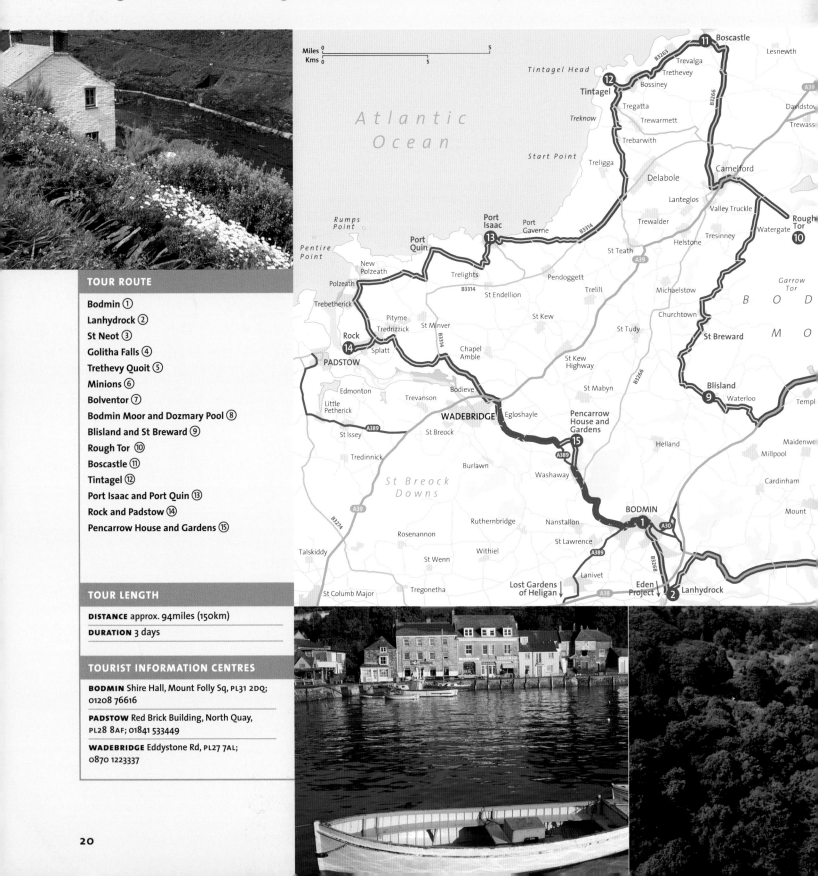

TOUR ROUTE

Bodmin ①
Lanhydrock ②
St Neot ③
Golitha Falls ④
Trethevy Quoit ⑤
Minions ⑥
Bolventor ⑦
Bodmin Moor and Dozmary Pool ⑧
Blisland and St Breward ⑨
Rough Tor ⑩
Boscastle ⑪
Tintagel ⑫
Port Isaac and Port Quin ⑬
Rock and Padstow ⑭
Pencarrow House and Gardens ⑮

TOUR LENGTH

DISTANCE approx. 94miles (150km)

DURATION 3 days

TOURIST INFORMATION CENTRES

BODMIN Shire Hall, Mount Folly Sq, PL31 2DQ; 01208 76616

PADSTOW Red Brick Building, North Quay, PL28 8AF; 01841 533449

WADEBRIDGE Eddystone Rd, PL27 7AL; 0870 1223337

Clockwise from far left:
cottage, Boscastle; Boscastle
village; gatehouse,
Lanhydrock; aerial view,
Lanhydrock; harbour, Padstow

1 BODMIN

Situated on the old trade route between Ireland and
the Continent, Bodmin was once an important resting
point for Christian pilgrims, including St Petroc who
founded a priory here in the 6th century. **St Petroc's
Church** houses the ornate cask that once contained his
relics and which has twice been stolen and returned.

Bodmin has many places to visit, including the
Military Museum, **Bodmin Town Museum** and **Bodmin
Jail**, where some of the nation's most precious posses-
sions, including the Crown Jewels and the Domesday
Book, were hidden during World War I. Grisly exhibits in
the gloomy underground passages and prison cells
recreate the unbearable conditions once endured here.
All those who met their end here were buried in its
grounds and an unmistakable air of despair still lingers.
Among them was Matthew Weeks who was executed
for murder in 1844. His trial can be relived at the
Courtroom Experience housed in the nearby Shire Hall.

*Take the B3268 south from
Bodmin and follow the signs
to **Lanhydrock**. Alternatively,
hop on the Bodmin and
Wenford Steam Railway
from Bodmin station to
Bodmin Parkway, from
where there is a pretty
walk to Lanhydrock.* **2**

2 LANHYDROCK

This beautiful 17th-century country house was once part
of St Petroc's Priory, and is set in 180ha (450 acres) of
woods and parkland, which descend to the River Fowey.
Magnificent formal gardens with clipped yews and
terraces, stunning magnolias and circular herbaceous
borders surround the house and the parish church. Fifty
rooms of the house are open to the public – from the
long gallery with its intricately carved plasterwork
ceiling to the kitchen complex recalling life 'downstairs'.

*Follow the unclassified road
north east to join the A38
and turn right heading
east, then turn left after
about 6 miles onto
unclassified roads to **St Neot**.*

3

5 TRETHEVY QUOIT

This imposing Bronze Age burial chamber is known locally as the Giant's House and dates from about 3500BC. The megalithic chamber is constructed from five huge granite slabs surmounted by a capstone. A small natural hole in the capstone may have been used for astronomical observations, while the rectangular hole chiselled out of the entrance stone is thought to have been used to entomb the bodies.

6 MINIONS

The quiet moorland village of Minions, the highest in Cornwall, was once a thriving mining centre for granite, copper and lead. Its history is explained in the **Minions Heritage Centre**, housed in a former engine house. A short walk west leads to the three stone circles of the **Hurlers**, which according to legend were men turned to stone for playing the Cornish sport of hurling on the Sabbath. Also within easy walking distance of the village is the **Cheesewring**, a strange granite formation reminiscent of a cheese press. Local folklore tells that it was home to a druid who provided thirsty passers-by with refreshment from a golden chalice that never ran dry.

7 BOLVENTOR

Situated at the heart of the moor, this tiny scenic hamlet is home to the old coaching inn immortalised in Daphne du Maurier's romantic novel *Jamaica Inn*. Sitting in the courtyard, supping a quiet pint, it is easy to see how du Maurier was inspired by the wild, windswept landscapes all around. The inn also houses a small **Smugglers' Museum**.

8 BODMIN MOOR AND DOZMARY POOL

The stillness of the bleak open moorland enfolds you in a blanket of silence as you turn off the A30. Although **Bodmin Moor** is comparatively small, the open, gently curving nature of the landscape, combined with the relative lack of features, creates a surprising sense of scale, remoteness and desolation. The quiet, brooding lake of **Dozmary Pool** lies in one of the most remote parts of the moor. It is here that Sir Bedevere is reputed to have thrown Excalibur, sword of King Arthur, as Arthur lay dying from wounds inflicted by his wicked nephew Mordred. A white hand is said to have arisen from the lake to take it to its depths.

Folklore also has it that Dozmary Pool is a bottomless lake (although it completely dried up during a drought in 1869), which the ghost of the infamous Cornish villain Jan Tregeagle was forced to empty with a leaky limpet shell as punishment for his wicked ways. Even today, there are those who believe the sound of the wind is Tregeagle moaning as demons chase him across the moor.

Follow the unclassified road east to **④ Golitha Falls**.

Continue on the unclassified road east towards Minions, turning right to Darite for **⑤ Trethevy Quoit**.

Return to Darite and proceed on unclassified roads west, then **⑥** *north to* **Minions**.

Return past the turn off for Darite and turn right following the River Fowey **⑦** *north to* **Bolventor**.

From the centre of Bolventor turn south onto the unclassified road to **⑧ Dozmary Pool**.

Loop around Colliford Lake and head north to the A30, then turn left. After about 5 miles turn right following unclassified roads to **Blisland**. *Then follow the unclassified roads north to* **St Breward**.

→ • • • • • • • • • • ⑨

3 ST NEOT

This pretty little village is worth a detour for its 15th-century **church**, which contains the most complete set of medieval stained-glass windows in England. Perhaps the most interesting is the one depicting St Neot, the kindly dwarf after whom the village was named. Standing only 1.2m (4ft) tall, the saint was famed for the miracles he performed involving animals, several of which are illustrated in the stained glass. Look for the oak branch on the roof of the tower, which is renewed every Oak Apple Day to commemorate the village's support of the royalist cause during the Civil War. In the churchyard stand five historic carved crosses. The oldest dates from the 9th century and is one of the best preserved Cornish crosses. Also worth a look before leaving is **St Neot Pottery**.

4 GOLITHA FALLS

An ideal spot to stop and stretch your legs, this nature reserve is set around an area of ancient woodland, which clings to the sides of a steep gorge where the River Fowey tumbles down a series of cascades. The scenery here is beautiful at any time of the year, but the falls are at their best after a bout of heavy rain. There are plenty of waymarked walks to follow through the oak and ash woods.

WARLEGGAN'S MAD MINISTER

A detour to Warleggan's squat little church recalls the intriguing story of the eccentric Reverend Frederick Densham. As the story goes, on taking up his post in this lonely moorland hamlet in 1931, the minister surrounded the rectory with barbed wire, patrolled the grounds with a pack of dogs and fitted the doors and windows with locks and bolts in order to alienate his parishioners. The villagers stayed away, and one entry in the register reads 'No fog. No wind. No rain. No congregation.' In response, the minister fashioned his own congregation from cardboard and preached undisturbed!

9 BLISLAND AND ST BREWARD

The pretty village of **Blisland** with its manor house, inn and old cottages set around a village green was much-loved by the poet John Betjeman. The parish church is mostly Norman with some 15th-century additions, and it features a beautiful colourful rood screen. Neighbouring **St Breward** is known for its granite quarries, and its stone has been used for national landmarks such as London's Tower Bridge. The church tower here, soaring to some 230m (750ft) above sea level, is the highest in Cornwall. The surrounding area is rich in reminders of past inhabitants with an ancient clapper bridge over the River De Lank and several prehistoric hut and stone circles within easy walking distance. Among them is the impressive **King Arthur's Hall**, a rectangular enclosure edged with upright stones. The site in fact has nothing to do with King Arthur but earned its name from the stones, which have the appearance of chairbacks.

Clockwise from far left: Golitha Falls; walkers, near Boscastle; Rough Tor

10 ROUGH TOR

The prominent heap of rocks known as Rough Tor forms the second-highest summit on Bodmin Moor, and the walk to its peak rewards the energetic with far-reaching views. Near the footbridge leading to the tor is a monument to 18-year-old Charlotte Dymond, who was murdered on the moor by her beau, crippled farm hand Matthew Weeks *(see p21).*

*Continue north on un-classified roads to Watergate and turn right after the village to the car park for **Rough Tor**.* ⑩

11 BOSCASTLE

This stunning village clings to the side of the beautiful Valency Valley at the mouth of a natural harbour. It's a place to explore the pretty streets with their craft shops and higgledy-piggledy cottages, pay a visit to the intriguing **Museum of Witchcraft** and then drink in the atmosphere at one of the characterful old inns. Novelist Thomas Hardy met his wife, Emma, here and much of his novel *A Pair of Blue Eyes* is set in Boscastle. A lovely walk up the valley leads to **St Juliot Church**, which was restored by Hardy when he was working as an architect.

As you ramble around Boscastle's quiet streets it's difficult to imagine the horrendous flash floods that hit the village in August 2004. Although many homes and businesses suffered severe damage, most have now been fully rebuilt. The tourist information centre shows news footage from the fateful day.

*Drive north west to Camelford, turn left on the A39 then right soon after onto the B3266 to **Boscastle**.* ⑪

*Head west on the B3263 to **Tintagel**.*
→ • • • • • • • • • • ⑫

⊕ *Head out of Tintagel on the B3263 and turn right onto unclassified roads to the B3314. Turn right, then after about 2 miles turn right again onto the unclassified road through Port Gaverne to* **Port Isaac**. *Continue on*
⑬ *the same road to* **Port Quin**.

12   TINTAGEL

To fully appreciate the atmosphere of King Arthur's legendary birthplace, climb the steps to ruined **Tintagel Castle**, perched high above the sea, and let your imagination run riot as the wind buffets you and the salt-spray flies in your face. From here, it's easy to visualise the stories of the gallant Knights of the Round Table and the cave beneath the castle where the magician Merlin lived. Back in the village there are a whole host of attractions given over to the legend, as well as the **Tintagel Old Post Office**, a tiny medieval manor house owned by the National Trust.

⊕ *From Port Quin head south and take the unclassified roads through Polzeath and Trebetherick to* **Rock**.
⑭ *Visit* **Padstow** *by ferry.*

THE CAMEL TRAIL

This scenic cycle/walking route follows the disused railway alongside the River Camel from Padstow to Poley's Bridge on Bodmin Moor, via Wadebridge and Bodmin. The railway originally formed the final leg of the Atlantic Coast Express line from London's Waterloo and was immortalised in John Betjeman's poem *Cornwall* as 'the most beautiful train journey I know'. Bikes can be rented from several hire shops along the trail, including Bridge Bike Hire in Wadebridge and Padstow Cycle Hire in Padstow.

Clockwise from below: Tintagel Castle; boat, Port Isaac; fishing boats, Port Isaac; harbour, Padstow

13   PORT ISAAC AND PORT QUIN

Port Isaac is a lovely old fishing village full of character, with narrow streets – such as the aptly named Squeeze-ee-belly Alley – an inn and closely packed cottages. A twisting lane leads out of the village to **Port Quin**, a tiny hamlet that suffered greatly when the railways stole the slate trade from its once bustling quay. Its demise was so swift that outsiders were led to believe the entire population had been swept away in a great storm. Nearby, at **Pentire Point**, there are scenic headland walks once frequented by John Betjeman.

14 ROCK AND PADSTOW

Boasting wide, beautiful stretches of sand, the former fishing village of **Rock** is beloved by artists and yachtsmen and is now a major watersports centre. From the village you can walk across the golf course to **St Enodoc Church** where John Betjeman is buried *(see right)*.

Just across the Camel Estuary lies the scenic seaside town of **Padstow**. Since parking is difficult and it's quite a detour by road, abandon the car in Rock and take the ferry across. Padstow is famous for Rick Stein's award-wining **Seafood Restaurant**, which overlooks the harbour, and also for its colourful May Day 'Obby 'Oss Festival, when villagers follow the 'oss along the narrow streets and in and out of houses. Wander round the Old Quarter with its meandering streets and visit the **National Lobster Hatchery**, a marine conservation centre explaining how scientists are working to preserve the Cornish fishing tradition. Towering above the village is **Prideaux Place**, an Elizabethan gem filled with fine furniture, superb plasterwork and paintings, including a mid-18th-century portrait of Humphrey Prideaux by the Italian artist Rosalba Carriera. The artist hid a love letter to Humphrey in the canvas, but sadly he never discovered the letter or knew of her affections.

POETIC INSPIRATION

From childhood holidays spent at Trebetherick on the Camel Estuary, poet laureate Sir John Betjeman developed a deep connection to this part of Cornwall, lovingly evoking its landscape in *Old Friends*, *Summoned by Bells* and *Seaside Golf*. On summer evenings, recitals of his poems are held on Brae Hill, overlooking **St Enodoc Church** where he is buried. For a glimpse of his personal artefacts, visit the **Betjeman Centre**, housed in the old railway station at Wadebridge.

15 PENCARROW HOUSE AND GARDENS

This fine historic house, still very much lived in and loved by its present owners, contains a superb collection of pictures, furniture, porcelain and a number of antique dolls. Spring is a particularly lovely time to visit when the azaleas, camellias and rhododendrons in the 20-ha gardens (50 acres) are in bloom.

*From Rock, continue east on unclassified roads to the B3314 and turn right. Cross the A39 and continue on the A389 and follow signs left to **Pencarrow House and Gardens**.* 15

*Drive back to the A389 and turn left to return to **Bodmin**.* 1

WITH MORE TIME

With an extra day, you can add on a fabulous loop to visit the extraordinary **Eden Project** *(left)* near St Austell. The huge biomes here – the largest conservatories in the world – tell the story of man's relationship with plants and celebrate the diversity of earth's flora. You can wander among olive groves and citrus trees, marvel at tropical orchids and cocoa plants or explore the outdoor gardens planted with tea, hemp, bamboo and tobacco. A short drive further south are the **Lost Gardens of Heligan**, which have been beautifully restored after 70 years of neglect.

Beneath Dartmoor's craggy heights

Dotted with mysterious standing stones and bisected by sparkling streams, the bracken-covered expanse of Dartmoor forms southern England's last great wilderness. Here seekers of solitude can explore more than 600 miles of public footpaths across some of the loneliest tracts in England. There is often no human life for miles: just Dartmoor ponies grazing freely and birds of prey circling overhead. On the western fringes of the moor lies the tranquil Tamar Valley, where a river flows through a landscape scattered with ruined chimneys and abandoned quays that hark back to an era when this was one of England's richest mining regions.

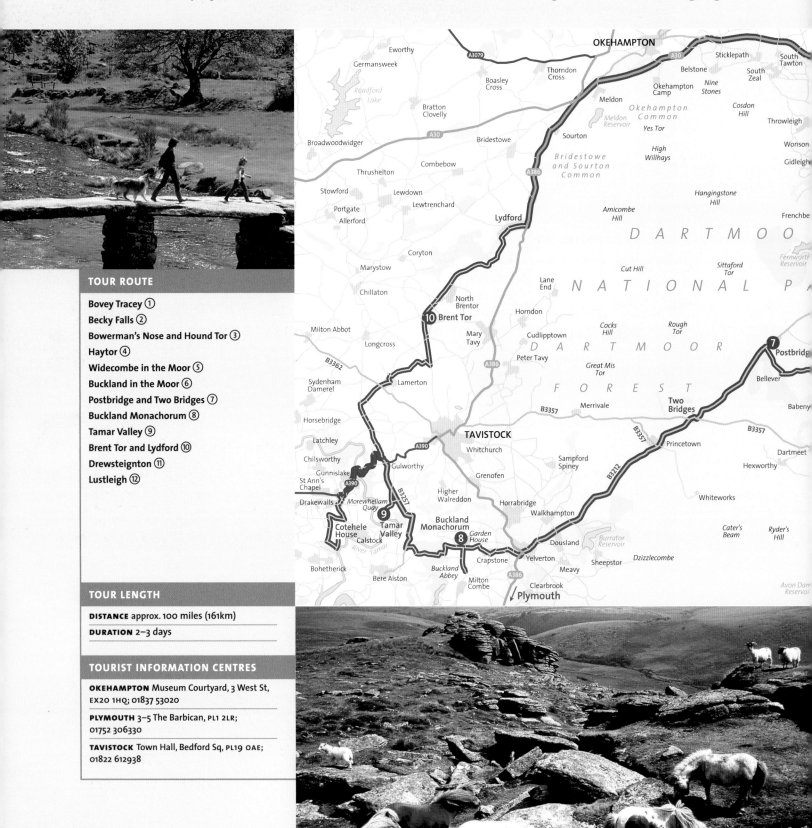

TOUR ROUTE

Bovey Tracey ①
Becky Falls ②
Bowerman's Nose and Hound Tor ③
Haytor ④
Widecombe in the Moor ⑤
Buckland in the Moor ⑥
Postbridge and Two Bridges ⑦
Buckland Monachorum ⑧
Tamar Valley ⑨
Brent Tor and Lydford ⑩
Drewsteignton ⑪
Lustleigh ⑫

TOUR LENGTH

DISTANCE approx. 100 miles (161km)

DURATION 2–3 days

TOURIST INFORMATION CENTRES

OKEHAMPTON Museum Courtyard, 3 West St, EX20 1HQ; 01837 53020

PLYMOUTH 3–5 The Barbican, PL1 2LR; 01752 306330

TAVISTOCK Town Hall, Bedford Sq, PL19 0AE; 01822 612938

Clockwise from far left:
clapper bridge, Postbridge;
view towards Widecombe in
the Moor; Sheepstor,
Dartmoor; Dartmoor ponies

1 BOVEY TRACEY

The River Bovey meanders right through this friendly
old market town on Dartmoor's eastern edge. On its
banks is the picturesque **Riverside Mill**, showcasing the
work of more than 230 members of the Devon Guild of
Craftsmen. More crafts await at the **Cardew Teapottery**,
where you can see a variety of teapots being
handcrafted, and at the **House of Marbles**, home to all
manner of glass and marbles, complete with a shop,
museum and regular glass-blowing demonstrations.

Bovey's most famous son was the wicked William de
Tracey, one of the knights who murdered Thomas à
Becket at Canterbury Cathedral in 1170 *(see p133)*. As
penance, he built Bovey's **church**, dedicated to the saint,
which houses a beautiful rood screen. Just outside the
town is **Parke**, administrative headquarters of the
Dartmoor National Park, from where you can enjoy
some excellent woodland and riverside walks.

From Bovey Tracey take the
B3387 west and turn right
after half a mile onto un-
*classified roads to **Becky Falls**.* **2**

2 BECKY FALLS

A choice of trails through this lovely woodland park
follow the picturesque Becka Brook as it tumbles 21m
(70ft) down a series of giant boulders. It is the perfect
spot for a picnic and a good place to get up close to
some of Dartmoor's more reserved residents, including
Dartmoor ponies and rescued birds of prey.

Continue north west past
Manaton and turn left onto
the unclassified road heading
*south past **Bowerman's Nose***
on your left. Continue south
*on this road to the **Hound***
***Tor** car park from where*
you can walk to both tors. **3**

3 BOWERMAN'S NOSE AND HOUND TOR

Eroded by wind and rain into strange shapes, these
rocky outcrops are associated with a plethora of myths.
Bowerman's Nose is the most intriguing, resembling a
human head in profile. The most popular legend has it
that the bowerman (hunter) disturbed a secret gathering of witches, who then petrified him and his hounds
(of **Hound Tor** fame). Tales such as this inspired Sir
Conan Doyle's story *Hound of the Baskervilles* in 1902.
Whether these tales have any truth or not, it's an
isolated spot, indescribably bleak even on the sunniest
day. South east of Hound Tor are the ruins of a
medieval village, well worth the extra walk.

Continue south on the
same road to the B3387,
*then turn left to **Haytor**.*

4

⤵
Return west on the B3387
to **Widecombe**
5 **in the Moor**.

⤵
Take the unclassified
roads south to **Buckland**
6 **in the Moor**.

4 HAYTOR

Its accessible location close to the road makes Haytor arguably the most visited of Dartmoor's tors. Climb to the top of this rugged rockpile for views that stretch as far as the coast on a clear day. Behind the tor you can see evidence of the old railway along which sturdy Dartmoor ponies used to haul granite from the nearby quarries to then be used in famous structures such as London Bridge. The National Park Information Centre in the lower car park on the main road stocks a good selection of leaflets and maps detailing further walks in the vicinity.

5 WIDECOMBE IN THE MOOR

Widecombe's grand 14th-century **church** has been dubbed the 'cathedral of the moor' and it is an impressive sight as you drop down into the village from the moorland above. The village makes for a pleasant stopping off point to wander the pretty streets lined with whitewashed houses and tearooms, and enjoy a hearty lunch at one of the two pubs. Widecombe is best known for its annual fair in September, which includes such traditional country events as sheep shearing, bale tossing and a tug of war.

Clockwise from far left:
Haytor; church, Widecombe
in the Moor; mural,
Buckland Abbey; cottages,
Buckland in the Moor

6 BUCKLAND IN THE MOOR

Tucked away down a maze of country lanes, this miniscule hamlet is famous for its picture-book thatched cottages, which have appeared on countless chocolate boxes and calendars. Look out for the clock on the church tower, which has the words 'MY DEAR MOTHER' instead of numbers on its face. The clock was a tribute by the local lord of the manor, William Whitley, to his mother on her death in the 1930s. He also inscribed two tablets on the summit of nearby **Buckland Beacon** with the words of the Ten Commandments. The lettering is much weathered but the views alone are worth the climb.

7 POSTBRIDGE AND TWO BRIDGES

The best preserved of Dartmoor's 30 or so clapper bridges crosses the East Dart at **Postbridge**. It is a popular spot, with a useful visitor information centre, so try to visit early or late to fully appreciate the lovely setting. From here the road winds across the lonely sheep-studded moor, through **Two Bridges** where residents tell of a phantom pair of 'hairy hands' that have forced many drivers off the road. The area has long been feared by locals.

8 BUCKLAND MONACHORUM

One of England's best-loved gardens awaits in this photogenic village nestling on the edge of Dartmoor. The **Garden House** is renowned for the naturalistic style of its 3ha (8 acres) including a stunning walled garden set around the ruins of a medieval vicarage. Just outside the village is **Buckland Abbey**, a former Cistercian abbey, famed as the home of Sir Francis Drake. The house contains some fascinating exhibits of the great explorer's colourful exploits, including Drake's drum, which, it is said, will beat of its own accord to summon the great man should England ever need his help. The village church contains a tribute to the generations of Drakes who lived here; look out for the carving of Drake's ship, the *Golden Hind*, on the family pew.

DARTMOOR 'LETTERBOXES'

From small beginnings in 1854, the pursuit of 'letterboxing' has escalated to enormous proportions. Today, there are more than 3,000 'letterboxes' of all shapes and sizes hidden across the moor. Each contains a rubber stamp pertinent to the location, which dedicated followers can use to stamp their own books or cards as proof of their visit. The boxes are almost impossible to find without some inside knowledge, but you can purchase clue sheets and there are also some books available.

*Drive on unclassified roads north west to **Postbridge**, then turn left on the B3212 to **Two Bridges**.* 7

*Take the B3212 south west to Yelverton. Cross the A386 and continue west on unclassified roads to **Buckland Monachorum**.* 8

*Continue west to the B3257 and turn right. After about 2 miles, turn left to **Morwhellam Quay**. Return to the B3257 and turn left. Turn left again onto the A390 and just past Gunnislake turn left and follow the unclassified roads for 4 miles to **Cotehele**.* 9

Clockwise from above:
aqueduct, Tamar Valley;
White Lady Waterfall,
Lydford; Castle Drogo,
Drewsteignton; Cotehele,
Tamar Valley

*From Cotehele, return to
the A390 and turn right.
At Gulworthy turn left
and follow the unclassified
roads across the B3362
to **Brent Tor** car park just
south of North Brentor.
Continue north east
to **Lydford**.*

9 TAMAR VALLEY

It is hard to imagine, but during its mining heyday this
tranquil valley was one of the busiest waterways in the
country and the quaysides bristled with ships' masts.
The museum village of **Morwhellam Quay** gives you
the opportunity to step back in time and experience
what it must have been like. Costumed staff
accompany you round the riverside trams, miners'
cottages and underground into the old copper mine.
Across the river at Cotehele Quay, the restored sailing
barge *Shamrock* is moored alongside the **Cotehele
Quay Museum**, which tells the story of the River Tamar.
Set in beautiful terraced gardens above the quay is the
medieval stately home of **Cotehele**, which includes a
magnificent Great Hall and some fine tapestries.

A WALK THROUGH HISTORY

A wealth of ancient remains – many of which are
accessible only on foot – are testimony to more
than 4,500 years of human habitation on
Dartmoor. Just south of Okehampton, a half-mile
climb leads up onto the moors from Belstone
Church to the atmospheric **Nine Stones** stone
circle, which despite its name is made up of 11
stones out of the original 40 or so that must have
been here. Another memorable climb is from
Sheepstor to **Drizzlecombe**, where a collection
of standing stones, cairns, stone circles and long
rows are sited in classic moorland surroundings.

If you're after a more substantial trek, the
circular **Dartmoor Way** traces a 90-mile route
linking Dartmoor's historic small towns and
villages including Okehampton, Bovey Tracey
and Princetown, taking in wild moorland
scenery, clapper bridges and tors along the
way. Alternatively you can explore the **Two
Moors Way**, which begins in Ivybridge before
traversing some of the remotest sections of
the moor en route to Exmoor, passing
prehistoric stones, abandoned mine buildings
and a section of disused tramway.

10 BRENT TOR AND LYDFORD

On the way to Lydford, stop off at **Brent Tor** and climb the footpath to the summit, where the squat little **Church of St Michael** surveys the lonely moorland below. Though sometimes shrouded in cloud, the views on a clear day are outstanding and the stillness is broken only by the cries of the birds wheeling overhead.

Lydford's main claim to fame is its spectacular wooded gorge, home in the 17th century to a band of outlaws whose exploits are recalled in Charles Kingsley's *Westward Ho!* Follow the circular path from the National Trust centre south to the impressive 27-m **White Lady Waterfall** (90ft) and **Devil's Cauldron**, where the thundering water hisses and spits through a series of whirlpools. Lydford itself is a quiet little place, dominated by its forbidding **castle**, once a prison. Pay a visit to the lovely **church**, with its carved pews and peaceful churchyard. For centuries, Dartmoor's dead were brought down from the moor along the ancient Lych Way to be buried here.

11 DREWSTEIGNTON

Thatched cottages and a medieval granite church cluster round the green in this picturesque hilltop village with its inviting pub. From the village, a footpath leads down to Fingle Bridge, which spans the River Teign in an idyllic setting. Perched on a rocky crag high above the river, with marvellous views, is **Castle Drogo**; behind its austere exterior lies a veritable treasure-trove of rich furnishings and tapestries.

12 LUSTLEIGH

This is one of Dartmoor's loveliest villages with cottages and a thatched pub grouped around a pretty 13th-century church. It is a perfect stopping-off point to enjoy a traditional Devonshire cream tea. A short walk across the clapper bridge leads to the hamlet of **Wreyland**, where thatched cottages are set in exquisite gardens.

*Continue through Lydford to the A386 and turn left, then turn right onto the A30. After about 8 miles, turn right onto the A382 then left on unclassified roads to **Drewsteignton**.* ⑪

*Head west on the unclassified road past Castle Drogo to the A382. Cross over the A382 and continue on unclassified roads and the B2206 through Chagford and North Bovey to **Lustleigh**.* ⑫

*Drive north east half a mile and turn right on the A382 to return to **Bovey Tracey**.*

← • • • • • • • • • • • ①

WITH MORE TIME

South of Dartmoor is **Plymouth**, a town steeped in maritime history. Among its attractions are the Hoe where Sir Francis Drake *(left)* finished his game of bowls before confronting the Spanish Armada; the historic Barbican quarter from where the Pilgrim Fathers set sail to America; and the excellent Plymouth Dome, which recounts Plymouth's seafaring past. Regular boat trips from the Barbican take in the waterfront sights, including the warships and submarines on the River Tamar and the Tudor Mount Edgcumbe House set in a vast country park.

The English Riviera and the sleepy South Hams

Chic, cosmopolitan Torquay lies at the northern end of the 'English Riviera', the cluster of seaside resorts around Tor Bay. Each has its own character: from nautical Brixham and kiss-me-quick Paignton to Torquay, the undisputed 'queen', with her luxury hotels and sparkling marina. From here, wind south into the tranquil, rural landscape of the South Hams where patchwork fields drop down to estuaries thronged with boats.

TOUR ROUTE

Torquay ①
Brixham ②
Coleton Fishacre ③
Dartmouth ④
Start Bay ⑤
Start Point ⑥
Kingsbridge and Salcombe ⑦
Overbeck's Museum and Garden ⑧
Bigbury-on-Sea and Burgh Island ⑨
Dittisham ⑩
Totnes ⑪
Berry Pomeroy Castle ⑫

TOUR LENGTH

DISTANCE approx. 95 miles (150 km)

DURATION 2–3 days

TOURIST INFORMATION CENTRES

DARTMOUTH The Engine House, Mayor's Ave, TQ6 9YY; 01803 834224

EXETER Civic Centre, Dix's Field, EX1 1RQ; 01392 265700

TORQUAY The Tourist Centre, Vaughan Parade, TQ2 5JG; 0870 70 70 010

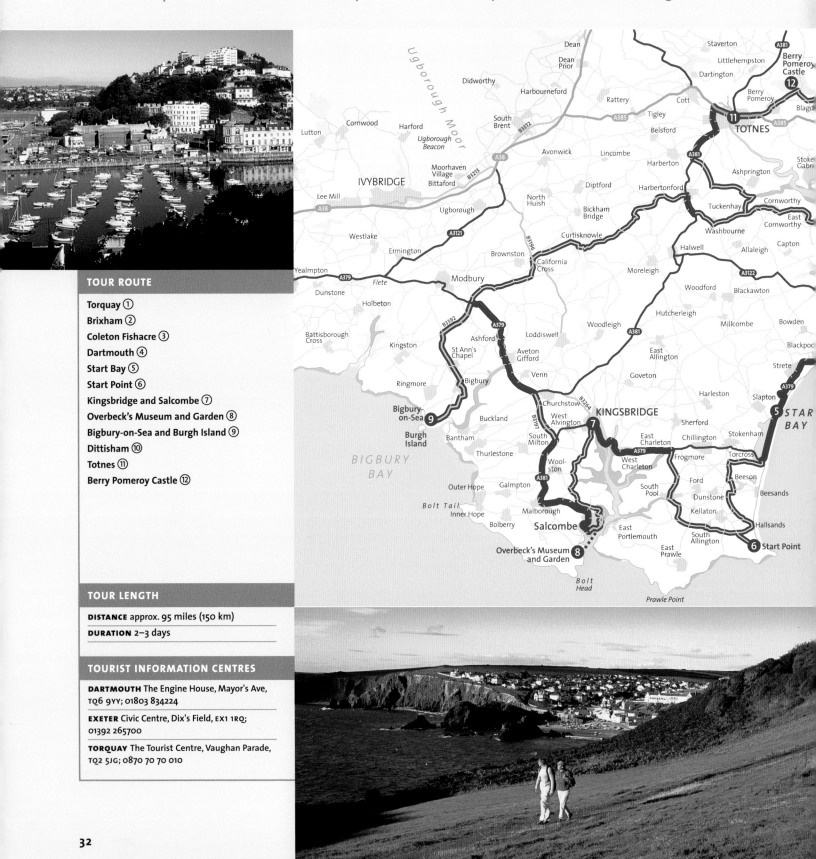

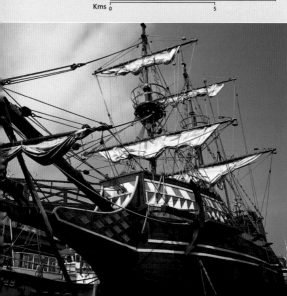

Clockwise from far left:
harbour, Torquay; Blackpool
Sands, Start Bay; Golden
Hind, Brixham; coastal
path, Hope Cove

1 TORQUAY

With its villa-clad hillsides, palm-lined promenades and millionaires' yachts bobbing in the marina, Torquay is a slice of the continent in England's south west. The old harbour brims with shops and lively waterfront cafes and has a particularly Mediterranean feel. Here you'll find **Living Coasts**, an aquatic attraction devoted to the conservation of coastal flora and fauna. A few minutes north of the harbour, **Torquay Museum** houses a gallery devoted to the crime writer Agatha Christie, one of Torquay's most famous residents. It also includes prehistoric archaeological finds from **Kents Cavern**, one mile out of town, which is open for underground tours.

A stroll west along the seafront brings you to Torquay's oldest building, **Torre Abbey**, dating from 1196, and its adjacent medieval Spanish Barn that is named after the Armada prisoners held here in 1588. Although both are closed for refurbishment until 2008, you can still walk around the exotic gardens, complete with Victorian palmhouse. The abbey lies just inland from Torquay's largest and most popular beach, the gently sloping **Torre Abbey Sands**, one of 20 beaches along Tor Bay's 22 miles of coast. If you prefer to escape the crowds, there are plenty of other sunspots, including the picturesque **Meadfoot Beach** with its views of Thatcher Rock.

Also worth a visit is chocolate-box-pretty **Cockington**, a thatched village nestled somewhat incongruously in Torquay's western suburbs. Visit the craft workshops at **Cockington Court** or picnic in the landscaped grounds, which feature lakes and woodland walks.

From Torquay's seafront
follow the A379/
A3022 to **Brixham**. ②

2 BRIXHAM

This intimate little town was once one of Britain's largest fishing ports, and the sea remains its lifeblood. Follow the quayside past the fish stalls and climb aboard the reconstructed *Golden Hind* to experience the cramped conditions faced by Sir Francis Drake when he circumnavigated the world between 1577 and 1580. Then, find out more about the town's seafaring past at the **Brixham Heritage Museum**. For panoramic sea views, take a walk east to **Berry Head**, where the clifftop lighthouse, at only 4.5m (15ft) tall, is both the highest and shortest in Britain.

Return on the A3022 to the
junction with the A379 and
turn left. Soon after, turn
left onto the B3205 then
left again on unclassified
roads following signs to
Coleton Fishacre.

→ • • • • • • • • • • • ③

⊕ Return to the B3205 and
turn left towards
Kingswear. Remain on
this road following signs
for the Lower Ferry to
④ cross to *Dartmouth*.

⊕ Head south on the B3205
and turn left on the A379
to *Start Bay* via Stoke
Fleming and then
⑤ continue to Torcross.

*From Torcross' seafront
proceed on unclassified
roads via Hallsands
to* **Start Point**.

→ • • • • • • • • • • ⑥

Clockwise from below left:
Dartmouth; lighthouse, Start
Point; Salcombe castle; pub
sign, Salcombe

3 COLETON FISHACRE

Opera lovers and garden enthusiasts will both enjoy a visit to this stunning seaside home of the famous operatic D'Oyly Carte family. As you wander round the beautiful gardens, familiar Gilbert and Sullivan melodies spill from the windows of the Arts and Crafts-styled house. Below, the garden plunges down into a steeply wooded coombe to the cliff's edge and is magnificent in spring when the camellias, rhododendrons and magnolias are a blaze of colour.

4 DARTMOUTH

The car ferry from Kingswear to Dartmouth takes only a few minutes, so have your camera at the ready as you cross the Dart Estuary to reach this picturesque town clinging to the hillside. Wander round the old streets and along the historic cobbled quayside lined with elegant 18th-century houses to **Bayard's Cove**, where the Pilgrim Fathers repaired their ships before hoisting sail to the New World. From here it's a 20-minute walk south along the river to **Dartmouth Castle**, which, together with Kingswear Castle on the opposite bank, guards the entrance to the estuary. To best appreciate the town's magical setting, join a scenic boat cruise or take a trip on the **Dart Valley Railway**, which runs north to the resort of Paignton. Look out for the impressive Britannia Royal Naval College, dominating the skyline above Dartmouth.

THE CHRISTIE CONNECTION

Agatha Christie (previously Agatha Mary Clarissa Miller) was born in Torquay in 1890 and lived much of her life in the area. Fans of her crime novels will recognise many of the places woven into her stories including Kents Cavern, setting for Hempsley Cavern in *The Man in the Brown Suit,* and Torquay's Imperial Hotel – the Majestic in *The Body in the Library*. Plans are afoot to open a Christie visitor centre, but in the meantime you can follow the **Christie Mile** walk along the seafront, which takes in buildings and sites associated with the writer including the Torquay Museum *(see p33)*. A leaflet is available from local tourist information centres.

5 START BAY

The scenic A379 sweeps south from Dartmouth to join the sea at the pretty village of **Stoke Fleming** overlooking Start Bay. One mile south is **Blackpool Sands**, one of the best beaches in the country with clean, clear water. Further on, the road winds down to **Slapton Sands**, a three-mile sand and shingle bar used by the Allied Troops as a practice area for the D-Day landings in World War II. Tragically, they were attacked by an enemy E-boat and more than 600 soldiers were killed. A memorial at **Torcross**, alongside the Sherman tank recovered from the sea, commemorates their lives. Behind Slapton Sands, the freshwater lake at **Slapton Ley National Nature Reserve** is a prime spot for birdwatching.

6 START POINT

As you stand at Start Point, pummelled by the wind, with the waves thundering below, it is easy to appreciate how the treacherous seas around this exposed peninsula have claimed so many lives. In the past, captured pirates were hung in chains here as a warning to their fellow brigands. Nowadays, the only warning is the reassuring beam from the lighthouse, open to visitors, which affords stunning views. A further reminder of the power of the sea can be found a few miles north at **Hallsands**. Today, only a hotel and a few cottages remain of this once-thriving fishing community, which collapsed into the sea one stormy night in 1917. Many of the now-ruined houses are still in evidence.

Head north west on unclassified roads through South Pool to Frogmore and turn left onto the A379 to **Kingsbridge**. *From Kingsbridge turn south on unclassified roads to* **Salcombe**. *(Alternatively take the ferry from Kingsbridge in summer.)* ⑦

7 KINGSBRIDGE AND SALCOMBE

The bustling market town of **Kingsbridge** lies in an attractive setting at the head of its tidal estuary. Handsome Tudor and Georgian houses characterise the town, in particular along steep, shop-lined Fore Street, which includes the colonnaded Shambles, once the market arcade. The **Cookworthy Museum** contains a number of fascinating photographs of the now-abandoned village of Hallsands *(see left)*.

   The pretty riverside town of **Salcombe**, hugging a hillside three miles downstream, is a favourite destination with visiting yachtsmen. There is an array of chandlery shops as well as a plethora of chic boutiques and restaurants, in addition to lovely estuary views.

Take the ferry from Salcombe to South Sands (about one mile south) and walk up the steep hill to **Overbeck's Museum and Garden.** *(Alternatively, follow the signs by car from Salcombe along the steep single track road.)*

→ • • • • • • • • • • • ⑧

⤓
Head north on the A381
and turn left onto the
B3197, then turn left again
onto the A379. Before
Modbury take another
left onto the B3392 to
⑨ *Bigbury-on-Sea*.

COASTAL WALKS

The long-distance **South West Coast Path** traces the same coast covered by this driving tour, so there are opportunities aplenty to don your hiking books and take to the paths. One of the most strenuous, but exhilarating sections of the path in this area is from Bolt Head, south of Salcombe, west to Bolt Tail; the path meanders along precipitous cliffs where gulls and cormorants wheel and scream, and views, on a clear day, reach as far as Burgh Island. For a gentler – but equally beautiful – stroll, walk north from the sandy beach at pretty Hope Cove to Bantham beach via thatched Thurlestone *(below)*, with its natural arched rock.

Return on the B3392 to the
A379 and cross over.
Continue on unclassified
roads through California
Cross to Harbertonford.
Turn right onto the A381
then left onto unclassified
roads through Cornworthy
to *Dittisham*.
→ • • • • • • • • • ⑩

8 **OVERBECK'S MUSEUM AND GARDEN**

This hidden gem is well worth a visit for the rather bizarre legacy of eccentric scientist Otto Overbeck, who lived here from 1928 to 1937. These include his collections of shipbuilding tools and natural history artefacts, as well as some of his inventions. Among them is an electrical rejuvenator, patented in 1924, that was supposed to extend human life to the age of 350. The house is set in 2.5ha (6 acres) of tropical gardens with fabulous vistas of the estuary.

9 **BIGBURY-ON-SEA AND BURGH ISLAND**

Deservedly popular for its acres of sandy beach, **Bigbury-on-Sea**'s star attraction is **Burgh Island**, accessible on foot at low tide or by a giant sea tractor when the tide is in. The island is dominated by its extravagant Art-Deco hotel, which has attracted many famous patrons including Agatha Christie, who set several of her stories here. After climbing to the top of the island, indulge in a cream tea at the hotel, or sup a pint at the Pilchard Inn and drink in the views.

Clockwise from below:
Burgh Island; Totnes Castle;
River Dart, Totnes

10 DITTISHAM

Narrow streets lined with stone and thatched cottages drop steeply to the River Dart in this atmospheric yachting village, featuring a lovely church. Ring the bell near the Ferry Boat Inn to summon the passenger ferry to **Greenway** across the river, to visit the gardens at the former country home of Agatha Christie. In the middle of the river you will see the Anchor Stone, where, legend has it, the unfaithful wives of the village were tied up as punishment.

11 TOTNES

Strategically located at the highest navigable limit and lowest crossing point of the River Dart, this ancient and virtually unspoiled hillside town has been an important settlement since Saxon times and is packed with archaeological remains. Today, Totnes is widely known for its diverse, creative community that gives the town quite a distinct atmosphere. The town boasts a particularly fine selection of wholefood shops, boutiques, secondhand bookstores and centres offering complimentary therapies. There's also a good range of arts and crafts on offer in the numerous galleries dotted around and at the local market held on Fridays and Saturdays throughout the year in the Civic Square.

Begin an exploration at the Old Steamer Quay, where the Dartmouth cruises put to shore. From here, Fore Street, lined with fine old merchants' houses, rises steeply. One house accommodates the **Elizabethan Museum** where items of local historical interest, including displays on Victorian mathematician Charles Babbage, inventor of the forerunner of the computer, are exhibited. Pass through the handsome medieval East Gate arch and turn right to the 11th-century **Guildhall**, where you can visit the old jail and see the table where Oliver Cromwell sat in 1646.

On the main High Street, look out for the columned arcades of Poultry Walk and the Butterwalk, which stand in sharp contrast to the modern façade of the **Civic Hall** opposite; the latter is the venue on Tuesdays during the summer for Totnes' Elizabethan market, where traders dress up in period costume. At the top of the hill the Norman **castle** boasts one of the best-preserved keeps in the country.

12 BERRY POMEROY CASTLE

Perched high above a romantic, wooded gorge, Berry Pomeroy is unusual in consisting of two sets of ruins, with the remains of an Elizabethan mansion set inside the old castle walls. It is also reputed to be one of the most haunted places in Britain. According to legend, the White Lady is the spirit of Margaret Pomeroy, starved to death here by her sister Eleanor, and it is said that all who see her meet an untimely end.

*Return west to Cornworthy and continue on unclassified roads via Tuckenhay to the A381. Turn right and then turn right again onto the A385 and continue to **Totnes**.* 11

*Leave Totnes heading east on the A385. Just out of town turn left to Berry Pomeroy and follow signs to **Berry Pomeroy Castle**.* 12

*Travel east on unclassified roads to the A380. Continue across, heading east, then turn left onto the A3022 and then right on the A379 to return to **Torquay**.* 1

WITH MORE TIME

The historic city of **Exeter**, with its timbered buildings and cobbled streets, makes for an absorbing day out. Begin at the medieval cathedral *(left)*, which has a magnificent fan-vaulted ceiling and carved Bishop's Throne, then wander round the close and explore the shops and 14th-century Guildhall on the High Street. Just north are the trendy boutiques and wine bars of Gandy Street and the Royal Albert Memorial Museum and Art Gallery, worth a visit for its eclectic displays. Finish at the old quayside, which buzzes with stylish shops and restaurants.

Rural backwaters of North Devon

Far from the honeypots of Devon's south and the county's two alluring national parks, this tranquil enclave dotted with historic market towns and little-known attractions is, for many, the quintessential Devon. Inland, steep, narrow lanes wind through a rural landscape characterised by undulating hills, ancient villages and isolated farmsteads. To the north lies Devon's most spectacular sweep of coast – a string of rugged cliffs eroded by the ferocious sea and interspersed with wide sandy beaches – where windswept footpaths, historic ports and time-forgotten villages invite exploration far off the beaten track.

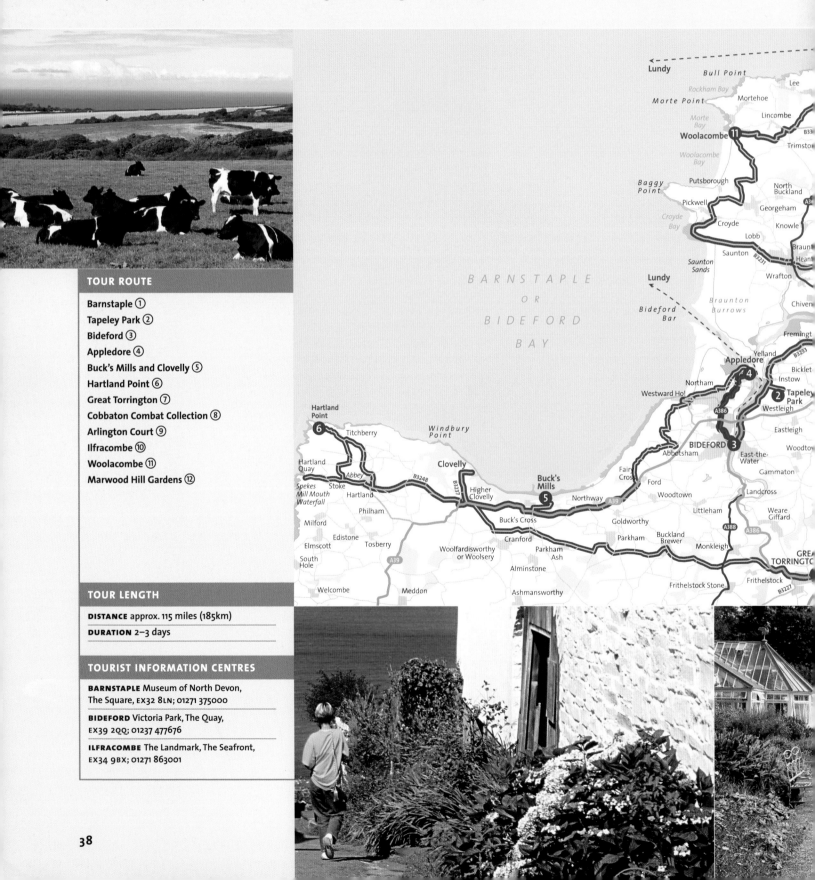

TOUR ROUTE

Barnstaple ①
Tapeley Park ②
Bideford ③
Appledore ④
Buck's Mills and Clovelly ⑤
Hartland Point ⑥
Great Torrington ⑦
Cobbaton Combat Collection ⑧
Arlington Court ⑨
Ilfracombe ⑩
Woolacombe ⑪
Marwood Hill Gardens ⑫

TOUR LENGTH

DISTANCE approx. 115 miles (185km)

DURATION 2–3 days

TOURIST INFORMATION CENTRES

BARNSTAPLE Museum of North Devon, The Square, EX32 8LN; 01271 375000

BIDEFORD Victoria Park, The Quay, EX39 2QQ; 01237 477676

ILFRACOMBE The Landmark, The Seafront, EX34 9BX; 01271 863001

Clockwise from far left:
countryside, near Buck's
Mills; harbour, Clovelly;
Arlington Court; cottage,
Buck's Mills

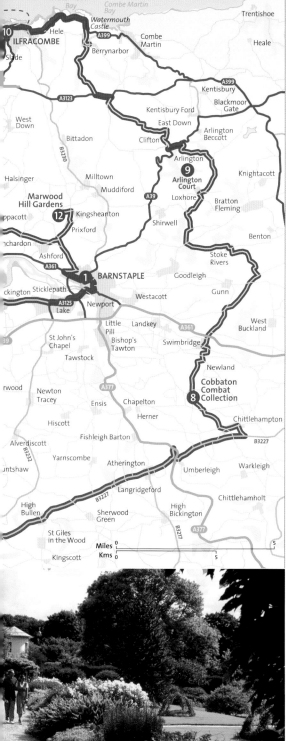

1 BARNSTAPLE

Many fine buildings remain from the days when
Barnstaple was a prosperous port, including the
colonnaded Queen Anne's Walk on the old quayside.
Built as a merchants' exchange, it now houses the
Barnstaple Heritage Centre, which explores the key
events in Barnstaple's history through a wealth of
audio-visual and interactive displays. From here, a
riverside walk follows part of the long-distance Tarka
Trail *(see p40)* under the 13th-century Long Bridge to the
Museum of Barnstaple and North Devon, where there's an
impressive display of 18th-century North Devon pottery.

Barnstaple's huge covered **Pannier Market** (daily
except Sundays) is the largest market in Devon, well
worth a visit as much for its grand wrought iron
architecture as for the range of crafts and produce for
sale. Its name derives from the wicker baskets once
used to carry produce to the market in the 19th
century. **Butcher's Row**, nearby, is a series of archways
with brightly coloured canopies, built exclusively to
house butchers' shops. Many still trade here today
alongside fishmongers, delicatessens and other food
shops. Away from the market bustle, the **Penrose
Almshouses** in Litchdon Street are also worth seeking
out. Built in 1634 to house the poor of the town and
still fulfiling their original purpose, an atmosphere of
gentle calm pervades here.

*Head south west out of
Barnstaple on the B3125 to
join the B3233 heading
west. Shortly after Instow
turn left to Tapeley Park.* ②

2 TAPELEY PARK

Tapeley's 8-ha gardens (20 acres) descend from a
Georgian mansion in a series of Italianate terraces,
brimming with colours and aromas, and affording
stunning views over the Torridge Estuary below. The
gardens have been restored over recent years and
contain many rare and tender species including the
oldest *Thuja plicata* trees in England, which are set
around a tranquil lake.

*Return to the B3233,
turn left and continue
to Bideford.* ③

Clockwise from above:
quay, Bideford; lighthouse,
Hartland Point; Clovelly

Follow the
A386 north to
4 Appledore.

Travel south west on
unclassified roads through
Abbotsham to join the A39.
Turn right and continue
about 5 miles to the right-
hand turning to Buck's Mill.
Rejoin the A39 and turn
right, then turn right again
on the B3237 to Clovelly.

→ • • • • • • • • • • 5

THE TARKA TRAIL

Henry Williamson's famous adventures of an
otter cub born on the banks of the River
Torridge infuse this part of North Devon. Many
of the places that feature in his evocative novel
Tarka the Otter (1927) remain remarkably
unchanged and can be seen on the **Tarka Trail**,
a 180-mile waymarked foot and cycle path that
tracks the otter's wanderings between the
valleys of the Taw and Torridge. Leaflets
covering certain sections of the trail are
available from local tourist offices. The book
has also given its name to the **Tarka Line**, the
picturesque rail route that follows the River
Taw south east from Barnstaple to Exeter.

3 BIDEFORD

Life in Bideford still centres around the old quayside,
where vessels laden with tobacco from the New World
once docked and from where valiant little ships set sail
to challenge the Spanish Armada in 1588. From the quay,
the ancient Long Bridge straddles the Torridge Estuary
across to the Royal Hotel, where Charles Kingsley
penned much of his famous novel *Westward Ho!*
Another of Bideford's famous sons was naval commander
Sir Richard Grenville, the man who brought back one of
the first native Americans ever to walk on English soil,
who was baptised at Bideford church in 1585. Grenville's
portrait and information on his various exploits can be
found at the **Burton Art Gallery and Museum**, situated
adjacent to Victoria Park close to the bridge. Behind the
park, streets of fine merchants' houses climb the steep
hillside to the splendid **Market Hall**, which houses the
Pannier Market on Tuesdays and Saturdays.

4 APPLEDORE

A maze of narrow lanes lined with sturdy, flower-
bedecked fishermen's cottages rise steeply from
Appledore's old quay. Shipbuilding still continues
here, though today this pretty village is more of a
haunt for visiting yachtsmen and tourists who come to
browse in the galleries and craft shops, or to sample
the tantalisingly fresh seafood. You can soak up
Appledore's seafaring past at the **North Devon
Maritime Museum**, where assorted nautical artefacts
range from cannons to World War II memorabilia.

5 BUCK'S MILLS AND CLOVELLY

A steep, hidden lane through a beautiful wooded valley leads to the tiny village of **Buck's Mills**, which clings to a hillside above the sea. You have to park at the top of the village and walk down the sloping main street lined with traditional whitewashed cottages to the stony beach, with its old limekiln.

Along the coast is Buck's more famous neighbour, Clovelly (no cars are allowed here either). It is an impossibly pretty place: flower-festooned cottages flank the steep cobbled main street, known as Up-a-long or Down-a-long depending on which way you're going. At the bottom is the sheltered harbour from where there are good views of the village rising steeply above. Charles Kingsley went to school here when his father was rector at the church, and it was Clovelly that inspired him to write his enduring classic *The Water Babies*. The **Kingsley Museum** explores the writer's association with the village. If you don't fancy the uphill haul back to your car, a Land Rover service operates from the Red Lion pub.

6 HARTLAND POINT

The relentless pounding of the sea on this wild stretch of coastline has undermined the rocks beneath **Hartland Point's** sturdy lighthouse to such an extent that a sea wall had to be built to protect it from further damage. From here, the South West Coast Path scrambles south over the jagged cliffs, popular with abseilers, to **Hartland Quay** on what is one of the most rewarding coastal walks in England. Despite being exposed to the full fury of the Atlantic, this was once a busy quay until it was swept away in 1887. The old quayside buildings are house a hotel and **The Hartland Quay Museum** displaying salvage from the ships that have foundered here over the centuries. Twenty minutes walk south along the coast brings you to **Spekes Mill Mouth Waterfall** where a stream cascades down a sheer rock face to the sea.

Just inland, at the pretty hamlet of **Stoke**, the tower of **St Nectan's Church**, the tallest in Devon, warns ships of the perilous rocks on this stretch of coast. Inside is a painted wagon-roof ceiling and intricately carved 15th-century screen. Nearby, **Hartland Abbey** once housed the monks who worshipped at the church; today it is a historic home containing a superb collection of porcelain, paintings and furniture, all set in beautiful gardens with scenic walks leading down to the sea.

*Return to the A39 and turn right to join the B3248 west to Hartland, then continue north on unclassified roads to **Hartland Point**. From here drive south on unclassified roads via Hartland Abbey to Stoke and Hartland Quay.* 6

*Return via Hartland and join the B3248 east. Turn left onto the A39 and right almost immediately onto unclassified roads through Buckland Brewer to join the A386 in to **Great Torrington**.*

7

↓
Take the B3227 north east and turn left after about 9 miles onto the unclassified road through Chittlehampton to the Cobbaton Combat (8) Collection.

↓
Continue north on unclassified roads through Swimbridge and Stoke (9) Rivers to Arlington Court.

Drive north on unclassified roads through East Down to the A3123 and turn left. Shortly after, turn right to Berrynarbor. Continue north, turning left onto the A399 to Watermouth Bay. From here continue west on the A399 to Ilfracombe.

→ • • • • • • • • • • • (10)

7 GREAT TORRINGTON

Strategically positioned above the River Torridge, it was at Great Torrington that one of the last great battles of the English Civil War took place in 1646. More than 17,000 troops fought in the streets and 200 royalist soldiers were blown up along with St Michael's Church, which was being used as a gunpowder store at the time. Costumed characters replay the events at the **Torrington 1646** museum, located on Castle Hill from where there are fabulous views of the River Torridge below.

Aside from its pretty main square and refurbished Pannier Market, Torrington is best known for the **Dartington Crystal Visitor Centre**, where you can take a tour and observe the stages of crystal production, and for the RHS **Rosemoor** garden with its impressive collection of more than 2,000 roses.

Clockwise from below:
Rosemoor, Great Torrington;
Croyde Bay

CATCHING THE PERFECT WAVE

Lashed by Atlantic rollers, North Devon boasts some of the best surfing beaches in England. Top of the list with experienced surfers is **Croyde Bay** *(below)*, where powerful waves have enticed some of the sport's top competitors including former British champion Richard Carter. **Westward Ho!, Woolacombe Bay** and nearby **Putsborough** are also popular surfing spots, while the gentler sloping beach at **Saunton Sands** is a favourite with beginners and longboarders. Boards, wetsuits and expert tuition are available at most beaches. For more information on surfing in the UK contact the British Surfing Association.

8 COBBATON COMBAT COLLECTION

One of Devon's most unlikely attractions awaits in the tiny farming community of Cobbaton. The Cobbaton Combat Collection is the work of Preston Isaac, who began amassing wartime memorabilia as a schoolboy. Today, his cluttered and ever-growing collection includes over 50 military vehicles and artillery pieces together with thousands of smaller items.

9 ARLINGTON COURT

The featureless exterior of Arlington Court belies the wealth of riches that lie within. Beautifully appointed rooms display the remarkable collection of Miss Rosalie Chichester, who lived here until 1949. Among the treasures are numerous model ships, more than 50 cabinets of shells and hundreds of snuff boxes and trinkets gathered on her travels round the world. Outside, a walk through attractive parkland leads to the stables, which house the National Trust's collection of some 50 horse-drawn carriages. Rides are available in the summer.

10 ILFRACOMBE

This popular resort has changed little since its Victorian heyday. On a rock above the pretty harbour, which is thronged with fishing boats and pleasure craft, stands the tiny **Chapel of St Nicholas**. Once a refuge for pilgrims travelling to Hartland Abbey, the church has shone a light from its window to guide boats into the harbour since the Middle Ages. On the seafront are the famous **Tunnel Beaches**, with four hand-carved tunnels leading through the cliff face to beaches and a tidal bathing pool. To the east, the rocky coastline is studded with sheltered inlets including the sandy cove of **Watermouth Bay** guarded by the imposing Victorian **Watermouth Castle**, now a family attraction with a theme park. Inland lies the picturesque village of **Berrynarbour**, with its quaint cottages and well-tended gardens, that nestles at the foot of the beautiful Sterridge Valley.

11 WOOLACOMBE

Woolacombe's wide sweep of sand is sprinkled with rock pools and scoured clean by Atlantic rollers, making it a popular choice with families and surfers alike. Follow the coastal footpath north to **Morte Point** and soak up the wild beauty of this glorious stretch of coastline with views extending to Lundy Island *(see below)*, 12 miles out to sea. Along the coast, the lighthouse at **Bull Point** warns of treacherous rocks where ships have come to grief. Further south the beaches at **Croyde** are a surfers' paradise *(see left)*. With its thatched cottages and tearooms, the village here still retains much of its old world charm.

12 MARWOOD HILL GARDENS

This 7-ha garden (18 acres) is built around three lakes with a range of trees, shrubs and herbaceous plants that guarantee colour all year round, from drifts of winter snowdrops to summer's vibrant hues. If you can, visit in the late spring when the waxy show of the rhododendrons and camellias is simply spectacular.

Follow the unclassified roads south west to join the B3343 and turn right to Woolacombe then drive south on unclassified roads to Croyde. ⑪

Take the B3231 south east to Braunton then follow unclassified roads east to Marwood Hill Gardens. ⑫

Travel south on unclassified roads to join the A361 to return to Barnstaple. ①

WITH MORE TIME

Take a day trip to tiny **Lundy Island** *(left)* on the *MS Oldenburg*, which sails from Ilfracombe and Bideford from March to October. This rocky outcrop, just three and a half miles long by half a mile wide and with a population of around 18, is a world apart, tranquil and unspoilt. Owned by the National Trust, it is home to a handful of houses, one shop, one pub and thousands of seabirds, including puffins, which can be sighted from April to May during mating season. It also offers plentiful opportunities for walking, climbing and snorkelling.

Somerset, Dorset
and Wiltshire

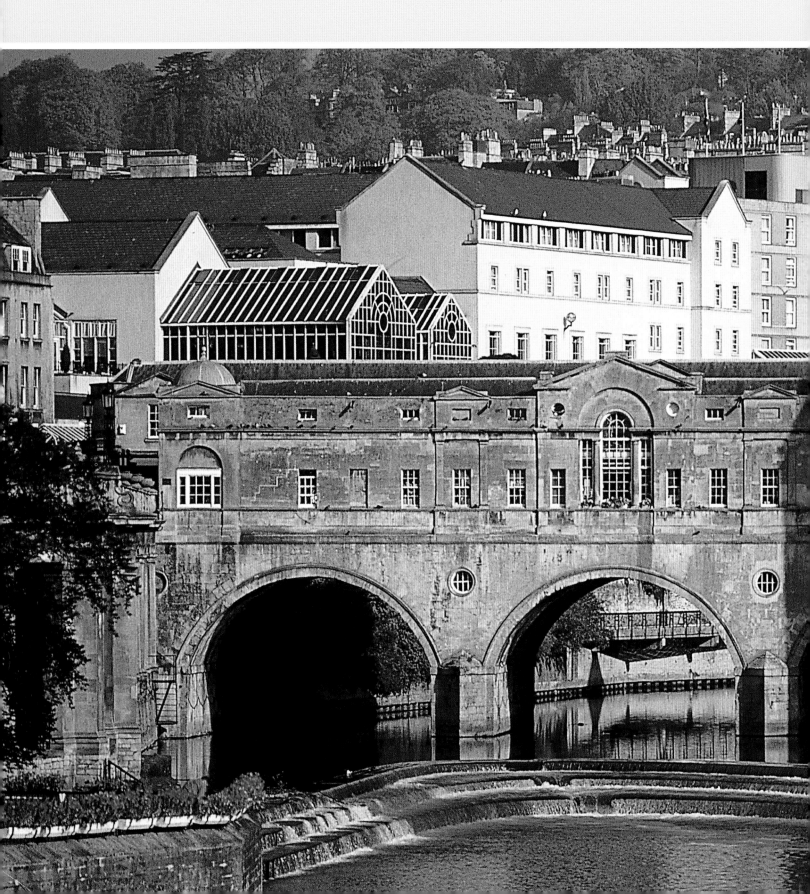

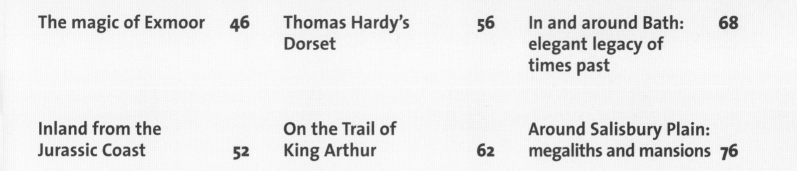

The magic of Exmoor

Straddling the boundary between Somerset and Devon, Exmoor is a wild, remote expanse of heather-clad moorland, deep wooded coombes sliced with sparkling streams and a spectacular coastline that is second to none. One of Britain's least discovered national parks, it spans 267 sq miles with over 620 miles of scenic footpaths and an astonishing diversity of flora and fauna, including shy Exmoor ponies and England's only herd of wild red deer. Landscape and literature are inextricably linked here, and the irresistibly romantic landscape has been the source of inspiration for many a literary masterpiece.

TOUR ROUTE

Dunster ①
Minehead ②
Selworthy ③
Porlock and Porlock Weir ④
Doone Country ⑤
Watersmeet ⑥
Lynmouth and Lynton ⑦
Valley of the Rocks and Woody Bay ⑧
Simonsbath ⑨
Exford and Withypool ⑩
Tarr Steps ⑪
Winsford ⑫
Dunkery Beacon ⑬

TOUR LENGTH

DISTANCE approx. 76 miles (122km)

DURATION 3 days

TOURIST INFORMATION CENTRES

LYNTON Town Hall, Lee Rd, EX35 6BT; 0845 660 3232

MINEHEAD 17 Friday St, TA24 5UB; 01643 702624

Clockwise from far left:
sheep, near Porlock; walker,
near Dunkery Beacon;
Dunster; cottage, Selworthy

Miles 0 ————————————— 5
Kms 0 ————————————— 5

1 DUNSTER

This picturesque medieval village nestles between two wooded hills, one topped by the huge Norman **Dunster Castle** with its sub-tropical terraced gardens and Jacobean interiors, the other by a folly. It is the perfect spot to stop for a traditional cream tea in one of the quaint tearooms and to browse the pretty shops. At the town's centre is the octagonal Yarn Market, built in 1609 for the sale of the celebrated Dunster cloth. A short stroll south leads to the **Dunster Working Watermill** and picturesque Gallox Bridge, once used by packhorses. On the way look out for the 14th-century Nunnery and St George's Church, which houses an impressive rood screen.

*From Dunster, take the A396 north to the junction with the A39 and turn left. At the first roundabout turn right to **Minehead** seafront.* **2**

2 MINEHEAD

This handsome seaside resort combines a long sandy beach with an attractive harbour and a charming old town characterised by thatched cottages and narrow alleyways. Walk down the steep Church Steps below St Michael's Church on North Hill to the esplanade and stroll around the harbour, a landing stage for boat trips including the Bristol Channel steam cruisers *Waverley* and *Balmoral*. The seafront marks the start of the long-distance South West Coast Path, which traces the jagged coastline westwards. East along the seafront is the terminus for the **West Somerset Railway**, where you can board a steam train on a nostalgic 40-mile round trip through the scenic Quantock Hills.

*Rejoin the A39 travelling west. After about 2 miles turn right to **Selworthy**.* **3**

3 SELWORTHY

Walk through the gate to the National Trust information centre and you'll soon see why this village commands so much attention. Here, hidden from the road by tall hedgerows, cream-coloured thatched cottages with neat gardens cluster photogenically round a village green, overlooked by a pretty church. Built in 1828 for the retired workers of the Holnicote Estate, the village has a delightful homogeny. Above, lies a footpath climbing a mile north to **Selworthy Beacon** from where there are commanding views across the Bristol Channel and Exmoor.

*Return to the A39 and turn right. After about a mile turn left into **Porlock**. Return to the A39 and turn left, then immediately right onto the B3225 through West Porlock to **Porlock Weir**.* **4**

*From Porlock Weir take the unclassified toll road west to the A39 and turn left. After about half a mile turn right to **Oare** and continue on unclassified roads to **Malmsmead**
❺ and **Rockford**.*

*From Rockford continue west on unclassified roads to the B3223. Turn right, then almost immediately right again onto the
❻ A39 to **Watersmeet**.*

*Continue on the A39 north west to Lynmouth. Take the B3234 out of the town and then the right-hand
❼ turn to **Lynton**.*

*Continue from Lynton on the unclassified toll road west into the **Valley of the Rocks** and on to **Woody Bay**.*

→ • • • • • • • • • • • ❽

4 PORLOCK AND PORLOCK WEIR

More thatched roofs await in **Porlock**, a quaint village tucked in a hollow between the hills, which invites you to browse the shops and while away the time in tearooms. Porlock is famous for its treacherously steep hill, which leads westwards out of the village; today's cars can negotiate it, but years ago vehicles regularly had to be towed to the top. Instead, head north west to the tiny hamlet of **Porlock Weir,** where a sleepy harbour belies its once vital role as the main route in and out of the area. From here a scenic toll road leads west through the woods to rejoin the main road. At the tollgate there's the start of a one-mile walk west to **Culbone Church**, the smallest parish church in England, set in a peaceful wooded valley.

5 DOONE COUNTRY

The villages of Oare, Malmsmead, Brendon and Rockford lie at the heart of 'Doone Country', the setting for R D Blackmore's famous 1869 novel *Lorna Doone* about a family of outlaws. At **Oare**, you can visit the tiny church where Blackmore's father was rector and where the fictional Lorna was shot at the altar on her wedding day. From here drive west along a scenic road, which hugs the wooded East Lyn Valley towards **Rockford**. Get out of the car en-route at **Malmsmead**, put on your walking boots and take a lovely walk up isolated **Doone Valley** along Badgworthy Water. As you amble through this ancient woodland where silent crooked oaks tower above the tiny stream, it is easy to believe in the colourful stories of the outlaws who lived here and who gave Blackmore inspiration for his novel.

6 WATERSMEET

The thickly wooded beauty spot known as Watersmeet stands at the confluence of two rivers that tumble through a steep gorge in a series of rapids. There are plenty of riverside paths to choose from, or you can simply sit on the veranda of the old fishing lodge (now a National Trust centre) and enjoy a cream tea while watching the water thunder past.

7 LYNMOUTH AND LYNTON

Scenically located at the mouth of the East Lyn River, **Lynmouth** is a traditional fishing village with a cluster of gift shops, a thatched pub and a charming little harbour. The town's tranquil atmosphere was shattered one night in 1952 when torrential rain falling on Exmoor raged down the valley causing much of the village to be washed away. It is hard to imagine such devastation as you wander round the centre today.

Twin town Lynton lies in the upper valley above **Lynmouth** hemmed in by towering cliffs and wooded gorges. The two towns are linked by the ingenious water-powered **Lynton and Lynmouth Cliff Railway**, which affords amazing views. In Lynton, the **Lyn and Exmoor Museum** houses some interesting displays about the area including photos of the flood.

Clockwise from far left:
Valley of the Rocks; Porlock
Bay; harbour, Lynmouth;
horseriders, near Porlock

LITERARY LINKS

Exmoor is best known for its association with R D Blackmore's novel *Lorna Doone*, but during the 18th century many writers, including the poets Wordsworth, Coleridge and Shelley, sought inspiration from Exmoor's wild and romantic landscapes. **Lynmouth** is particularly rich with literary association; it was here that Coleridge would often walk with Wordsworth, and where he conceived his *Rime of the Ancient Mariner*, inspired by Watchet harbour. Shelley also stayed here with his wife in 1812 in what is now called **Shelley's Cottage**.

Porlock was a favourite spot of the Wordsworths, as well as of Robert Southey and Coleridge, who famously caroused together at Porlock Weir's Ship Inn. **Ash Farm**, near the tiny hamlet of Culbone *(below)*, is where Coleridge is said to have been staying when he wrote his incomplete poem *Kubla Khan*.

8   VALLEY OF THE ROCKS AND WOODY BAY

West of Lynton the scenery becomes ever more impressive with jagged rock formations jutting skywards in the desolate **Valley of the Rocks**, which was described by Robert Southey as 'the very bones and skeleton of the earth'. Park the car and climb one of the strange shattered crags for the stunning sea views – you may even meet one of the resident wild goats. Back in the car, the narrow, winding toll road climbs away from the coast in a series of hairpin bends; it's slow going but the scenery is spectacular. On a fine day it's worth stopping at **Woody Bay** where the sheltered rocky beach is backed by steep wooded cliffs, through which a fast-flowing stream gushes down to the sea. From here there is a fabulous two-and-a-half mile cliff walk – not for the fainthearted – to Heddon's Mouth past one of the highest waterfalls on this stretch of coast.

*From Woody Bay follow unclassified roads south to rejoin the A39, and turn left heading east. At the junction with the B3223 turn right to **Simonsbath**.*

→ • • • • • • • • • • 9

Clockwise from above:
Tarr Steps; Winsford; Dunkery Beacon, Exmoor National Park; Withypool

Continue east on the B3223, then join the B3224 to Exford. From Exford take the unclassified road south west. Cross the B3223 and continue past Landacre Bridge to the junction, then turn
10 *left to Withypool.*

Drive east from Withypool to join the B3223. Turn right and after about 2 miles turn right on the unclassified
11 *road to Tarr Steps.*

Retrace your route to the B3223. Go straight across, and continue on this unclassified road to Winsford.

→ • • • • • • • • • • • • **12**

9 SIMONSBATH

The scenery changes dramatically as you climb up from the coast onto the wild moors and the pretty hamlet of Simonsbath. It consists of little more than a church, a handful of cottages and two hotels, but all around the views stretch endlessly across lonely open moorland strewn with heather and dotted with distant sheep. Keep your eyes peeled for the sturdy Exmoor ponies and wild red deer that roam free near here.

10 EXFORD AND WITHYPOOL

Old cottages cluster round the green in **Exford**, a popular centre for riders and walkers, situated on an ancient crossing point on the River Exe. Enjoy a refreshing drink at one of the quaint old inns before setting off to neighbouring **Withypool**, a tiny unspoilt village set around an old stone bridge. On the way, take a slight detour west to stop off at **Landacre Bridge**, a local beauty spot, ideal on a hot day for a picnic by the river and dipping your toes in the clear, icy water.

11 TARR STEPS

This ancient clapper bridge, believed to date from the Middle Ages, is the finest of its type in Britain, with huge stone slabs set across 17 spans. The stones look as though they have been here forever, but in fact they have been frequently replaced throughout their history. In the famous Lynmouth floods of 1952 all but one were washed away. Most days, it is a tranquil little spot, perfect for an afternoon snooze. The stunning moorland scenery all around makes this whole area hugely popular with horseriders. If you fancy a short trek, there are several stables in the vicinity offering rides for all levels of ability.

EXMOOR ON FOOT

The landscape of Exmoor is tremendously varied, from rolling farmland and high, wild moorland to a dramatic and tantalisingly beautiful coastline. Britain's longest national trail, the **South West Coast Path** *(below)*, follows the coast west from Minehead along lofty cliffs interspersed with isolated rocky coves, carved by wind and waves. It offers some of the most rewarding, and often challenging, coastal walking in Britain. Exmoor's other famous long-distance route, the **Two Moors Way**, begins at Lynmouth on its 102-mile journey south to Ivybridge on the southern edge of Dartmoor, crossing the high moors of Exmoor's remote and tranquil interior before dipping into its deep wooded fringes. There are also a plethora of shorter footpaths as well as a regular schedule of guided walks with park rangers. For more information contact the Exmoor National Park Authority.

12 WINSFORD

A scattering of thatched cottages around an attractive green and no fewer than eight bridges and a ford make this one of the most photographed villages on the moor. On the way here from Tarr Steps you will pass a footpath off to the right, leading to the **Caratacus Stone**, an ancient monolith bearing an inscription to Caratacus, the last great Celtic chieftain.

Take the unclassified road north east to the A396 and turn left to Wheddon Cross. Turn left in the village onto the B3224. At the bend take the second right turn and follow the unclassified road to *Dunkery Beacon* car park. 13

13 DUNKERY BEACON

It is a relatively easy half-mile walk from the car park up to the stone beacon that marks Exmoor's highest point at 519m (1700ft). On a clear day you can drink in views stretching across 16 counties from the Brecon Beacons in the north to Dartmoor in the south. You should also be able to make out the little church at Selworthy, a white silhouette clearly visible against the green bulk of Selworthy Hill.

Continue north on unclassified roads to Luccombe, then head east via Wootton Courtenay to return to *Dunster*.

WITH MORE TIME

South of Exmoor, two of the region's finest historic gems beckon. **Knightshayes Court** *(left)* is a Victorian Gothic mansion designed by flamboyant architect William Burges, with elegant formal terraces and topiary. To the east lies the beautiful medieval house of **Cothay Manor and Gardens**, which is set in romantic gardens. Further east near Taunton is another worthwhile visit, **Hestercombe Gardens**, where the fabulous grounds have been painstakingly restored and include a secret landscape garden complete with lake and temples.

Inland from the Jurassic Coast

Walk along the dramatic beaches of the West Dorset coast and 185 million years of history unfold before your eyes. This is part of the breathtakingly beautiful, 95-mile long Jurassic Coast, which was awarded World Heritage status in 2001. Once an area of swamp and lagoons where dinosaurs roamed at the end of the Jurassic period, it is now a rich hunting ground for fossils. Inland, hidden among the rolling hills, are lush gardens, gorgeous stone cottages and little-known treasure houses, as well as the opportunity to sample some of England's finest home-grown produce.

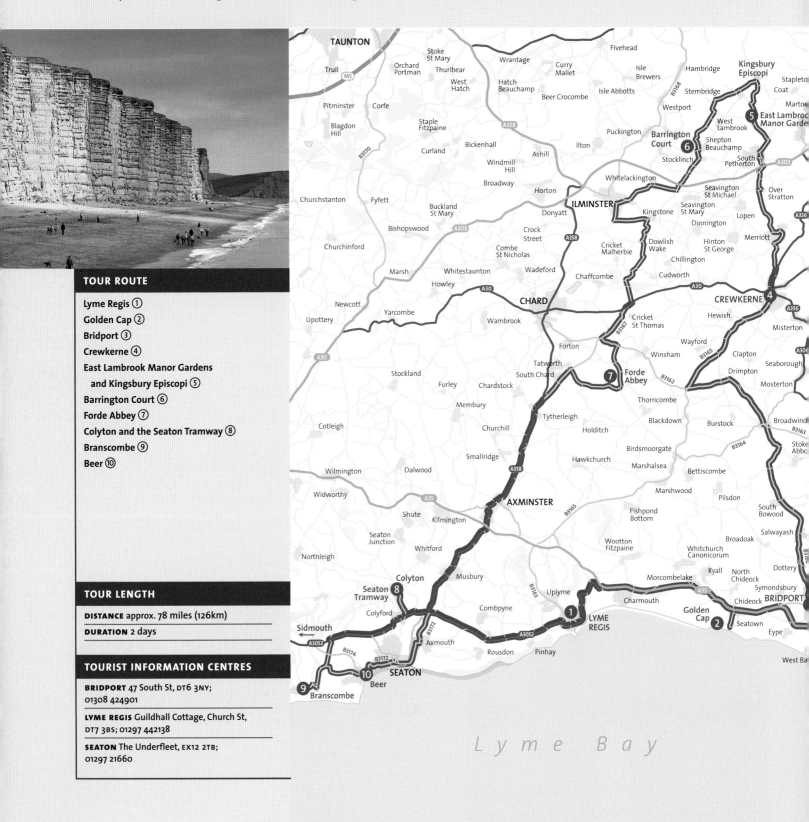

TOUR ROUTE

Lyme Regis ①
Golden Cap ②
Bridport ③
Crewkerne ④
East Lambrook Manor Gardens
    and Kingsbury Episcopi ⑤
Barrington Court ⑥
Forde Abbey ⑦
Colyton and the Seaton Tramway ⑧
Branscombe ⑨
Beer ⑩

TOUR LENGTH

DISTANCE approx. 78 miles (126km)

DURATION 2 days

TOURIST INFORMATION CENTRES

BRIDPORT 47 South St, DT6 3NY;
01308 424901

LYME REGIS Guildhall Cottage, Church St,
DT7 3BS; 01297 442138

SEATON The Underfleet, EX12 2TB;
01297 21660

Miles 0 ———— 5
Kms 0 ———— 5

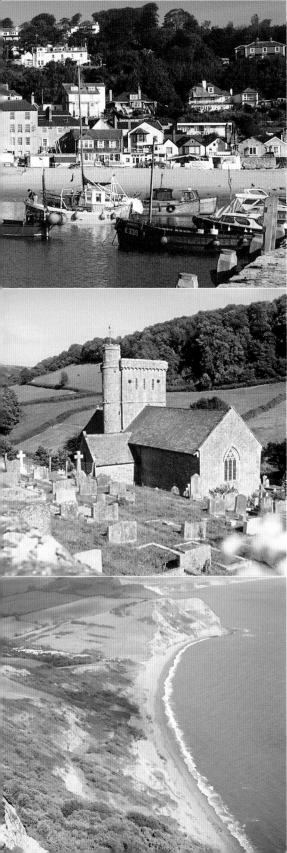

Clockwise from far left:
Jurassic Coast, near the
Golden Cap; The Cobb, Lyme
Regis; harbour, Lyme Regis;
church, Branscombe; view
from the Golden Cap

1 LYME REGIS

Narrow streets lined with shops, cafes and fine
Georgian houses rise steeply from the sea in this lovely
resort, best known as the setting for the film *The
French Lieutenant's Woman* (based on John Fowles'
novel). The handsome harbour, which huddles in the
shelter of its curved stone breakwater, known as **The
Cobb**, is where the cloaked heroine of the film famously
stood gazing out to sea. The breakwater is also a key
setting in Jane Austen's novel *Persuasion*.

Lyme Regis is world famous for its bountiful fossils,
which emerge with astonishing frequency from the
crumbling cliffs. The most famous find was in 1811
when 12-year-old Mary Anning uncovered a complete
6m (21ft) icthyosaurus skeleton, now on display in
London's Natural History Museum. You can find out
more at the excellent **Philpot Museum**, which houses
many finds. Or if you fancy fossil hunting yourself, one
of the best areas is the beach between Lyme Regis and
neighbouring **Charmouth**; but beware of the tide and
crumbling cliffs. The Philpot Museum together with the
Charmouth Heritage Coast Centre and **Dinosaurland**
(two other magnets for avid fossil collectors) give
advice and run regular guided fossil collecting walks.
Alternatively, you can always treat yourself to an
ammonite from one of the many shops selling fossils.

*From Lyme Regis head north
on the A3052 and turn right
onto the A35. Continue to
Chideock, then turn right
onto the steep, narrow
unclassified road to Seatown
and Golden Cap.* **2**

2 GOLDEN CAP

At a height of 190m (625ft), Golden Cap is the highest
sea cliff along the south coast – the far-reaching views
from the summit simply take the breath away. As you
climb the steep path west from the little hamlet of
Seatown, close your eyes for a moment and inhale the
heavy, sweet scent of gorse mingled with the
invigorating sea air. For an enjoyable round trip,
continue west to the abandoned hamlet of **Stanton St
Gabriel**: its now-ruined chapel was reputedly used by
smugglers to hide casks of brandy. Then return to
Seatown for a well-earned drink at the village inn.

*Return to the A35 and turn
right in to Bridport.*

→ • • • • • • • • • • • **3**

Clockwise from above:
Forde Abbey; gardens,
Barrington Court

⊘ *Take the B3162 north to the*
B3165 and turn right to
④ *Crewkerne.*

⊘ *Drive north on the A356*
out of Crewkerne for about
one mile then turn left on
unclassified roads via South
Petherton to East Lambrook
Manor Gardens and then
⑤ *on to Kingsbury Episcopi.*

From Kingsbury
Episcopi drive south west
on unclassified roads
through Stembridge to
Barrington Court.

→ • • • • • • • • • • ⑥

HOME GROWN

There is nothing that quite beats the taste of fresh home produce, and this part of England offers plenty of opportunities to buy some of the country's finest. **Brown and Forrest** *(below)*, a traditional family-run smokery in Langport, produces excellent smoked eel and salmon, as well as smoked chicken, duck, lamb and trout. For a real taste of Somerset cider visit **Perry's Cider** in the picturesque village of Dowlish Wake near Ilminster, where you can sample award-winning speciality ciders produced in the 16th-century thatched barn. And if you fancy picking your own fruit stop off at **Forde Abbey Fruit Farm**.

3 BRIDPORT

A vibrant and colourful town set amongst the West Dorset hills, Bridport is dominated by a Georgian town hall and broad, wide open streets offering views of the countryside beyond. The town's long history as the centre of the country's rope- and net-making industry is explored in the **Bridport Museum**.

4 CREWKERNE

The attractive market town of Crewkerne features many fine buildings, art, antique and book shops and a striking 15th-century church made from the locally quarried, honey-coloured hamstone. The town's history is recounted at the **Crewkerne Heritage Centre** with displays on the Saxon mint, the famous grammar school and the town's cloth-making past.

5 EAST LAMBROOK MANOR GARDENS AND KINGSBURY EPISCOPI

East Lambrook Manor Gardens is the quintessential English cottage garden, boasting colourful herbaceous borders, overspilling with flowers, set against the backdrop of a golden stone house. The garden was created by the late Margery Fish and houses a nursery selling many rare and unusual plants.

Just to the north lies the traditional hamstone village of **Kingsbury Episcopi**, where there's a lovely church and an ancient lock-up cell on the green. The village is set in the heart of cider country and you can visit **Somerset Cider Brandy**, one of the region's oldest producers, to see the old oak vats and copper stills, walk round the orchards and sample some of the delicious finished product.

6 BARRINGTON COURT

Garden lovers will want to linger in the beautiful and elegant gardens at Barrington Court, which are laid out as a series of themed 'rooms', including the enchanting lily garden and the white garden with its cool and carefully coordinated silvers and creams. The Tudor manor house now houses an antique furniture showroom.

7 FORDE ABBEY

Reached by winding country lanes, Forde Abbey is one of rural England's best-kept secrets. The house, dating from 1140, was once a Cistercian monastery and contains some magnificent tapestries depicting cartoons by Raphael. The gardens are equally impressive, set in 12ha (30 acres) and including five lakes, a bog garden and a wonderful working kitchen garden where serried rows of vegetables stand to attention.

8 COLYTON AND THE SEATON TRAMWAY

Tucked away at the head of the River Axe, the little Saxon town of **Colyton** lies at the start of the scenic narrow-gauge tram ride to the coast at Seaton. The three-mile **Seaton Tramway** runs alongside the verdant Axe Estuary, teeming with wading birds and other wildlife. As you set off look out for Colyton's landmark St Andrew's Church; its tower was once used to guide ships up the estuary. Seaton itself boasts a fine promenade, harbour and some lovely parks and gardens where you can stretch your legs before your return journey. On the way back, you could stop off at pretty **Colyford**, where there's an old petrol station housing a motor museum.

Continue south on unclassified roads across the A303 through Ilminster and Dowlish Wake to the A30. Turn right on the A30, then almost immediately left onto the B3167. After about one mile, turn left onto the B3162, then right onto the unclassified road to *Forde Abbey*. **7**

9 BRANSCOMBE

This idyllic coastal village, featuring pretty rows of rose-bedecked cottages, a church and fine pubs, is believed to be the longest village in Britain. A cluster of National Trust-owned buildings here include the old thatched **Forge** where blacksmiths can be seen at work, the restored water-powered **Manor Mill**, and the thatched **Old Bakery**, where you can enjoy a heavenly cream tea, by a roaring open fire in winter.

Travel west on unclassified roads to the B3167 and turn left to join the A358, heading south through Axminster to the junction with the A3052. Turn right then right again on the B3161 to *Colyton* and the *Seaton Tramway*. **8**

10 BEER

One of the scenic jewels of this stretch of coastline, the attractive little port of Beer nestles in a sheltered cove between tall chalk cliffs, with a tiny stream flowing through its centre. The village is renowned for its history of lacemaking, and you'll still find some lace for sale in the gift shops that line the main street. In 1839, 100 Beer lacemakers produced the trimmings for Queen Victoria's wedding dress for the princely cost of £1,000.

Wander down to the beach with its painted bathing huts and brightly coloured boats on the shingle, and then visit **Beer Quarry Caves**, where for 2,000 years chalk limestone has been hewn by hand – some of it used in notable buildings around the country including Westminster Abbey. The labyrinth of caverns hide a secret Catholic chapel used during times of religious persecution; the caves were also a favourite hiding spot for smugglers in the 18th and early 19th centuries, including the notorious Jack Rattenbury.

Return to the A3052 and turn right. After about 3 miles turn left on the unclassified road south to *Branscombe*. **9**

Continue on unclassified roads heading east to *Beer*. **10**

Take the B3172 east to the junction with the A3052, then turn right to return to *Lyme Regis*. **1**

WITH MORE TIME

Just along the coast from Beer is the genteel resort of **Sidmouth** *(left)*, characterised by elegant Regency architecture, beautiful gardens and a wide esplanade. The resort's picturesque setting between majestic red cliffs at the mouth of the River Sid and its inviting sand and pebble beach made it fashionable with the upper classes in the 19th century, many of whom built grand residences here. Just west of town is the popular Jacob's Ladder beach, while to the east, on Salcombe Hill is the Norman Lockyer Observatory, with its large telescopes and planetarium.

Thomas Hardy's Dorset

Associations with the novelist and poet Thomas Hardy are to be found at almost every twist and turn in his homeland of Wessex. The rolling hills, hedgerow-bordered lanes, quaint villages and historic market towns steeped in tales of intrigue all provide the backdrop against which Hardy's characters act out their fate. Serene country houses set in gorgeous gardens invite exploration, as does the dramatic World Heritage Coast, which reveals a succession of extraordinary rock formations created by the pounding of waves over millions of years.

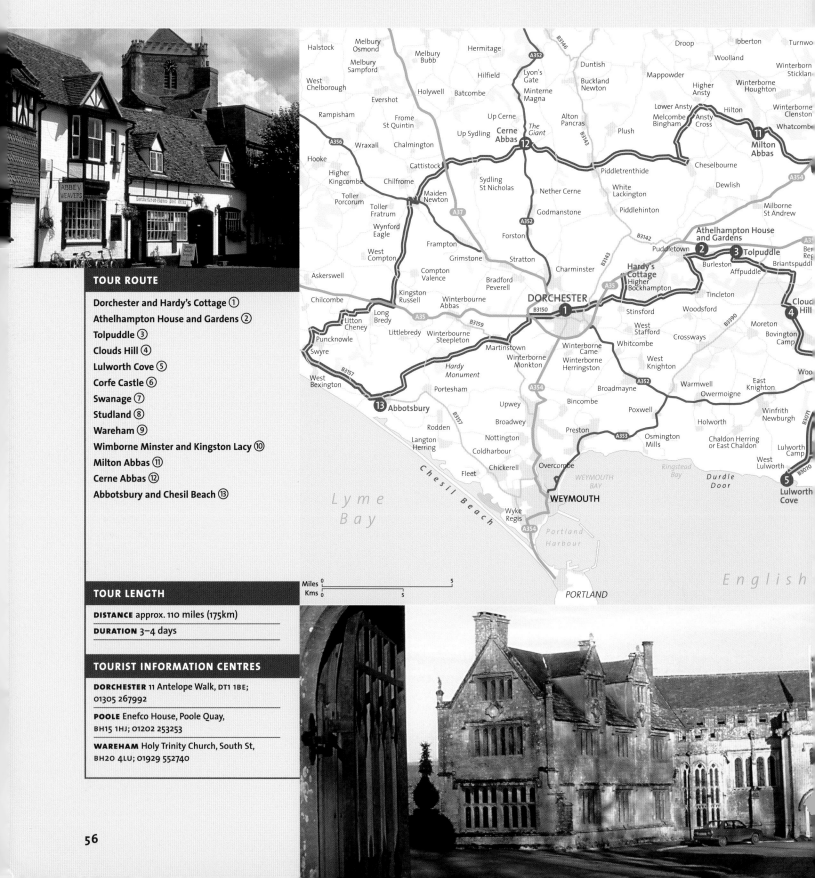

TOUR ROUTE

Dorchester and Hardy's Cottage ①
Athelhampton House and Gardens ②
Tolpuddle ③
Clouds Hill ④
Lulworth Cove ⑤
Corfe Castle ⑥
Swanage ⑦
Studland ⑧
Wareham ⑨
Wimborne Minster and Kingston Lacy ⑩
Milton Abbas ⑪
Cerne Abbas ⑫
Abbotsbury and Chesil Beach ⑬

TOUR LENGTH

DISTANCE approx. 110 miles (175km)

DURATION 3–4 days

TOURIST INFORMATION CENTRES

DORCHESTER 11 Antelope Walk, DT1 1BE;
01305 267992

POOLE Enefco House, Poole Quay,
BH15 1HJ; 01202 253253

WAREHAM Holy Trinity Church, South St,
BH20 4LU; 01929 552740

1 DORCHESTER AND HARDY'S COTTAGE

If Thomas Hardy's spirit roams anywhere, it is around this attractive old market town – the fictional Casterbridge of his famous novel *The Mayor of Casterbridge*. This is where he went to school, trained as an architect and lived for 40 years in the house he designed at **Max Gate**. Hardy's impressive legacy is highlighted in the **Dorset County Museum**, which has the largest collection of Hardy memorabilia in the world, and commemorated by a statue on High Street West, which portrays the writer as an elderly man. Just three miles north east of Dorchester, **Hardy's Cottage** at Higher Bockhampton is particularly popular with literary pilgrims. The pretty thatched cottage is where the writer was born and wrote many of his finest works.

Judge Jeffrey's Restaurant on High Street West is a reminder of Dorchester's chequered past. This is the former home of the infamous 'hanging judge', sent here to punish the supporters of the Duke of Monmouth's unsuccessful rebellion in 1685. A series of trials known as the Bloody Assizes saw 74 rebels hung, drawn and quartered and 175 transported to the West Indian colonies for slave labour. Almost as notorious was the fate of the Tolpuddle Martyrs *(see p58)* who were held in cells at the **Old Crown Court**, which can be visited by guided tour in summer. Behind the High Street you can visit the impressive **Roman Town House**, an excavated Roman villa with a preserved mosaic floor. Dorchester also boasts its own Roman amphitheatre, the **Maumbury Rings** on the southern edge of town, which is still used today for outdoor performances.

2 ATHELHAMPTON HOUSE AND GARDENS

The rooms inside this fine 15th-century house are magnificently furnished and brimming with architectural interest, particularly the Tudor Great Hall featuring a timbered roof, minstrels' gallery and richly detailed heraldic glass, and the oak-panelled Great Chamber with its secret passageway. Surrounding the house are 8ha (20 acres) of gardens with a series of lovely vistas; the Great Court contains 12 giant yew pyramids and eight walled gardens.

Clockwise from far left:
Dorchester; Hardy's Cottage; statue, Abbotsbury Sub-Tropical Gardens; Athelhampton House and Gardens

*Take the B3150 east out of Dorchester. At the junction with the A35 cross over onto the unclassified road to Stinsford and continue east. For **Hardy's Cottage**, detour left at the first crossroads after Stinsford. For **Athelhampton House and Gardens** turn left at Tincleton and then right.* **2**

*Continue east on unclassified roads through Burleston to **Tolpuddle**.*

→ • • • • • • • • • • • • **3**

⊕ Drive east on unclassified
roads through Affpuddle to
Briantspuddle. Turn right in
the village and continue
south for about 2 miles
④ to **Clouds Hill**.

3 TOLPUDDLE

The little village of Tolpuddle was put on the world map by six farm labourers who – in response to their intolerable living conditions – established a trade union here in 1883. Their actions led to their arrest and ultimately the foundation of modern-day trade unionism: their story is told at the **Tolpuddle Martyrs Museum**. Only one of the martyrs was ever to return here; the others, following their pardon, emigrated to Canada.

4 CLOUDS HILL

You can almost picture T E Lawrence in this tiny cottage, as the rooms remain just as he left them, filled with his simple furnishings and wartime photographs, the walls lined with books. The well-known soldier and author, better known as Lawrence of Arabia, rented Clouds Hill in 1923 as a retreat from army life while serving at nearby Bovington Camp. Tragically, he was killed in a motorbike accident on his way home here just five days after being discharged from the army.

⊕ Continue south on
unclassified roads through
Bovington Camp, and then
right onto the A352. Turn
left almost immediately
onto the B3071/B3070
to West Lulworth and
⑤ **Lulworth Cove**.

5 LULWORTH COVE

It is not just geologists who marvel over the graceful line of this natural horseshoe-shaped bay, which was formed some 10,000 years ago. Lulworth Cove sits at the western end of the Isle of Purbeck, where the spectacular coastline has been awarded World Heritage status. Bring a picnic and some walking boots and follow the coastal path one mile west to view the striking limestone archway of **Durdle Door**. Or for even better views, catch the motorboat launch, which sails in the summer from Lulworth beach to Mupe Bay and Durdle Door. You can find out more about the history and geology of the area at **Lulworth's Heritage Centre** in West Lulworth.

Drive north east on the
B3070, turn right just
before East Lulworth and
follow unclassified roads to
Corfe Castle.

→ • • • • • • • • • • • ⑥

THE HARDY TRAIL

Thomas Hardy's novels and poems are rich in depictions of rural life and the struggles of country folk set against the backdrop of his native land. A well-established trail explores the gentle Dorset countryside so beloved by the writer *(below)*, taking in many of the towns and villages that feature in his works. Among those identifiable are Dorchester (Casterbridge in *The Mayor of Casterbridge*), Bournemouth (Sandbourne in *Tess of the D'Urbervilles*), Bere Regis (Kingsbere in *Tess of the D'Urbervilles*) and Stinsford (Mellstock in *Under the Greenwood Tree*). Other Hardy landmarks forming part of the trail include Sturminster Newton where Hardy and his wife Emma had their first real home together, Stinsford's churchyard where Hardy's heart is buried in his wife's grave and Hardy's birthplace at Higher Bockhampton. A free leaflet outlining the trail is available from tourist information centres in the area.

6 CORFE CASTLE

Sweeping sea views will accompany your drive east from the coast up onto the chalk ridge of the Purbeck Hills, before dropping down to Corfe. The village is dominated by the majestic ruins of its castle, which once guarded a strategic gap in the hills. The history of the castle is a long and bloody one: the young King Edward was murdered by his stepmother here in AD978 and, in the 12th century, 22 knights were starved to death in the dungeons on the order of King John. Although blown up during the Civil War, the ruins still retain many fine features, in particular the Horseshoe Tower, which survives almost to its original height.

7 SWANAGE

Up until the 19th century, Swanage was the main centre for the transportation of Purbeck marble, used to decorate churches and cathedrals around the country. Today, it is a seaside town with a sandy beach and restored Victorian pier, and the terminus for the scenic **Swanage Railway** with steam trains huffing and puffing their way six miles inland past Corfe Castle. A leisurely stroll from the seafront towards the town centre brings you to the picturesque Mill Pond in the oldest and most attractive part of town.

On the clifftops above Swanage lies **Durlston Country Park**, 113 ha (280 acres) of land perfect for walking, picnicking or just taking in the fantastic views of the Isle of Wight across Swanage Bay. Its main man-made feature is the massive Great Globe, made from Portland limestone and carved with a world map. It was placed here in 1887 by John Mowlem, one of Swanage's most successful stone and building contractors.

Clockwise from far left:
Durlste Door, near Lulworth Cove; Great Globe, Durlston Country Park; castle ruins, Corfe Castle

8 STUDLAND

Much of this pretty village, which is clustered around a Norman church, lies in the hands of the National Trust. It is an ideal spot to take a break from driving and relax on its white, sandy, shell-strewn beach, which stretches for three miles from Shell Bay to the crumbling chalk stacks of Old Harry Rocks. Behind the beach, nature trails – rich in birdlife – lead through the sand dunes. For a particularly rewarding walk, climb to the Agglestone, a 5m-high boulder (16ft), which according to legend was hurled here by the Devil as he sat on the Needles on the Isle of Wight; his intended target was Salisbury Cathedral! The South West Coast Path also begins its 630-mile journey west from **Studland Bay** to Minehead *(see p47)* in north Somerset, offering stunning coastal walks.

Take the A351 south east to **Swanage.** 7

Drive north out of Swanage on the unclassified road and then turn right on the B3351 to **Studland.** 8

Head west on the B3351 to Corfe Castle then turn right onto the A351 and join the B3075 right to **Wareham.** 9

⊘ *Continue north on the A351
and then take the B3075
left to Winterbourne
Zelston. Turn right onto the
A31 to **Wimborne Minster**.
From Wimborne Minster
take the B3082 north west*
⑩ *to **Kingston Lacy**.*

9 WAREHAM

Wareham's old quay gives a clue to this inland town's former role as Dorset's principal port, and is a good place to begin a stroll round this charming town. Wareham has played an important part in Dorset's history: it was here that the boy King Edward was buried without ceremony after his murder at Corfe Castle, while the now-named Bloody Bank along the town walls was the spot chosen by Judge Jeffreys to hang some of the Monmouth rebels.

On the northern edge of town, the preserved Saxon **St Martin's Church** houses medieval wall paintings and a marble effigy of T E Lawrence *(see p58)*. Just south of Wareham (off the A351) is the **Blue Pool**, an idyllic beauty spot where the water changes colour according to variations in the weather, a phenomenon caused by the reflective properties of the clay in the water.

10 WIMBORNE MINSTER AND KINGSTON LACY

The delightful market town of Wimborne Minster is dominated by the twin spires of its medieval **minster**, which boasts a magnificent Norman nave and arches. Of particular interest is the Chained Library above the choir vestry, founded in 1686 as a free library for the townspeople. Look out for the Quarter Jack on the west tower – a brightly painted figure of a grenadier, which still strikes the quarter hours.

Just west of town lies the 17th-century estate of **Kingston Lacy**. This elegant country mansion owes its outstanding art collection to W J Bankes, a friend of Lord Byron. Shortly after inheriting the house, Bankes became involved in a sexual scandal and fled to Italy, from where he continued to send shipments of artefacts right up to his death. The treasures survive today and include paintings by Rubens, Titian and Van Dyck as well as ornate ceilings, Egyptian antiquities and a magnificent marble staircase. The house is set in attractive formal gardens and surrounded by 100ha (250 acres) of wooded parkland, with lovely waymarked walks and magnificent snowdrop displays in early spring.

*Continue north west on
the B3082, turn left on
unclassified roads through
Sturminster Marshall and
cross the A350 to the A31.
Turn right on the A31, and
after about 3 miles turn
right again following
unclassified roads through
Winterborne Kingston and
Whitechurch. Cross the
A354 and continue north
west to **Milton Abbas**.*
➔ • • • • • • • • • • • ⑪

Clockwise from right:
**Tithe Barn, Abbotsbury;
ceiling, Wimborne Minster;
St Catherine's Chapel,
Abbotsbury; Giant, Cerne
Abbas; Kingston Lacy**

Follow unclassified roads to Ansty Cross and then south to Cheselbourne and west via Piddletrenthide to **Cerne Abbas**. ⑫

11 MILTON ABBAS

Only the 15th-century **abbey** remains of the old town of Middleton, demolished in the 1770s by Lord Milton and rebuilt nearby as Milton Abbas in a place where it would not mar the view from his house. The 'new' village is an enchanting place to visit with its identical thatched cottages lining the main street.

12 CERNE ABBAS

Most people visit Cerne Abbas to see the **Giant**, a huge, naked, club-wielding figure cut into the chalk hillside above the town. His association with springtime fertility rites has led to the theory that he is a representation of the Roman hero-god Hercules, though no one knows for certain. In Victorian times, the grass was encouraged to grow over what were considered to be his offensive parts, but they have since been allowed to reappear. Little remains of the abbey that gave the village its name, but it's certainly worth wandering round the streets, which are full of old world charm. Look out for the **Pitchmarket**, opposite the church on Abbey Street, one in a row of fine Tudor houses and the purported home of Thomas Washington (uncle of the American president) in the 18th century.

13 ABBOTSBURY AND CHESIL BEACH

As you approach Abbotsbury from the west, the view of the village – nestling around its church in a patchwork of green with the great shingle ridge of Chesil Beach stretching endlessly beyond – is simply stunning. This is a gem of a village with picturesque thatched cottages and welcoming pubs and tearooms. The 11th-century Benedictine abbey is long gone, but the abbey gateway and **Abbotsbury Tithe Barn** still make an impressive sight, as does **St Catherine's Chapel**, which guards the village from its perch on a lonely hill. Down on the Fleet Lagoon is the famous **Abbotsbury Swannery**, where a huge colony of mute swans have been breeding in sheltered waters for over 600 years. Leave some time to visit the **Abbotsbury Sub-Tropical Gardens**, just outside the village, where palm trees flourish and camellias and magnolias create a blaze of colour in spring.

Continue on foot south east from Abbotsbury to Chesil Beach and explore this remarkable shingle spit, 12m-high (40ft) in places and stretching for 10 miles to the Isle of Portland. One of its most curious features is the gradual degradation in the size of the pebbles from east to west, which is so precise that local fishermen landing on the beach at night can tell where they are by the size of the stones.

Drive west on unclassified roads to Maiden Newton, turn right onto the A356 then almost immediately left, continuing south on unclassified roads to Kingston Russell. Turn briefly right onto the A35, then left following unclassified roads south west to Swyre. Turn left onto the B3157 to **Abbotsbury** and **Chesil Beach**. ⑬

Take the narrow unclassified road from Abbotsbury north east to the B3159. Turn right through Martinstown then shortly after turn left and continue to the A35 and follow the B3150 to return to **Dorchester**. ⓵

WITH MORE TIME

Sheltered by one of the largest natural harbours in the world, **Poole** is a busy port with an attractive quay lined with old houses, restaurants and pubs as well as the Poole Pottery Factory Outlet. From the quay, a regular ferry service sails to **Brownsea Island** *(left)*. Set at the entrance to Poole harbour, with spectacular views of the Purbeck Hills, this lovely wooded island is one of the few places where red squirrels still thrive, and it is an idyllic place to walk or picnic. The northern part of the island is a nature reserve, home to red deer and more than 200 bird species.

On the trail of King Arthur

The rolling hills of Somerset and Dorset are blanketed with a patchwork of pretty stone villages, stately homes and lovingly tended gardens, and their wonderful, sleepy back roads make them ideal for cycling and leisurely driving. Scattered with historic castles, glorious cathedrals and mysterious caves, the area is loaded with headline attractions. However, it is also awash with sacred sites, prehistoric hill forts and mystical ley lines, all of which gave rise to rich local lore offering strong links with the legend of King Arthur and his band of knights. Whether these tales have any historic truth or not, the area brims with intrigue.

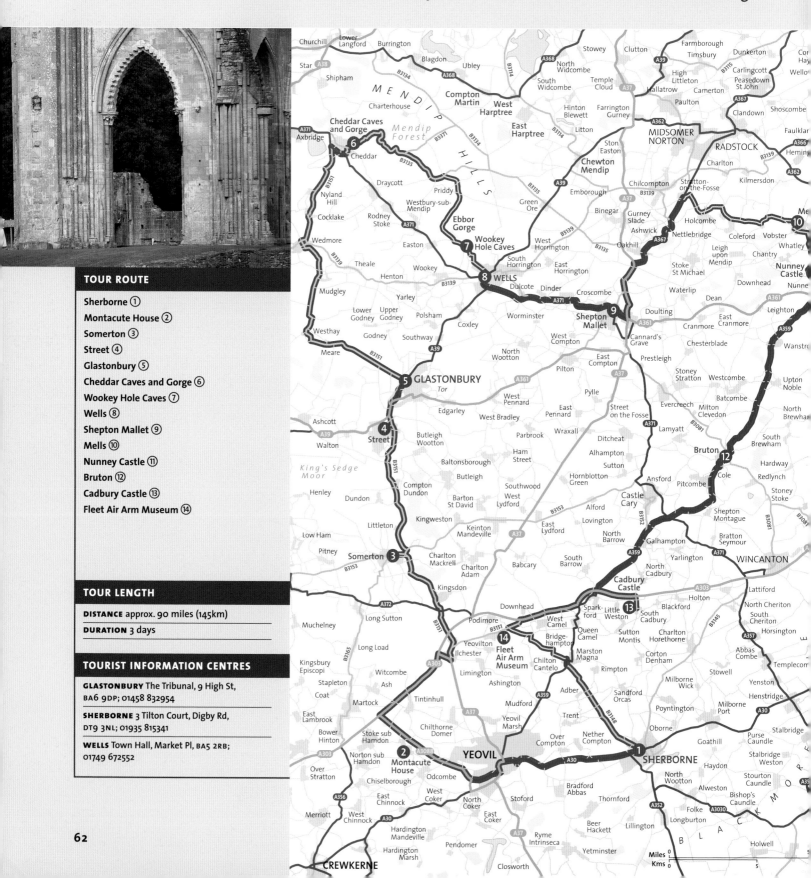

TOUR ROUTE

Sherborne ①
Montacute House ②
Somerton ③
Street ④
Glastonbury ⑤
Cheddar Caves and Gorge ⑥
Wookey Hole Caves ⑦
Wells ⑧
Shepton Mallet ⑨
Mells ⑩
Nunney Castle ⑪
Bruton ⑫
Cadbury Castle ⑬
Fleet Air Arm Museum ⑭

TOUR LENGTH

DISTANCE approx. 90 miles (145km)

DURATION 3 days

TOURIST INFORMATION CENTRES

GLASTONBURY The Tribunal, 9 High St,
BA6 9DP; 01458 832954

SHERBORNE 3 Tilton Court, Digby Rd,
DT9 3NL; 01935 815341

WELLS Town Hall, Market Pl, BA5 2RB;
01749 672552

Clockwise from far left:
Glastonbury Abbey;
Glastonbury Tor; Sherborne
Abbey; window, Wells
Cathedral; Wookey Hole Caves

1 SHERBORNE

Once the capital of Wessex, the pretty town of Sherborne, with its winding streets and red stone buildings, is a sleepy but charming place. Sherborne was a cathedral city until Old Sarum *(see p77)* took the honour in 1075, and its wonderful church, **Sherborne Abbey**, was built on the remains of the 8th-century cathedral. The church is a fine example of 15th-century Perpendicular style, and its most impressive features are the delicate fan vaulting – the oldest in the country – and a set of beautiful misericords on the choir stalls. The medieval **Almshouse** in the abbey close is one of only a few in the country that still fulfils its original role. Nearby on Church Lane, you'll find the **Sherborne Museum**, which chronicles the history of the town's fortunes.

Also worth visiting is **Sherborne House**, a Palladian mansion built in 1720, which is currently under restoration. The house is now used for local art exhibitions but its most glorious asset is the baroque mural of the Calydonian hunt and Goddess Diana in the hall, painted by Dorset artist Sir James Thornhill.

Sherborne is most famous for its two castles. **Sherborne Old Castle**, 'a malicious and malevolent' place according to Cromwell, was a much-coveted 12th-century fortress. Queen Elizabeth I granted it to Sir Walter Raleigh in the late 16th century, and although he spent a fortune on alterations, it never lived up to his lofty expectations and he soon moved across the river and began work on the new **Sherborne Castle**. When Raleigh fell out of favour with the court in 1617, the castle was sold to the Digby family who have been there ever since. Expect fine Gothic interiors brimming with artworks, period furniture and porcelain and – from the landscaped grounds – a view of the ruined old castle destroyed by Cromwellian troops in 1645.

Take the A30 west from
Sherborne and turn right
onto the A3088 south of
Yeovil, then follow the signs
*left to **Montacute House**.*

→ • • • • • • • • • • ❷

KING ARTHUR & THE ISLE OF AVALON

God-like king, parable of virtue or mythical hero, King Arthur and the tales of his legendary escapades have endured through the centuries and yet no one is sure whether he actually existed. Just as contentious is Glastonbury's claim to be the mythical Isle of Avalon where Excalibur (King Arthur's sword) was forged, where his sister Morgan le Fay lived and where Arthur was brought to die. It was only in the 12th century that Glastonbury came to be associated with Avalon. A great fire devastated the monastery, and just seven years later a band of resourceful monks 'found' Arthur's grave in the grounds. The streams of pilgrims that followed brought significant wealth to the abbey for its reconstruction. Additional local stories about Joseph of Arimathea, the Holy Grail, the healing well waters and the causeway to Cadbury Castle *(see p67)*, thought to be legendary Camelot, all support Glastonbury's claim to be the Isle of Avalon. Whether it is elaborate early spin or historical truth no one really knows; either way the town and its sacred sites continue to hold a mystical and powerful pull that is difficult to ignore.

⊕ *Continue north west on the A3088, then turn right onto the A303 in to central Ilchester and take the B3151* ③ *north to* **Somerton**.

⊕ *Continue north on the B3151* ④ *to* **Street**.

Drive further north on the B3151 to **Glastonbury**.

→ • • • • • • • • • • ⑤

2 MONTACUTE HOUSE

One of England's finest Elizabethan mansions, Montacute House was built in 1590 for Sir Edward Phelips, a lawyer and politician known for giving the prosecution's opening speech at the trial of Guy Fawkes. The stunning house with its carved parapets and elegant chimneys has equally impressive interiors with elaborate plasterwork, opulent textiles and period furniture, which made it an ideal location for the filming of *Sense and Sensibility*. The grand state rooms play host to a fine collection of Tudor and Elizabethan portraits on permanent loan from the National Portrait Gallery, and outside the impressive landscaped grounds include formal gardens.

3 SOMERTON

Somerton was the capital of Wessex in the 7th century until Alfred the Great established Winchester *(see p93)* as the new seat of government. Today it is a lovely, mellow town with a wide 17th-century square, an octagonal market cross, a town hall and some elegant houses and inns. The parish **church** contains one of the finest wooden roofs in the county, carved by the monks of nearby Muchelney Abbey. In summer, a programme of events includes the popular week-long Somerton Arts Festival, which takes place every July.

4 STREET

Local farmer and devout Quaker Cyrus Clark set up a sheepskin and shoe-making business in Street in 1825, and the town became internationally known as the home base of C & J Clark Ltd, whose headquarters still border the High Street. Street now boasts a major factory outlet shopping complex – **Clarks Village** – attracting visitors from far and wide with more than 75 individual shop units, many of which are household-name companies, selling quality goods at discount prices.

Clockwise from far left:
gardens, Montacute House;
Glastonbury Abbey;
Wookey Hole Caves;
market cross, Somerton

5 GLASTONBURY

Although more famous today for its music festival than its mystical connections, bohemian Glastonbury lies at the heart of numerous ancient legends and at the crossing point of powerful ley lines. The town has attracted those in search of spiritual enlightenment for centuries, and today it is bursting with wholefood, incense and healers.

The once majestic **Glastonbury Abbey** was allegedly founded by Joseph of Arimathea, a kinsman of Christ who owned mines in the nearby Mendip Hills. According to local legend he arrived here with the Holy Grail (the chalice used in the Last Supper), planted his staff in the earth, saw it sprout a thorn bush and began his quest to bring Christianity to England. Officially however, the abbey evolved out of a Celtic monastery, founded in the 4th or 5th century, and grew into a wealthy Benedictine abbey after the bodies of King Arthur and Queen Guinevere were allegedly found in the grounds. The abbey, however, was decimated during the Protestant Reformation and all that remains today are the evocative ruins. Joseph's Holy Grail was supposedly hidden in the nearby **Chalice Well**, an iron-red spring surrounded by tranquil gardens. The water from the well is unlikely to have been coloured by the blood of Christ as local legend suggests, but many believe it does have curative powers.

Just east of town, rising spectacularly above the plains is **Glastonbury Tor**, a conical hill topped by St Michael's Tower and the ruins of a 14th-century church. It is a truly mystical place with incredible views over the surrounding countryside that gives a real sense of why this town and area has inspired writers, poets and healers for centuries.

6 CHEDDAR CAVES AND GORGE

Known for its eponymous cheese, Cheddar pulls in the crowds who come to explore its dramatic gorge and limestone caves. The caves were formed during the last Ice Age creating amazing rock formations in **Gough's Cave**. A 40,000-year-old skeleton discovered in **Cox's Cave** has helped prove the theory that they were used as shelter for primitive families. Just outside the cave the steep steps of Jacob's Ladder lead to vantage points with stunning views of Exmoor, Glastonbury Tor and the sea. From here you can walk along the top of the spectacular steep-sided gorge – it is a far more peaceful route than the drive through the gorge on the narrow winding road below.

7 WOOKEY HOLE CAVES

The impressive series of caves at Wookey Hole were carved by the River Axe over millions of years. They feature some magnificent underground chambers with incredible stalactites and stalagmites, as well as an eerie subterranean lake where dramatic light and sound effects bring the caves' natural wonder to life. Here too, supposedly, is the final resting place of the Witch of Wookey Hole, a woman reputed to have cast her evil eye on locals. Legend has it, she was finally stopped in her tracks and turned to stone when a monk sprinkled her with holy water.

Travel north west on the B3151 to Cheddar, then turn right onto the A371 and left onto the B3135 to **Cheddar Caves and Gorge.** 6

Drive through the gorge on the B3135 and turn right on unclassified roads through the village of Priddy to Ebbor Gorge and **Wookey Hole Caves.** 7

From Wookey Hole, drive south east on unclassified roads to **Wells.**

 8

Clockwise from above:
nave, Wells Cathedral;
Nunney Castle; Fleet
Air Arm Museum; façade,
Wells Cathedral

⊘ *Drive east on the
A371 to Shepton*
⑨ *Mallet.*

8 WELLS

Charming, understated Wells hides its treasures from
prying eyes, and it is only when you walk from the
Market Square into the Cathedral Close that you spy
the magnificent Early English Gothic **cathedral** for the
first time. Set back on the green lawns and presiding
over the surrounding medieval buildings in the close, the
cathedral reveals a fanfare of 300 figures on the recently
restored west front. Inside, giant scissor arches take the
weight of the central tower and wonderful capitals and
corbels line the nave. Look out for the astronomical
clock dating from 1392, and then climb the stone steps
to the stunning Chapter House.

Before leaving the close stroll around to the **Vicar's Close,**
a gorgeous lane said to be the oldest continually inhabited street in Europe. Next to the cathedral on Market
Square is the imposing **Bishop's Palace**, a 13th-century
monument with Gothic state rooms, a moat fed by the
springs that give the town its name and its own bevy of
swans trained to ring a bell whenever they need feeding.

*Head north on the A37 and
turn right onto the A367 to
Stratton-on-the-Fosse, then
drive east on unclassified
roads through Holcombe
and Vobster to Mells.*

➔ • • • • • • • • • • ⑩

9 SHEPTON MALLET

Nestling in a fold of the Mendip Hills, the historic market
town of Shepton Mallet dates back to Roman times.
From the 15th to the 17th centuries, it became a significant market and wool-trading centre, and many fine
examples of cloth merchants' houses still remain.

10 MELLS

A cluster of listed buildings, thatched cottages and an imposing 15th-century **church** make up the gorgeous village of Mells. The church has a lovely tower with diagonally-set pinnacles and a cemetery containing the grave of World War I poet Siegfried Sassoon. Mells is also known for its beautiful 14th-century manor house, seat of the Horner family whose ancestor supposedly gave rise to the childhood rhyme 'Little Jack Horner', after finding the deeds of the house hidden in a pie.

11 NUNNEY CASTLE

Dominating the attractive town of Nunney is this remarkable 14th-century moated castle built by John de la Mere after his return from the Hundred Years War. Designed to impress rather than defend, the fortified mansion borrows heavily from French style with closely spaced towers adorning a central townhouse. The castle suffered badly when it was attacked by Cromwellian forces during the Civil War, and the damage sustained eventually caused the complete collapse of the north wall.

12 BRUTON

It is worth stopping off at the sleepy town of Bruton for its lovely collection of buildings, which range from Jacobean almshouses to the wonderful Perpendicular church with its twin towers. A network of narrow alleyways or 'bartons' link Bruton with the River Brue and an unusual 16th-century dovecote that sits on a hill overlooking the town.

Head south on unclassified roads through Whatley to **Nunney Castle.** 11

Take the A359 south from Nunney to **Bruton.** 12

Continue south on the A359, then turn left onto the A303 and then quickly right to South Cadbury and **Cadbury Castle.** 13

13 CADBURY CASTLE

The massive banks and ditches that surround the limestone hill at South Cadbury make it the largest hill fort in Somerset and certainly the kind of fortification that only a chieftain could afford to build. The site was probably first occupied about 5,000 years ago, but it is most famous for its connection to King Arthur. Although hotly disputed, many believe that this is the site of the legendary Camelot (Arthur's fortress and site of many of his most famous battles). A raised causeway called King Arthur's Hunting Track links the site to Glastonbury and adds credence to the claim. Either way, the impressive earthworks and stunning views make it an excellent spot for a walk and some fanciful musing.

Return to the A303 and turn left, heading west through Sparkford. After Downhead, turn left onto the B3151 and follow signs left to the **Fleet Air Arm Museum.** 14

14 FLEET AIR ARM MUSEUM

Highlights of this museum's large aircraft and military collection include the second prototype of Concorde and a simulated helicopter ride onto the flight deck of a 1970s aircraft carrier. The displays also cover aircraft from World War I, World War II and the Falklands, as well as up-to-date exhibitions on the latest airforce technology.

Take the unclassified road just east of the museum, signposted for Bridge-hampton, to the A359, turn right and shortly after turn left on the B3148 to return to **Sherborne.** 1

WITH MORE TIME

Drive east onto the limestone ridge that forms the Mendip Hills *(left)* and you'll be rewarded with far-reaching views over the low-lying land below. The hills are littered with prehistoric earthworks, forts, barrows and the remains of the mining industry, and they offer great walks with a host of pretty villages and cosy pubs for excellent pit stops. By car, take a detour from Cheddar Gorge through **Compton Martin, West Harptree** and **East Harptree** and then on to **Chewton Mendip** before dropping down through unspoilt **Ebbor Gorge** to Wookey Hole.

In and around Bath: elegant legacy of times past

The glorious countryside surrounding the elegant World Heritage city of Bath has attracted man since prehistoric times. Littered with ancient monuments, magnificent medieval villages, gorgeous gardens and gracious stately homes, this region is a microcosm of all that is best in England's green and pleasant land. Ramble through river valleys, clamber over castle walls or take in the beautiful Georgian city of Bath.

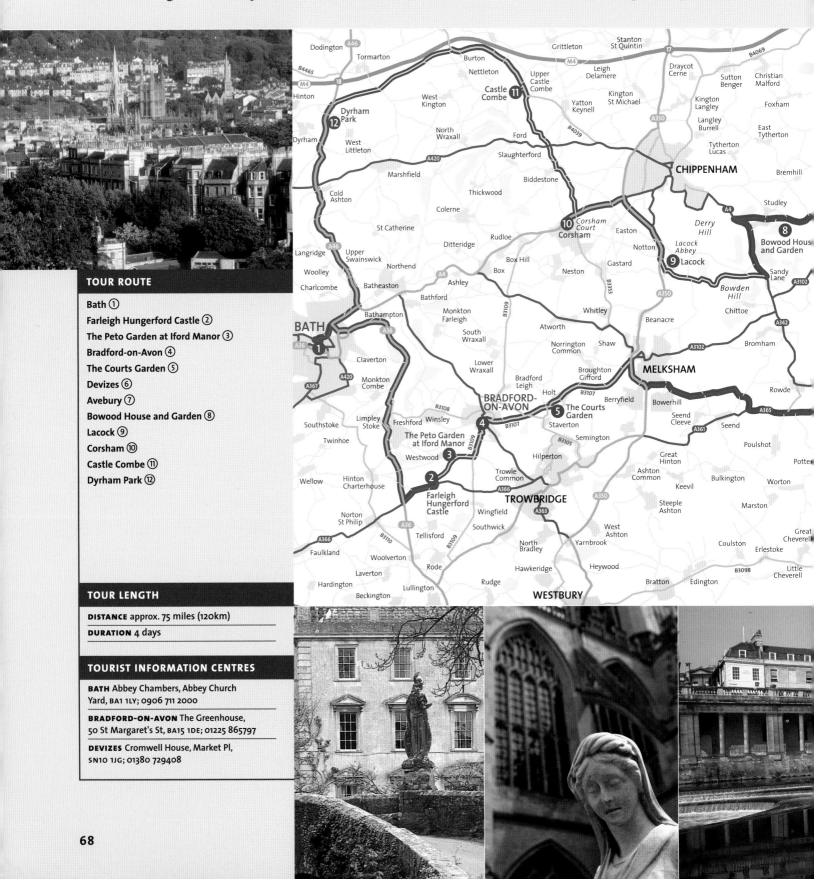

TOUR ROUTE

Bath ①
Farleigh Hungerford Castle ②
The Peto Garden at Iford Manor ③
Bradford-on-Avon ④
The Courts Garden ⑤
Devizes ⑥
Avebury ⑦
Bowood House and Garden ⑧
Lacock ⑨
Corsham ⑩
Castle Combe ⑪
Dyrham Park ⑫

TOUR LENGTH

DISTANCE approx. 75 miles (120km)

DURATION 4 days

TOURIST INFORMATION CENTRES

BATH Abbey Chambers, Abbey Church Yard, BA1 1LY; 0906 711 2000

BRADFORD-ON-AVON The Greenhouse, 50 St Margaret's St, BA15 1DE; 01225 865797

DEVIZES Cromwell House, Market Pl, SN10 1JG; 01380 729408

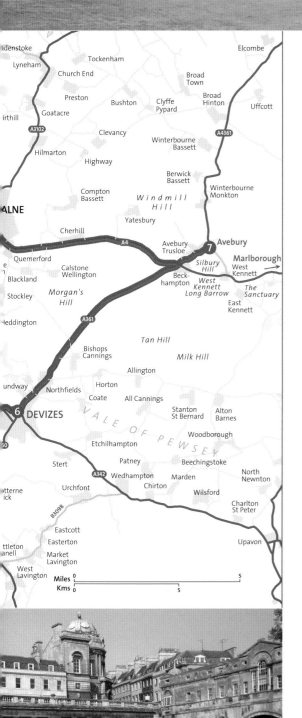

1 BATH

Cultivated and ever-so-elite, Bath has never lost its air of 18th-century exclusivity. Today the city streets are lined with chi-chi boutiques, expensive galleries, antique shops and fine restaurants, and it makes a fascinating place to just stroll around and soak up the atmosphere. Wander from one architectural gem to another, take in some of the museums and then lose yourself in a daydream of Georgian high society.

The city has traded on the presence of Britain's only hot springs since Celtic times, but it was the Romans who had the engineering skills to create the great bathing complex you see today. Bath's real heyday, however, was as a spa resort in the 18th century when artists, writers and the moneyed flocked here to join fashionable society in its never-ending round of socialising. The **Roman Baths** *(see p70)* got a neo-classical makeover at this time, and the city enjoyed a period of unprecedented building work. Bath now boasts more than 5,000 listed buildings and the gracious, sweeping, honey-coloured curves of **The Circus** and the **Royal Crescent** are the elegant highlights of a city heaving with Palladian mansions and stunning townhouses. To peek inside one of the city's treasures visit **No. 1 Royal Crescent**, which has been restored to its original glory. Many of the city's famous buildings, such as the grand **Bath Assembly Rooms**, are mentioned in Jane Austen's *Northanger Abbey* and *Persuasion*. To gain insight into the Bath of her time, visit the **Jane Austen Centre**, where you can see period prints and displays on her personal life.

Spanning the River Avon, Italianate **Pulteney Bridge** is another top attraction. Lined with shops, it presides over the beautiful V-shaped weir on the river below and affords wonderful views of the **Holburne Museum of Art**, home to a stunning collection of furniture, porcelain and paintings. Bath is one of Britain's top tourist cities and can be overrun in summer, but throw away your map, wander the side streets and you'll soon be transported back in time and away from the crowds.

Take the A36 south from Bath and turn left onto the A366 to Farleigh Hungerford Castle.

Clockwise from above:
stained-glass windows, Bath
Abbey; Roman Baths; The
Peto Garden at Iford Manor;
Roman mosaic, Bath

ROMAN BATHS AND PUMP ROOM

Britain's only hot springs drew the Romans to Bath, and
the magnificent remains of their bathing complex are
now one of England's most popular attractions. The
baths fell into decline after the departure of the Romans,
but a visit by Queen Anne sealed their status as the
fashionable place to 'take the cure' in the 18th century.
The grandiose main pool or Great Bath is surrounded
by statues of famous emperors and governors and is
overlooked by a Victorian gallery. Every day, some one
million litres (220,000 gallons) of hot water still flow
through the complex from the Sacred Spring, and it is
this water that fills the pools to this day. The Romans
believed the incredible surging water was the work of
the gods, and a temple to the local goddess, Sulis
Minerva, was built on the site in her honour.

You can walk though the warren of underground
passages and chambers and inspect the sophisticated
pumping and draining systems created by the Roman
engineers. Two other baths, the Cross Bath and the Hot
Bath, were connected to the main baths by a covered
walkway and today have been incorporated into a long-
awaited state-of-the-art spa complex (the opening of
which has been delayed due to legal problems). It is also
worth visiting the museum, which displays artefacts
found on the site and gives an intriguing insight into
the lives of the Romans who lived and worked in the
area. Next door, the late 18th-century Pump Room, which
overlooks the King's Bath, was the epicentre of Bath's
high society. The hall now houses a restaurant and the
Pump Room Trio play music here most mornings.

BATH ABBEY

Built on the site of a Norman cathedral where the
first king of a united England was crowned, Bath
Abbey is a superlative example of Perpendicular style
with slender pillars and soaring vertical lines. The
present abbey was begun in 1499, after a dream
inspired the then bishop, Oliver King, to raze the ruined
church and build a monument to the glory of God. The
west front depicts his vision of angels climbing up a
ladder to heaven. Inside elaborate monuments and
memorials, including the tomb of the city's Victorian
society dandy, Beau Nash, line a nave illuminated
by magnificent stained-glass windows and decorated
with incredible fan vaulting.

2 FARLEIGH HUNGERFORD CASTLE

The atmospheric ruins of two towers, part of a curtain wall, the outer gatehouse and the chapel are all that remain of the 14th-century bastion of Sir Thomas Hungerford, first speaker of the House of Commons. The surviving chapel is of particular interest and features a 14th-century wall painting of St George slaying the dragon, as well as the fine tomb of Sir Thomas Hungerford. Beneath the chapel is a small, dark crypt dating from the 14th-century, where a collection of lead coffins containing family remains are located. The priest's house at the east end of the chapel holds a small museum with displays on the history of the castle, a collection of Civil War armour and the artefacts recovered during digs on the site.

3 THE PETO GARDEN AT IFORD MANOR

Ilford Manor was home to architect and landscape gardener Harold Peto in the early 20th century, and he wasted no time in transforming the gardens into his very own Italianate creation. Peto used the steep sides of the Frome Valley to structure his stunning terraced garden. Dotted with classical sculptures and ornamental buildings, the gardens offer stunning views across the valley, and in summer the Romanesque cloisters play host to recitals and operas. The original house – now closed to the public – is medieval, but a classical façade was added in the 18th century.

WILTSHIRE'S WHITE HORSES

The steep hills of the chalk downs of central Wiltshire have proved to be ideal for hill carvings, and the county boasts the largest concentration of white horses *(below)* in the country. Contrary to popular opinion, the white horses generally date only from the 18th century, and though there were originally 13, now only eight are visible, five of which lie within a five-mile radius of Avebury. Horses are not the only theme, and many other figures were dug out by World War I troops. Among those that have been maintained are eight regimental badges near Fovant, a giant kiwi in Bulford near Salisbury and the Codford Rising Sun near Warminster.

Drive north on the unclassified road from Farleigh Hungerford to Westwood. Turn left in the village and follow the signs to **The Peto Garden at Iford Manor**. ❸

Drive east to the B3109 and turn left to **Bradford-on-Avon**. ❹

5 THE COURTS GARDEN

Set in an arboretum around an 18th-century house closely associated with the wool trade, the National Trust gardens at The Courts are a culmination of work by several centuries of loving owners. Classical statues, a stone temple and a conservatory adorn the colourful garden, while unusual topiary and a water garden of irises and lilies encompass the original wool dyeing pond and the stone pillars used for drying wool.

6 DEVIZES

The elegant town of Devizes is anchored by a sweeping semi-circular market place surrounded by fine Georgian houses, but its legendary market cross tells a cautionary tale for traders. According to the inscription, Ruth Pierce promptly fell to the ground here after she asked God to strike her dead if she lied about the price of a corn deal. Undeterred, traders still gather here four days a week to sell everything from traditional country foods to antiques. The town also boasts two Norman churches and in St John's Avenue, Elizabethan timbered houses with overhanging upper storeys. Also worth a look is the **Wiltshire Heritage Museum**, an incredible place heaving with prehistoric finds and local artefacts. Just outside town, the **Caen Hill** flight of 29 locks on the Kennet and Avon Canal is a glorious testimony to the feats of Victorian engineering.

⊕ *Take the B3107 east out of Bradford and follow the signs right for* ➎ *The Courts Garden*.

⊕ *Return to the B3107 and turn right to Melksham. Turn right onto the A350 and then left onto the* ➏ *A365 east to Devizes*.

Take the A361 north east to Avebury.

↪ • • • • • • • • • • • ➐

4 BRADFORD-ON-AVON

The graceful, honey-coloured town of Bradford owes much of its charm to the fine houses of wealthy 17th-century weavers that still line its winding streets. A prosperous town with fine food shops and interesting boutiques, Bradford makes a great place for a ramble. At the top of the hill to the west of the centre the medieval **Chapel of St Mary's Tory** is an atmospheric spot with fine views over the town, while at the bottom of the hill is the remarkably well-preserved 10th-century **Church of St Laurence**. Cross the old stone bridge with its overhanging room, originally a pilgrim's chapel and later a lock-up, to call into the quirky **Bradford Museum** where you'll find a reconstructed Victorian pharmacy, and then stroll on to visit the medieval **Tithe Barn** near the river. Then catch a boat or follow the tow path along the canal to the Victorian **aqueduct** at Avoncliff.

Clockwise from top left:
Tithe Barn, Bradford-on-Avon;
stone circle, Avebury; Bowood
House; statue, Devizes;
bridge, Bradford-on-Avon

PREHISTORIC PROMENADES

To really appreciate the significance of the Avebury site and to get a sense of its scale, walk south east from the stone circle between the two parallel rows of 100 standing stones known as **West Kennett Avenue**. The one-and-a-half mile path leads to the **Sanctuary**, an ancient stone circle with two concentric rings. From here you can hike to the **West Kennett Long Barrow**, a huge burial chamber dating from about 3,500BC, which contained the remains of almost 50 people. Overlooking the valley below, the site commands excellent views over Avebury and the brooding **Silbury Hill** *(below)* the largest artificial Bronze Age mound in Europe. Probably used originally as a burial chamber, the 40-m (130-ft) mound is now off limits to hikers due to the erosion caused by thousands of feet.

7 AVEBURY

Eerily quiet by comparison to Stonehenge, and far more mysterious and atmospheric, Avebury's **stone circle** is far larger than its more famous neighbour and visitors have free access to wander round the giant standing stones. The circle and surrounding earthworks date from 4,500BC and cover a huge area, completely encompassing the pretty village of Avebury. In the village, the **Alexander Keiller Museum** explains the various theories about the history of the site, while an interactive exhibition at the thatched **Great Barn** explores the construction of the circle and the significance of the artefacts found there. Also worth a visit is **Avebury Manor and Garden**, which has beautiful Queen Anne interiors and a restored walled garden.

8 BOWOOD HOUSE AND GARDEN

Built and subsequently improved upon by a clutch of famous architects and designers, Bowood House is a grand 18th-century mansion with magnificent interiors. Among a collection of palatial rooms you'll find a fine sculpture gallery and the laboratory where Dr Joseph Priestly discovered oxygen in 1774. Outside, the stunning grounds were landscaped by 'Capability' Brown and include a Doric temple by a lake and gorgeous rhododendron gardens.

*Head south west on the A361 and turn right onto the A4 past Calne, then follow the signs left for **Bowood House and Garden**.* **8**

*Return to the A4 and turn left, then turn left again onto the A342. Turn right onto unclassified roads in the village of Sandy Lane and follow the signs to **Lacock**.* **9**

Clockwise from above:
Lacock Abbey; grounds of
Manor House, Castle Combe;
cottages, Castle Combe

*Drive north west to the
A350 and turn right heading
north, then turn left onto
⑩ the A4 to **Corsham**.*

*Head north on unclassified
roads via Biddestone to
Castle Combe.*

⑪

9 LACOCK

Largely untouched by time, the picturesque feudal village of Lacock is a favourite of film location scouts and has starred in *Harry Potter* films and the BBC's *Pride and Prejudice*. **Lacock Abbey** still maintains some traces of its original 13th-century structure, but has seen many additions since the Dissolution in 1539, when it became home to Sir William Sharington, vice-treasurer of the Bristol mint who was disgraced by charges of embezzlement in 1549. His descendent, William Henry Fox Talbot discovered the process of producing a photographic negative here in the early 19th century, an achievement celebrated in the **Fox Talbot Museum** of photography. Fox Talbot is buried in the village cemetery while his infamous relative, Sharington, managed to secure a tomb under the wonderful barrel-vaulted roof of the **Church of St Cyriac**. Lacock can be besieged by visitors in summer so it's a good idea to visit early in the morning or late in the evening to enjoy it at its most tranquil.

10 CORSHAM

The dignified town of Corsham was once a wealthy centre of the cloth-making industry, and it boasts a remarkable collection of fine buildings including some beautiful gabled weavers' cottages and almshouses. Next to the almshouses is the local school, which still has the original master's pulpit desk intact, and in the church graveyard is the final resting place of Sarah Jarvis, who died in 1753 at the grand old age of 107. Something of a local legend, she was renowned for having grown a new set of teeth soon after her hundred birthday, as well as *'a new set of toes, her former ones having rotted off about 16 years ago',* according to the *Worcester Journal* of 1752.

The town's highlight, however, is **Corsham Court**, a grand Elizabethan mansion dating from 1582. Used as a film location in *Remains of the Day*, the house is famous for its stunning art collection, which includes the work of Caravaggio, Rubens and Michelangelo. Outside, peacocks roam the magnificent grounds and around the gorgeous Gothic bathhouse.

12 DYRHAM PARK

Nestled in its own deer park and formal gardens, this late 17th-century Baroque mansion was designed for William Blathwayt, secretary at war during the reign of William III. The house is filled with a fine collection of Dutch decorative arts, elaborate wood panelling and antique furniture, while its restored domestic quarters offer an insight into life below stairs. The grounds offer superb views of the surrounding countryside and are passed by the long-distance walking path, the Cotswold Way, on its route between Chipping Campden and Bath.

Take the B4039 north to Burton, turning left onto an unclassified road just before the M4 overpass. Continue west until the A46, then turn left and follow the signs left to Dyrham Park. 12

11 CASTLE COMBE

Looking much as it would have hundreds of years ago, Castle Combe must surely be a contender for the prettiest village in England. Here, lovely stone cottages line a narrow street that opens onto an attractive market place with a medieval church and views across to the elegant Manor House (now a luxury hotel). An old stone bridge crosses a trickling brook on the far side of the road, and without street lighting or TV aerials to mar its image as rural idyll, it is the implausibly perfect picture of medieval Britain.

CROP CIRCLES

Wiltshire is crop circle central, and each summer complex designs appear in the fields of barley and wheat across the county. Tourists, scientists and journalists are drawn to the phenomenon that some say is the work of extraterrestrial visitors; however, the giant geometric patterns are more likely a form of public art practised by conceptual artists. Either way the designs can be simply stunning. The largest crop circle recorded in 2001 measured 239m-long (787ft) and featured 409 spiralling circles.

Take the A46 south and follow the signs into Bath. 1

WITH MORE TIME

A sleepy market town with an impressive array of traditional shops and picturesque cottages, **Marlborough** *(left)* has one of the widest high streets in England. A fire destroyed much of the town in 1653, prompting parliament to ban the use of thatch and leaving the town free to rebuild the colonnaded high street in stunning Georgian style. The town also boasts a solid Victorian town hall, a fine Perpendicular church and rambling lanes still flanked by original half-timbered cottages. Elite Marlborough College is also here, and in its grounds is a mound said to be Merlin's tomb.

Around Salisbury Plain: megaliths and mansions

Mysterious ancient monuments, picture-postcard villages, rolling chalk hills and numerous stately homes dot the landscape around Salisbury Plain, a sweeping plateau of grassland anchored by graceful Salisbury. Home to a spectacular cathedral and a labyrinth of medieval streets, Salisbury is the perfect starting point for a trip to enigmatic Stonehenge, and the ancient hill forts and romantic castle ruins that litter the area.

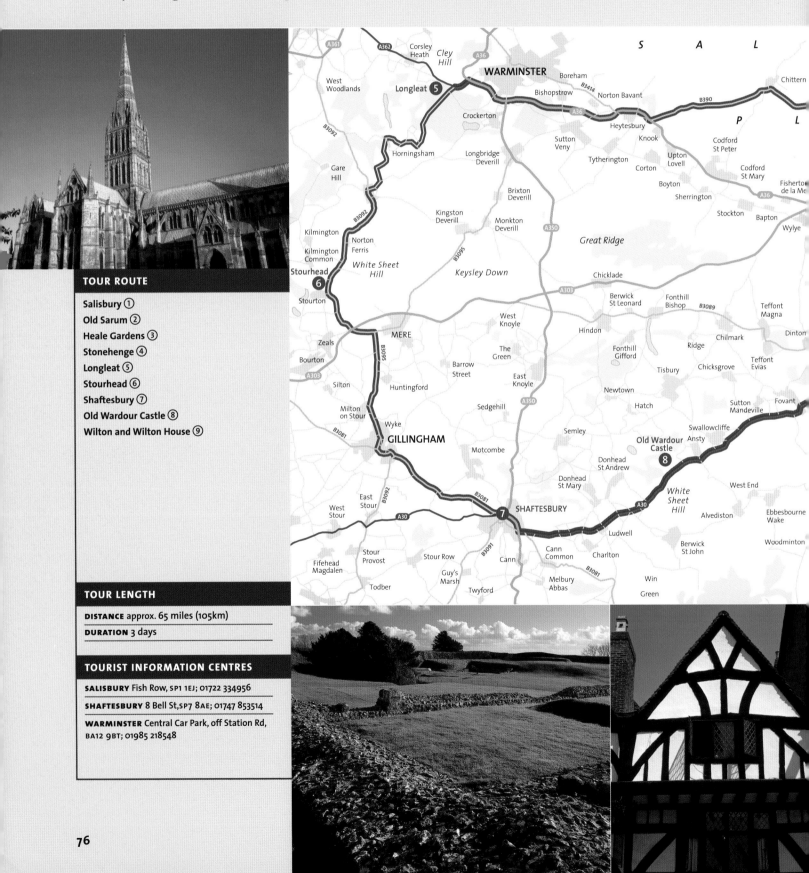

TOUR ROUTE

Salisbury ①
Old Sarum ②
Heale Gardens ③
Stonehenge ④
Longleat ⑤
Stourhead ⑥
Shaftesbury ⑦
Old Wardour Castle ⑧
Wilton and Wilton House ⑨

TOUR LENGTH

DISTANCE approx. 65 miles (105km)

DURATION 3 days

TOURIST INFORMATION CENTRES

SALISBURY Fish Row, SP1 1EJ; 01722 334956

SHAFTESBURY 8 Bell St, SP7 8AE; 01747 853514

WARMINSTER Central Car Park, off Station Rd, BA12 9BT; 01985 218548

Clockwise from far left:
Salisbury Cathedral;
Stonehenge; Stourhead;
Tudor House, Salisbury; Old
Sarum, Wiltshire

1 SALISBURY

Dominated by the soaring spire of its majestic
cathedral, Salisbury is an atmospheric market town
boasting everything from medieval halls to half-
timbered Tudor townhouses. The jewel in its crown is
the stunning cathedral, a showpiece of Early English
Gothic style complete with pointed arches, flying
buttresses and a serene sense of light and space.
Inside, a host of interesting tombs line the austere
nave, including that of a boy-bishop. In the north aisle
you'll also find what is thought to be the oldest
working clock in the world, while behind the high altar
is the modern and striking *Prisoners of Conscience*
stained-glass window. The four central columns of the
nave are visibly buckled from the weight of the 125-m
spire (404ft), the tallest in Britain. Despite remedial
work, the tower leans precariously and a brass plate in
the floor of the nave measures the incline. Before
leaving the church via the tranquil cloister, visit the
octagonal Chapter House with its delicate fan vaulting
and one of only four original copies of the Magna Carta.

The **Cathedral Close** – lined with impressive buildings
and museums – is one of the largest and most
beautiful in the country. Look out for the 13th-century
Medieval Hall and the glorious Queen Anne-style
Mompesson House, used as a location in Ang Lee's film
Sense and Sensibility. Around the corner, the 15th-
century **St Thomas's Church** contains a bizarre
judgement day painting depicting naked bishops and
Christ sitting on a rainbow. Narrow lanes still bearing
their medieval names lead from here to the market
square where traders have convened since 1219; today,
markets are still held every Tuesday and Saturday.

Take the A345 north out of
Salisbury for 2 miles and
follow the signs left
to Old Sarum. **2**

2 OLD SARUM

First established in the Iron Age, the massive hill fort of
Old Sarum was continuously inhabited up until the
Middle Ages, when the pope decreed that its cathedral
could move down the hill and into the valley. All that
now remains on the site are the ruins of the castle,
cathedral and bishop's palace – and the stunning
views over the valley below.

Continue north west on
unclassified roads via Lower
Woodford to Middle
Woodford and follow the
signs right to Heale Gardens.

3

⊕ *Continue on unclassified roads north from Middle Woodford to the A303, turn left and drive west until the road forks. Take the right fork onto the A360 and **Stonehenge** is*

4 *off to the left.*

3 HEALE GARDENS

A secret 17th-century hideaway of Charles II, Carolean Heale House is an imposing manor surrounded by fine gardens. Although the house is closed to the public, the beautiful gardens, partly laid out by Harold Peto in 1910, are worth a visit for the stunning herbaceous borders, shrub roses and the serene water garden with its Japanese tea-house and Nikko bridge.

4 STONEHENGE

Instantly recognisable and thronged with visitors, Stonehenge is Europe's most famous prehistoric monument. The mysterious stone circle was built by one of the world's earliest cultures, and work on the site began more than 5,000 years ago. Experts cannot agree on the original purpose of the stone circle, but the alignment of the inner horseshoe of stones with the rising sun at the summer solstice has lead to speculation that the site may have been used as a place of worship or ritual sacrifice or may even have been an astronomical clock. Everyone agrees, however, that the site was of incredible importance to the people of the time. Work continued on the site for 1,500 years, and the inner circle is made up of four-tonne megaliths that were dragged 250 miles from the Preseli Mountains in south Wales. The largest standing stones (each weighing about 50 tonnes) came from the Marlborough Downs, 20 miles away, and it is estimated some 600 men were needed to move each one.

*Head north west along the A360 across the Salisbury Plain, then turn right onto the A36. After 6 miles turn left onto the A362 and shortly after follow the signs left to **Longleat**.*

→ **5**

Clockwise from below: **Stonehenge; Wiltshire, Longleat safari park; the Pantheon and lake, Stourhead; Temple of Apollo, Stourhead**

5 LONGLEAT

The first British stately home to open its doors to the paying public, Longleat has wholeheartedly embraced the concept of commercialism and makes for an absorbing day out. It now flaunts everything from a drive-through safari park to a Postman Pat village and the world's largest hedge maze, where the average person gets lost for an hour and a half. It is somewhat astonishing to see giraffes, rhinos and lions roaming the grounds landscaped by 'Capability' Brown. The beautiful, highly ornate Elizabethan house contains many fine treasures, as well as the erotic paintings of the famously eccentric owner, Lord Bath.

*Head south on unclassified roads via Horningsham to the B3092. Turn left and drive south for 4 miles, then follow the signs right to **Stourhead**.* 6

6 STOURHEAD

The grand Palladian mansion at Stourhead is filled with Chippendale furniture and paintings by the Old Masters, and yet it pales in comparison to the gorgeous gardens that surround it. Laid out between 1741 and 1780, the landscaped grounds are heaving with neoclassical monuments and follies set around a large lake. A lakeside path meanders through mature growths of exotic trees and over ornamental bridges giving constantly changing views of the monuments and their rippling reflections. A longer walk leads to King Alfred's Tower, a 50m-high brick folly (165ft) affording great views over the estate and surrounding countryside.

*Continue south on the B3092 over the junction with the A303 and join the B3095 south through Gillingham and left onto the B3081 to **Shaftesbury**.* 7

⊕
Take the A350 south and
turn left onto the A30. Head
east for 6 miles until the
signposted turning on the
8 *left to Old Wardour Castle.*

Continue travelling north
*east on the A30 to **Wilton**.*
***Wilton House** is signposted*
to the right off the round-
about on Minster Street.

→ • • • • • • • • • • **9**

7 SHAFTESBURY

Lording it over the surrounding plains, the town of Shaftesbury is perched on an outcrop of sandstone and offers brilliant views over Blackmore Vale. At the height of its fortunes, the town boasted a castle, 12 churches and four market crosses. Its most famous attraction today is charming **Gold Hill**, a steep, curving cobbled street of thatched cottages used as a film location in *Far from the Madding Crowd* and in the classic Hovis bread advert. To see inside one of the quaint cottages pop into the **Shaftesbury Town Museum**, where you can also gain insight on the history of the town and its abbey. Once the richest nunnery in England, **Shaftesbury Abbey** was founded by Alfred the Great in AD888 and razed by Henry VIII 650 years later. Today only the foundations remain.

8 OLD WARDOUR CASTLE

One of the most romantic ruins in England, Old Wardour Castle has a stunning lakeside setting and a bloody, tormented past. Made famous by Kevin Costner's *Robin Hood: Prince of Thieves*, the unique six-sided castle was originally built by Lord Lovel in the 14th century and took its inspiration from French chateaux. By the early 17th century, it was the royalist Arundell family who ruled the roost, and in 1643 some 1,300 advancing Parliamentarians besieged the castle with only Lady Blanche Arundell and 25 men to defend it. They managed to hold out for almost one month before the castle was captured; the lady of the house was imprisoned and later executed. Six months on, a countersiege began, which ended only when gunpowder mines under the castle exploded and destroyed it beyond repair. The ruined castle soon became a backdrop for a new house, but to this day Lady Arundell's ghost is said to wander the castle ruins at twilight.

WOODFORD VALLEY TRAIL

North of Salisbury lies the Woodford Valley, renowned for its charming, riverside thatched cottages. Though it makes a pleasant drive, it is best appreciated on foot, and there is an easy, circular waymarked route that wanders through the valley from Upper Woodford, taking about three hours to complete. Head north from the Bridge Inn in **Upper Woodford** through a small wood and along the river to the picturesque villages of **Great Durnford** and **Wilsford**. From here the trail leads to **Normanton Down** where you can explore ancient burial mounds and take in fabulous views over Stonehenge. The route then circles back to Upper Woodford. A second, shorter trail starts in **Lower Woodford** and explores the lower river valley passing thatched homes, quaint estate cottages and a manor house en route.

Clockwise from far left:
Gold Hill, Shaftesbury;
Cube Room, Wilton House;
Palladian bridge,
Wilton House

9 WILTON AND WILTON HOUSE

Renowned for its carpet industry, the quaint market town of **Wilton** was once the ancient capital of Wessex and today makes a pleasant stopping-off point for its Georgian houses, riverside walk and numerous antique shops. Its real gem, however, is the exquisite **Wilton House**, home to the earls of Pembroke since 1542. The house was rebuilt by Indigo Jones after a major fire in 1647, and its sumptuous interiors feature elaborate plasterwork, ornate ceilings and a host of paintings by Van Dyck, Rembrandt, Poussin and Tintoretto. The beautiful gardens have attracted numerous film-makers: scenes from *The Madness of King George* and *Mrs Brown* were shot here, and the stunning Double Cube Room appears as the ballroom in *Sense and Sensibility*.

Leave Wilton heading
east on the A36 to
*return to **Salisbury**.*

WITH MORE TIME

If time permits, extend your route north via the sleepy village of **Tilshead** to look at its distinctive flint and stone buildings. Continue to **Edington**, where the priory – all that is left of a 14th-century Augustinian monastery – beautifully exemplifies the architectural transition from Decorated to Perpendicular style, with an unusual two-storey porch, medieval marble floors, Victorian mosaics and fine plaster ceilings. To the west in Bratton, you can stretch your legs on a steep climb to the **Westbury White Horse** *(left; see p77)*, which dates from the 18th century.

Hampshire and Surrey

'The Island' and its idyllic pleasures

Less than one mile from Hampshire's coast, yet half a world away, the Isle of Wight is a treasure-trove of sleepy thatched villages, rolling hills, rambling cliff-top walks, and medieval castles and manor houses. Its stunning scenery and tranquil atmosphere made the island a favourite haunt of Queen Victoria, Alfred, Lord Tennyson and Julia Margaret Cameron. It retains much of its Victorian character today. From the towering cliffs on its westernmost tip to the immaculately kept greens of the inland villages, the island is an enchanting enclave promising lazy summer days and rustic charm.

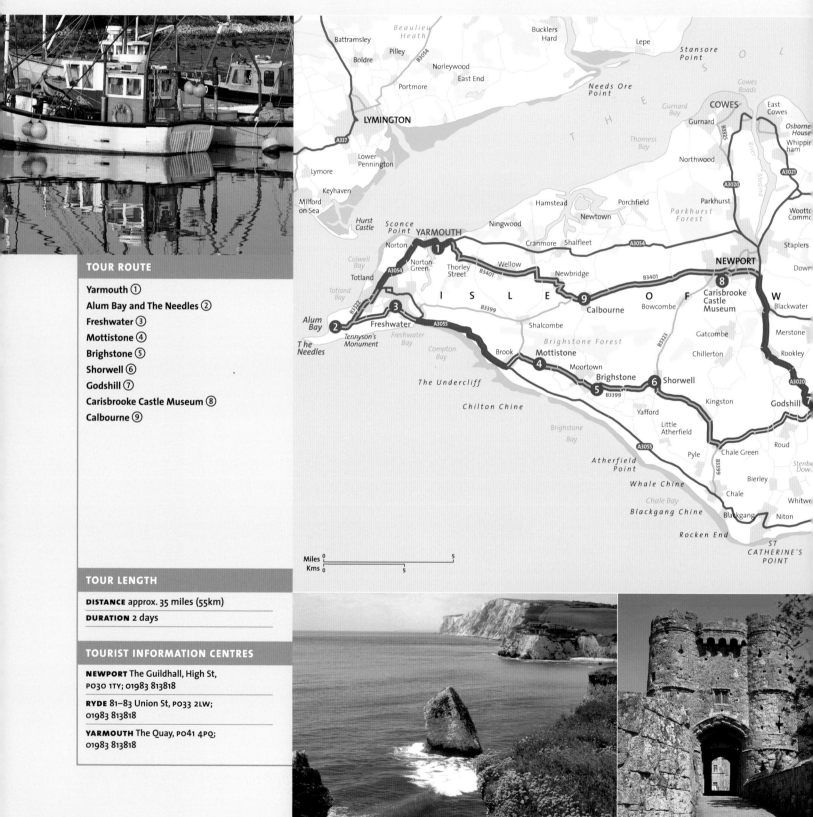

TOUR ROUTE

Yarmouth ①

Alum Bay and The Needles ②

Freshwater ③

Mottistone ④

Brighstone ⑤

Shorwell ⑥

Godshill ⑦

Carisbrooke Castle Museum ⑧

Calbourne ⑨

TOUR LENGTH

DISTANCE approx. 35 miles (55km)

DURATION 2 days

TOURIST INFORMATION CENTRES

NEWPORT The Guildhall, High St, PO30 1TY; 01983 813818

RYDE 81–83 Union St, PO33 2LW; 01983 813818

YARMOUTH The Quay, PO41 4PQ; 01983 813818

Clockwise from far left:
fishing boats, Yarmouth; The
Needles; Alum Bay; cottages,
Godshill; Carisbrooke Castle
Museum; Freshwater Bay

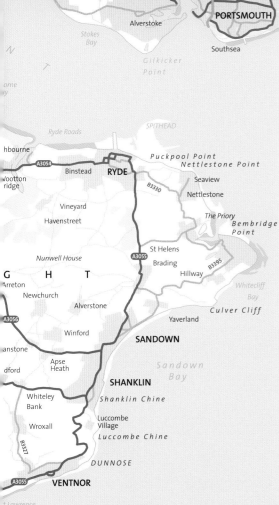

1 YARMOUTH

A short hop by car ferry from mainland Lymington *(see p91)*, the picturesque yachting centre of Yarmouth makes an attractive introduction to the Isle of Wight. The town was one of the earliest settlements on the island and still maintains an old-world aura long lost in other areas. Tucked between the quay and the pier, and lapped on two sides by the sea, is **Yarmouth Castle**, Henry VIII's final coastal fortification, hastily built in 1547 to improve defences after his beloved *Mary Rose* was attacked and sunk in the Solent. Conveniently, the king had recently dissolved two Hampshire monasteries and the stone was brought here to quickly construct the castle. Its design was pioneering, foregoing the traditional central tower for a square battery and gabled, arrow-head bastion. The castle houses exhibitions of paintings and photographs of the Isle of Wight, and the battery makes an excellent spot for a picnic on a fine summer's day.

*From Yarmouth, drive south west on the A3054 to Totland and continue on the B3322 to **Alum Bay** and **The Needles**.*

2 ALUM BAY AND THE NEEDLES

Famous for its multicoloured sandstone cliffs, sweeping **Alum Bay** is a stunning spot with an amusement park and souvenir shops on the cliff top. Take the chair lift down to the beach below to fully appreciate the spectacular views of the jagged chalk cliffs that lead out to The Needles, three towering chalk stacks rising from the sea. From Alum Bay a one-mile walk leads to the top of **The Needles** and the **Needles Old Battery**, a fort built on the cliffs in 1862. Used as a secret rocket testing site in the 1970s, its 60m (200ft) tunnel leads to a lookout point on the cliffs offering incredible views over the Needles and lighthouse below.

*Head north east out of Alum Bay on the B3322 and then turn right onto unclassified roads east to **Freshwater**.*

Take the A3055 4 miles
east, then turn left at Brook
and right onto the B3399
④ to *Mottistone*.

3 FRESHWATER

Extending east from The Needles, the impressive white cliffs of Freshwater lord it over the south of the peninsula as far as the quiet cove at Freshwater Bay. There's an exhilarating two-mile stretch of the Tennyson Trail *(see right)*, running east from The Needles to Freshwater Bay.

FAMOUS FACES AT DIMBOLA LODGE

It was in 1860, during a visit to poet Alfred, Lord Tennyson's home in Freshwater, that pioneering Victorian photographer Julia Margaret Cameron *(below)* fell in love with the area. She immediately bought two cottages in Freshwater, which she knocked together to form **Dimbola Lodge**. Having turned the coalhouse into a darkroom and the chicken coup into a conservatory, she set upon photographing Victorian VIPs with vigour, '...*all hands and hearts sympathised in my new labour, since the society of hens and chickens was soon changed for that of poets, prophets, painters and lovely maidens...*'. The house now contains a fascinating photographic museum starring Cameron's otherworldly portraits.

4 MOTTISTONE

Mottistone ('speaker's stone' in Old English) is the stuff of legend. Depending on whom you believe, it was the site of supernatural clashes or a place of ritual sacrifice. Either way, all that now remains are the two sandstone megaliths, probably once part of a Neolithic long barrow, and believed to be the oldest objects on the island. The larger standing stone was supposedly thrown here by a giant, while the smaller recumbent stone is apparently the mark of the devil. From Mottistone Common, where the stones are found, there are far-reaching views across to Freshwater Bay and down to the tenanted Elizabethan **Mottistone Manor Garden**. The superb gardens are well worth a visit for their colourful herbaceous borders and a beautiful organic kitchen garden.

5 BRIGHSTONE

Nestled in the lee of a forested hill, Brighstone is a pretty, little village with a stunning row of thatched cottages and a beautiful medieval church. Nearby is the quirky **Dinosaur Farm Museum**, which explains the island's geological history including why the swamps and ponds of the area were such perfect environments for the preservation of fossils and why, as a result, the island is one of Europe's top spots for dinosaur remains.

6 SHORWELL

Another picture-postcard village, with a placid cluster of ancient houses and thatched cottages surrounding the village green, Shorwell is a stunning place that makes a great base for walking. It is also less over-run with tourists than the island's coastal towns and villages. In the ancient church a massive 15th-century painting of St Christopher adorns the wall. North of the village, a wooden footbridge leads to a path through the woodlands up to **Chillerton Downs**, which makes a great setting for an afternoon stroll.

Continue driving south
east on the B3399 for
⑤ 2 miles to *Brighstone*.

Continue driving south east
along the B3399 for another
⑥ 2 miles to *Shorwell*.

Head south along the
B3399 to Chale Green and
turn left along unclassified
roads to *Godshill*.

→ • • • • • • • • • • • ⑦

7 GODSHILL

The implausibly picturesque village of Godshill is one of the island's most popular attractions with its gorgeous thatched cottages, meandering lanes and cosy coffee shops serving enormous cream teas to the summertime crowds. It was supposedly divine intervention that gave the town its name. Legend suggests that a mysterious force began moving the stones for the planned church from their original location to the top of the hill each night, and when two guards were placed on duty to solve the mystery, they saw the stones move of their own accord. Taking this as a sign from God, the **Church of All Saints** was built on the hilltop and the town was renamed in its honour. Inside the unusual church there are a variety of ornate tombs dating back as far as Tudor times and a stunning Lily Crucifix mural from 1440. Slightly younger and less divine, the **Model Village** in the gardens of the old vicarage captures life from times past in miniature.

Clockwise from far left: coastline, near Freshwater Bay; the Arch, Freshwater Bay; view through window, Carisbrooke Castle Museum; thatched cottage, Calbourne

TENNYSON TRAIL

The poet Alfred, Lord Tennyson lived at **Farringdon House** in Freshwater from 1853 to 1869, and the Tennyson Trail commemorates his connection with the island, linking some of his favourite spots. Possibly the best inland trail on the island, the 14-mile waymarked path wanders west from **Carisbrooke Castle** though hilly beech woods and along the ridge of the downs to the white cliffs at Freshwater, ending at The Needles. Here a summit monument *(below)* to the writer commands stunning views over the downs.

8 CARISBROOKE CASTLE MUSEUM

Imposing Carisbrooke Castle commands a strategic position on a hilltop and provides panoramic views from its battlements. Originally a Norman castle, it was extended, developed and many times fortified over the years, even though it saw little battle action. It was mainly used as a royal prison, its most famous inmate being King Charles I, who was imprisoned here for over one year. Despite having comfortable chambers and a bowling green built for his use, Charles made an abortive attempt to escape and became wedged in the bars of his window. One of the most interesting aspects of the castle is the opulent 13th-century chapel designed by Countess Isabella, who ruled the castle and the island for 30 years. The castle is also home to a team of donkeys, which demonstrate how barrels of water were raised from the depths of the 49m (160ft) well shaft.

9 CALBOURNE

Worth a quick stop off, the photogenic town of Calbourne is a tourist honeypot and much of its charm lies in Winkle Street, a curving row of stone houses and thatched cottages. The town also boasts the **Calbourne Water Mill and Museum**, with grinding demonstrations daily and punting on the mill pond.

Drive north on the A3020 towards Newport and turn left onto the B3401 on the outskirts of town. **Carisbrooke Castle Museum** *is on the left about one mile from this junction.* ⑧

Drive west along the B3401 to **Calbourne**. ⑨

Continue west on the B3401, then turn left on the A3054 to return to **Yarmouth**. ①

WITH MORE TIME

The magnificent Italianate villa at **Osborne House** *(left)* was built as a modest country retreat for Queen Victoria, and it was here that she retired to grieve when her beloved Albert died in 1861. Lavish, gilt furnishings and statues abound in the grandiose state rooms, while the intimate private quarters give a touching glimpse of royal family life. Surrounded by cascading fountains, terraced gardens and rolling parkland, it is well worth the detour north from Newport. It is a short hop from here to Georgian **Cowes**, the epicentre of British yachting since Regency times.

The New Forest's atmospheric woods and heathland

A patchwork of open heathland, ancient forest and Victorian ornamental drives make up England's most recent national park, a haven of tranquillity and a place still ruled by ancient laws and privileges. Almost untouched since it became the personal hunting ground of William the Conqueror in 1079, the leafy glades, picturesque villages and roaming wild ponies are a far cry from the bustling resorts of the south coast.

TOUR ROUTE

Christchurch ①
Brockenhurst ②
The Rufus Stone ③
Minstead ④
Lyndhurst ⑤
Beaulieu ⑥
Buckler's Hard ⑦
Lymington ⑧
Milford on Sea ⑨

TOUR LENGTH

DISTANCE approx. 55 miles (90km)

TIME 2 days

TOURIST INFORMATION CENTRES

CHRISTCHURCH 49 High St, BH23 1AS;
01202 471780

LYMINGTON New St, SO41 9BH;
01590 689000

LYNDHURST Main Car Park, SO43 7NY;
023 8028 2269

Miles 0 _____ 5
Kms 0 _____ 5

Clockwise from far left:
autumnal scene, New
Forest; ponies, New Forest;
pony trekking, near
Brockenhurst; typical
thatched cottage, New
Forest; tavern and Priory
Church, Christchurch

1 CHRISTCHURCH

Christchurch, with its beautiful harbour and enormous 11th-century **Priory Church**, is a little-known gem. According to local legend, its church was to be built in a different location, but each time the building materials were delivered, they were mysteriously moved overnight to the present site of the church. Now the longest-established parish church in the country, this spectacular Norman building boasts a glorious fan-vaulted porch, lovely medieval stone carvings, one of the oldest misericords in England and a stunning north transept. For some background on the church and town's heritage the nearby **Red House Museum** is worth a visit before strolling along the mill stream on Convent Walk to **Place Mill** on Christchurch Quay. The 900-year-old mill has been beautifully restored to display the ancient machinery as well as showcase local arts and crafts.

Take the A35 north east out
of Christchurch and turn
right onto the B3055 to
Brockenhurst.

2 BROCKENHURST

With a menagerie of ponies, donkeys and cows wandering freely through the village, drinking from the stream at the bottom of the high street and grazing on the surrounding heathland, Brockenhurst appears to have one foot firmly in the past. Situated at the heart of the New Forest, it makes an ideal base for exploration. To fully experience the serenity of the park, abandon the car and explore the network of gravel trails on foot or by bike. Brockenhurst also makes an ideal location for pony-treks into the forest, with several nearby stables offering trips.

Head west out of
Brockenhurst on the
Rhinefield Road, crossing
over the A35 and driving on
to the A31. Turn right and
head north east on the dual
carriageway for two-and-a-
half miles and then follow
the sign left for
The Rufus Stone.

Clockwise from above:
lake and village, Beaulieu;
Beaulieu Palace House;
National Motor
Museum, Beaulieu

⬇ *Return to the A31 and turn
left, almost immediately
turn right on unclassified
roads following the signs*
④ *to Minstead.*

⬇ *Drive 1 mile south
east out of Minstead on
the Lyndhurst Road
and turn right onto the*
⑤ *A337 to Lyndhurst.*

SCENIC DRIVES

The New Forest *(below)* is peppered with scenic drives and walks, but one of the best areas to roam is the section just north of Brockenhurst known as the **Rhinefield Ornamental Drive**. Here, the dappled light, majestic redwoods and giant Douglas firs re-create scenes from the enchanted forests of childhood stories. In spring the road is ablaze with rhododendrons, and you can walk from the Blackwater car park along a three-mile circular walk through a gorgeous avenue of the oldest and tallest redwoods in the forest, planted in Victorian times. Further on, across the A35 is the **Bolderwood Arboretum Ornamental Drive,** where you can see the fenced-off, 400-year-old Knightwood Oak, the forest's largest and most famous tree with a whopping girth of 7.4m (25ft). Just past here, at Bolderwood Green, the shy herds of deer that persuaded William the Conqueror to make the forest his hunting ground can be seen from a special viewing platform.

*Drive 8 miles south
east on the B3056
to Beaulieu.*

→ • • • • • • • • ⑥

3 THE RUFUS STONE

Cruel, greedy, manipulative and unjust, William the Conqueror's son, King William II, was neither respected nor well-liked among his peers and was nicknamed Rufus either for his red hair or his fiery temper. While out hunting one day, an arrow shot by one of his party glanced off a tree and fatally stabbed him in the eye. The Rufus Stone commemorates the spot where he fell; whether his death was by accident or intent no one knows.

4 MINSTEAD

A picture-postcard cluster of thatched cottages hugs the village green at Minstead, the former home and final resting place of Sir Arthur Conan Doyle, famed for his creation of detective Sherlock Holmes. Plucked from his upright grave in the garden of his East Sussex home, he was reinterred with his second wife, Jean, at the churchyard in Minstead in 1955. Nearby, the beautiful **Furzey Gardens** are famous for their year-round colour and a delightful thatched cottage.

5 LYNDHURST

Ancient rules setting down commoners' rights to turbary (peat cutting) and pannage (pig grazing) are discussed in the **Queen's House** in Lyndhurst, 'capital' of the New Forest and home to the Verderer's Court, the statutory body that regulates forest development. The tiny town is more famous, however, for its connection to *Alice in Wonderland*. Alice Liddell, the inspiration for Lewis Carroll's famous book, is buried in the churchyard here. Just on the edge of town is the picturesque Swan Green, a cluster of quintessential thatched cottages, which have appeared on many a chocolate box.

6 BEAULIEU

Now part of the Montagu family's sprawling estate, the quaint village of Beaulieu is set in the grounds of what was originally one of England's most influential monasteries. Little of the glory days of 13th-century **Beaulieu Abbey** remain except for the refectory, which is now the parish church and supposedly one of the most haunted places in Britain. The elaborate Gothic gatehouse, or **Palace House**, also survived and is now the Montagu family home. The most famous attraction here, though, is the **National Motor Museum** and its collection of 250 cars spanning the decades. Among them is landspeed racer *Bluebird* and a McLaren F1.

7 BUCKLER'S HARD

From Beaulieu it's worth abandoning the car and the crowds and making your way south on foot for a scenic four-mile round trip to the heritage town of Buckler's Hard. This pretty 18th-century village was originally a sugar port but soon became a naval shipyard and birth place of some of Nelson's most favoured vessels. For an interesting overview of village history visit the **Buckler's Hard Story**, a maritime museum with reconstructions of village life in the restored cottages along the quay. From Buckler's Hard you can take a relaxing cruise across the river to **Exbury Gardens**, which are famed for their rhododendrons, azaleas and camellias.

8 LYMINGTON

The bustling town of Lymington is at its busiest on Saturday mornings when the beautiful Georgian high street is taken over by a lively market. Behind the main street, a network of cobbled lanes full of tea rooms, gift shops, and displays of beach balls and buckets and spades runs down the hill to the busy quay. Packed with leisure boats and strolling visitors, Lymington is also the port for the Isle of Wight ferry. Just a short walk from the quay, you'll find the outdoor 18th-century **Roman Seawater Baths**, which are still in use, and the **St Barbe Museum and Art Gallery**, which tells the sailing and smuggling history of the New Forest coast.

9 MILFORD ON SEA

If you fancy some activity after all the driving, the pretty coastal town of Milford on Sea has a lovely swimming beach and a great, if arduous, return walk along a shingle spit to the atmospheric **Hurst Castle**, one of Henry VIII's coastal fortifications. Charles I was held prisoner here in 1648 before his trial and execution.

Follow the unclassified road south from Beaulieu signposted for Buckler's Hard. 7

Return to Beaulieu and turn left onto the B3054 to Lymington. 8

Drive southwest out of Lymington on the A337 and turn left after two miles onto the B3058 to Milford on Sea. 9

Drive west along the coastal B3058 until you rejoin the A337 and turn left to return to Christchurch.
← • • • • • • • • • • • • 1

WITH MORE TIME

Continue from Christchurch into **Bournemouth** to enjoy its sweeping seven miles of golden sands *(left)*. Relax on the beach, stroll through the gorgeous public gardens or take a tour of the Russell-Cotes Art Gallery and Museum, a fascinating place with a lavish collection of Japanese art and design, and Pre-Raphaelite paintings. For a little more excitement you could visit the flashy Oceanarium, with its flesh-eating piranhas and shark tunnels; or take a trip on the Bournemouth Eye, a giant, tethered balloon offering great views.

Around England's ancient capital

The capital of Alfred the Great's Wessex, Winchester is one of the country's most fascinating cathedral towns, with an extraordinary wealth of historic buildings and a delightful setting amid water meadows. Relics of its 2,000-year history are tucked away within a compact web of medieval streets, squares, gardens and alleys, making it an intriguing town to discover on foot. From Winchester, you can meander into the Hampshire countryside to explore rolling downland, sparkling trout-filled rivers and the ideally tranquil villages that provided the backdrop to the 19th-century novels of Jane Austen.

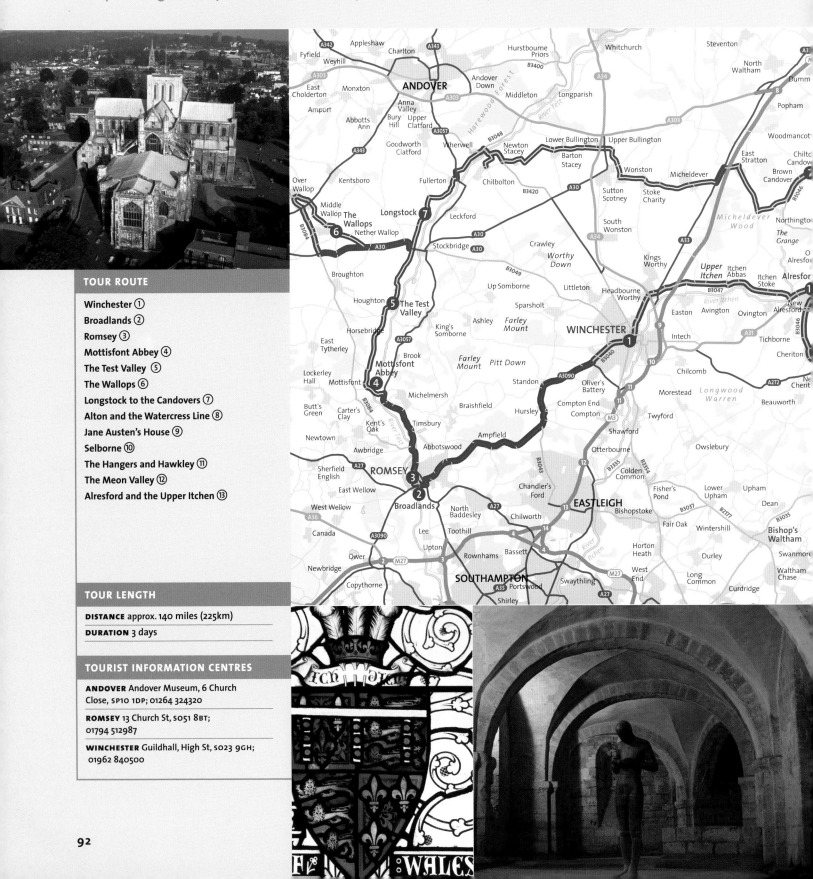

TOUR ROUTE

Winchester ①
Broadlands ②
Romsey ③
Mottisfont Abbey ④
The Test Valley ⑤
The Wallops ⑥
Longstock to the Candovers ⑦
Alton and the Watercress Line ⑧
Jane Austen's House ⑨
Selborne ⑩
The Hangers and Hawkley ⑪
The Meon Valley ⑫
Alresford and the Upper Itchen ⑬

TOUR LENGTH

DISTANCE approx. 140 miles (225km)

DURATION 3 days

TOURIST INFORMATION CENTRES

ANDOVER Andover Museum, 6 Church Close, SP10 1DP; 01264 324320

ROMSEY 13 Church St, SO51 8BT; 01794 512987

WINCHESTER Guildhall, High St, SO23 9GH; 01962 840500

1 WINCHESTER

Winchester's unique atmosphere is defined by a blend of historic charm, tranquillity and subtle stylishness. Forming a natural focus to the town is the majestic **Winchester Cathedral** and its grand close. The cathedral was begun in 1079, replacing an older Saxon version (the foundation outline of which is still marked out in stone slabs in the close). Inside, visit the library containing the astonishing Winchester Bible begun in 1160, and look out for the modest grave of Jane Austen in the north aisle.

The town's ancient alleyways are dotted with numerous smaller gems, including two exquisite Norman churches, **St Lawrence-in-the-Square** and tiny **St Swithun-upon-Kingsgate**. North of the close is the High Street, Winchester's main thoroughfare since Roman times, which runs uphill to belligerent-looking **Westgate**, where there are great views from the town's battlements as well as graffiti left by 17th-century prisoners. Beyond the gate is the **Great Hall** of Winchester's medieval royal castle, with its mysterious Round Table on one wall. Despite its associations with King Arthur, it actually dates to the Middle Ages, and was restored for Henry VIII in 1522.

South of the close are the imposing buildings of Winchester College, founded in 1382, as well as the house at 8 College Street where Jane Austen died in 1817 and the medieval ruins of **Wolvesey Castle**. From here, Keats' Walk – a lovely footpath beside the River Itchen that inspired John Keats to write his 1819 *Ode to Autumn* – leads south to the 12th-century **St Cross Hospital**, another of the town's impressive medieval monuments.

From Westgate roundabout in Winchester take the B3040 to join the A3090, Romsey Road heading south west. At the entrance to Romsey town, turn left into Broadlands. 2

2 BROADLANDS

This elegant Palladian-style mansion is famed as the birthplace and residence of the first Lord Palmerston and the former home of Lord Mountbatten. It was built in the 1730s amid stunning grounds designed by the great landscape artist 'Capability' Brown. Under the third Lord Palmerston, the Victorian prime minister, it became one of the most celebrated great houses in Britain, welcoming a flock of famous guests. You can tour Broadland's palatial rooms, see an exhibition on Mountbatten or linger in the lovely gardens.

Follow signs for Romsey town centre.
3

3 ROMSEY

This is perhaps the most charming of all Hampshire's small country towns, with a lovely square presided over by a statue of the great Lord Palmerston. Its jewel is **Romsey Abbey**, the finest purely Norman church in England, with a strikingly simple structure of towering columns and arches. The town residents bought the abbey from Henry VIII as their parish church in 1544 and so it survived the dissolution of the monasteries. Of note are the simple grave of Lord Mountbatten and the monument to Sir John and Grisell St Barbe of 1658, which features endearing effigies of the couple and their four sons. Nearby, the **King John's House and Heritage Centre** incorporates a carefully preserved Victorian gun shop in addition to a 13th-century residence featuring a remarkable room that was 'graffitied' with coats of arms by Edward I's nobles when they passed through Romsey in 1306.

Drive north on the A3057 Stockbridge road, and look out for a left turn signposted to
④ Mottisfont Abbey.

4 MOTTISFONT ABBEY

Mottisfont Abbey's distinction lies in its connection to a host of residents who have made their mark upon it. The house began as a 13th-century priory (the giant cellars of which can still be visited), but following the destruction of the monasteries it was acquired by the Sandys family, who built the present, unusual early-Georgian mansion. In the 1930s, Mottisfont was then bought by socialites Gilbert and Maud Russell, whose redecoration included a lovely room with whimsical trompe-l'œil murals by artist Rex Whistler (left unfinished when he joined the army in 1939). Also on show is the impressive art collection, bequeathed by painter Derek Hill, a friend of the Russells. It includes paintings by major artists such as Lowry and Dégas, which deviate from their usual artistic styles. Explore the delightful gardens to discover paths beside the River Test and an explosively fragrant national collection of old-fashioned roses in summer.

Drive into Mottisfont village and continue north on unclassified roads to Houghton and Stockbridge in **The Test Valley**.

⑤

Clockwise from below:
Mottisfont Abbey; The Test Valley; Romsey Abbey; cottages, Wherwell

5 THE TEST VALLEY

Celebrated for its trout fishing, the Test is one of England's prettiest rivers, flowing through lush meadows and between glittering 'bournes' or side-streams. The lane from Mottisfont runs through villages of heavy-lidded thatched roofs like **Houghton** and **Stockbridge**, once a crossing point for sheep and cattle drovers across the River Test. Lately Stockbridge has become a thriving centre for antiques, art and craft galleries, and it is known for its Michelin-starred restaurant, the **Greyhound**. For walkers, take the easy five-mile riverside stretch of the Test Way between Stockbridge and Mottisfont, passing through tiny Horsebridge with its fine old pub.

6 THE WALLOPS

West of Stockbridge are the three characterful Wallop villages. Tree-shrouded **Nether Wallop** has an entrancing partly Saxon church with wall paintings from the 10th to the 15th centuries, while just to the north is the brooding Iron Age hill fort of Danebury Hill. **Middle Wallop** is spread out across the downs and offers the **Museum of Army Flying** for military and aircraft buffs. **Over Wallop**, the smallest of the villages, is noted for its main street divided by flashing brooks and crossed by tiny bridges.

7 LONGSTOCK TO THE CANDOVERS

Meander east from lovely **Longstock** on minor roads stopping off en route at placid and picturesque villages that feel miles from anywhere. A lane north through Longstock leads to flower-bedecked, white-walled **Wherwell**, which along with its neighbour **Chilbolton** is one of the prettiest villages on the River Test. This is an area that can be explored on foot via the Test Way, which crosses Chilbolton Common, with its abundance of birds, and ancient Harewood Forest. From Chilbolton, still narrower lanes twist and turn through remote **Bullington** eventually to reach **Brown**, **Chilton** and **Preston Candover**, three attractive villages that thrived in the Middle Ages. Chilton Candover has a Norman underground crypt, buried and forgotten until the 1920s.

8 ALTON AND THE WATERCRESS LINE

The relaxing town of **Alton** has had a prominent market since Saxon times. It is also the eastern end of the **Watercress Line**, a 10-mile heritage railway line between Alton and Alresford. Run entirely by enthusiasts, it has steam and vintage diesel trains, operating regularly in season. Look out for 'special trains' – Victorian themed days, Christmas trains and more.

*In Stockbridge turn left onto the A30, then right on unclassified roads to **The Wallops**.* ⑥

*Drive south on the B3084 and turn left on the A30 to return to Stockbridge. Then take the unclassified road left to **Longstock** and wind eastwards along unclassified roads via Bullington to **The Candovers**.* ⑦

*From Preston Candover head east on unclassified roads through Bradley to meet the A339, then turn right to **Alton**.* ⑧

*Follow the A339 south out of Alton, cross over the A31 onto the B3006, then turn right to **Jane Austen's House** in Chawton.* ⑨

↓
Return to the
B3006 and turn
⑩ right for **Selborne**.

↓
Continue south on the
B3006 and turn right for
Empshott and continue to
⑪ **The Hangers** and **Hawkley**.

Follow signs south on
unclassified roads from
Hawkley via Steep to
Stroud, to meet the A272.
Turn right and then left in
Langrish for **East Meon**.
Continue south west from
here to **Droxford**, then turn
right and head north on
the A32 past **Exton** to
West Meon.

→ • • • • • • • • • • • • ⑫

9 JANE AUSTEN'S HOUSE

Jane Austen fans should not miss this charming house, where the writer lived with her mother and sister from 1809 to 1817, and wrote or completed all her novels. Its simple, snug and very feminine rooms and neat garden instantly recall the homes of the less wealthy characters in Austen's novels – those ladies who haven't ensnared a well-to-do husband – and the evocative furnishings include her tiny writing table. **Chawton** village too seems like a model for every Austen village, with its lines of old cottages, woods and rectory.

10 SELBORNE

No village in England has been more lovingly documented than Selborne. In 1789 the Reverend Gilbert White, the village rector and a pioneer naturalist, published his *Natural History of Selborne*, describing its plants, birds, animals and even folklore in great detail. **Gilbert White's House** – beautifully restored with the gardens he created – is a perfect example of a Georgian rectory, and has an inspiring display on White's work. Oddly, the house was bought for the nation by the family of the explorer Captain Oates, who died with Captain Scott in Antarctica in 1912, and so it also contains the **Oates Museum**. Selborne is one of Hampshire's loveliest villages, boasting a Norman church dating from 1180 atop a giant hill or 'hanger' *(see right)* with lovely views and the unusual zig-zag footpath laid out by White himself.

JANE AUSTEN'S HAMPSHIRE

Jane Austen's life was inextricably linked to her native county, and although she moved to Bath for a few years and gathered plenty of inspiration in the city, it was in Hampshire that she was happiest. Austen *(below)* was born in 1775 in Steventon, outside Basingstoke, where her father was rector, and she lived there until he decided to retire to Bath in 1801. Mr Austen's death left Jane, her mother and sister with a much reduced income, and they moved back to Hampshire, to Southampton in 1806, and in 1809 to the much-loved house at Chawton. Austen stayed here until May 1817, when her health deteriorated and she moved to 8 College Street in Winchester, to be nearer her doctor. She died there two months later and was buried in Winchester Cathedral beneath a stone that notoriously makes no mention of her extraordinary literary success.

11 THE HANGERS AND HAWKLEY

A series of surprisingly steep-sided hills in East Hampshire are known as **The Hangers**. Writer William Cobbett explained the name by describing them in 1830 as being so steep that 'the trees and underwood hang... to the ground, instead of standing on it'. Wander along the roads or paths between the Hangers and you feel as if you've entered Hampshire's own miniature rainforest, with dense vegetation soaring up around you. The most impressive and famous hangers are found around **Hawkley**, where there are many beautiful places for walking along paths trodden by Cobbett and Gilbert White.

12 THE MEON VALLEY

South west of The Hangers runs another superlative trout stream, the Meon, beloved by the great fishing writer Izaak Walton, who sang its praises in his *Compleat Angler* of 1653. Along the River Meon there are also beds for growing watercress – one of the region's foremost products. Some of the prettiest heart-of-England villages are located along this stretch. At **East Meon**, you'll find an 11th-century Saxon church and the great Ye Olde George pub. From here lanes lead south west towards the river at delightful **Droxford** – Walton's favourite fishing-spot – and then north to ravishing **Exton**. A little further north still, the South Downs Way leads up Old Winchester Hill, a giant grassy down with the remains of an Iron Age fort and fabulous views. Continuing north, **West Meon** has some of Hampshire's best fishing spots, and a churchyard with two notable graves: those of Thomas Lord, founder of Lord's cricket ground in 1814, and Soviet spy Guy Burgess, who was brought back here by his family after he died in Moscow in 1963.

13 ALRESFORD AND THE UPPER ITCHEN

'New' **Alresford**'s official title is somewhat well worn, since it dates from the 12th century when the town was created by the Bishop of Winchester as an extension of Saxon Old Alresford, which lies one mile to the north. Today, Alresford is a strikingly pretty, mostly Georgian country town, with an unusually wide main street that was built for medieval sheep trading and appropriately named Broad Street. Considered one of the finest streets in England, it leads to a delightful riverside walk. From Alresford follow the road or St Swithun's Way footpath along the **Upper Itchen** back to Winchester through more watercress villages, such as charming **Itchen Abbas** and leafy **Easton**, a great base for invigorating walks.

Clockwise from far left: dining room, Jane Austen's House; Upper Itchen Valley; Gilbert White's House, Selborne

WALKING IN HAMPSHIRE

Hampshire has an exceptionally good network of long-distance footpaths, many of them also cycle and bridle paths. The **Test Way** is one of the prettiest and one of the easiest to explore in a few short 'chunks' of a couple of hours' walk. It runs the length of the Test Valley from Eling, near Southampton, to Inkpen Beacon near Newbury, passing through many lovely, tree-shrouded spots along the glistening river. Other walking highlights are the long paths that run west to east across the county: the **Clarendon Way** from Salisbury to Winchester; **St Swithun's Way**, north east from Winchester through Alresford towards Canterbury; and the superb **South Downs Way** south east from Winchester to Eastbourne, crossing Old Winchester Hill and the tops of the downs, affording fabulous views. Shorter paths include the **Hangers Way** south of Alton, and the **Meon Valley Trail** along a disused rail track from Wickham to West Meon. All the footpaths can be broken up into easy-to-handle stretches of a few miles or less, and leaflets with maps and details are available from all local information offices.

Continue north on the A32 and turn left onto the A272, then right onto the B3046 to Alresford and The Upper Itchen. **13**

Follow signs westwards on the B3047 to return to Winchester.

1

WITH MORE TIME

A detour south east of Winchester takes you to the charming old market town of **Bishop's Waltham**, centred around the atmospheric stone ruins of a palace. Begun in the 12th century by one of Winchester's wealthy bishops, this was one of the most opulent medieval residences in England. Further east near Petersfield, over 575ha (1,400 acres) of the South Downs have been made into the **Queen Elizabeth Country Park** *(left)* a magnificent expanse of woods and downland with great walking, cycling and riding trails as well as countless fine picnic spots.

Stately mansions and picture-perfect villages of the Surrey Hills

The beautiful countryside, picturesque villages and magnificent country houses and gardens of Surrey seem a world away from the nearby suburban sprawl of Greater London. You won't have to look far to discover Norman churches, snug country pubs, appealing market towns and gracious architecture, while the delightful woods and trails of the North Downs beckon the walker at almost every turn.

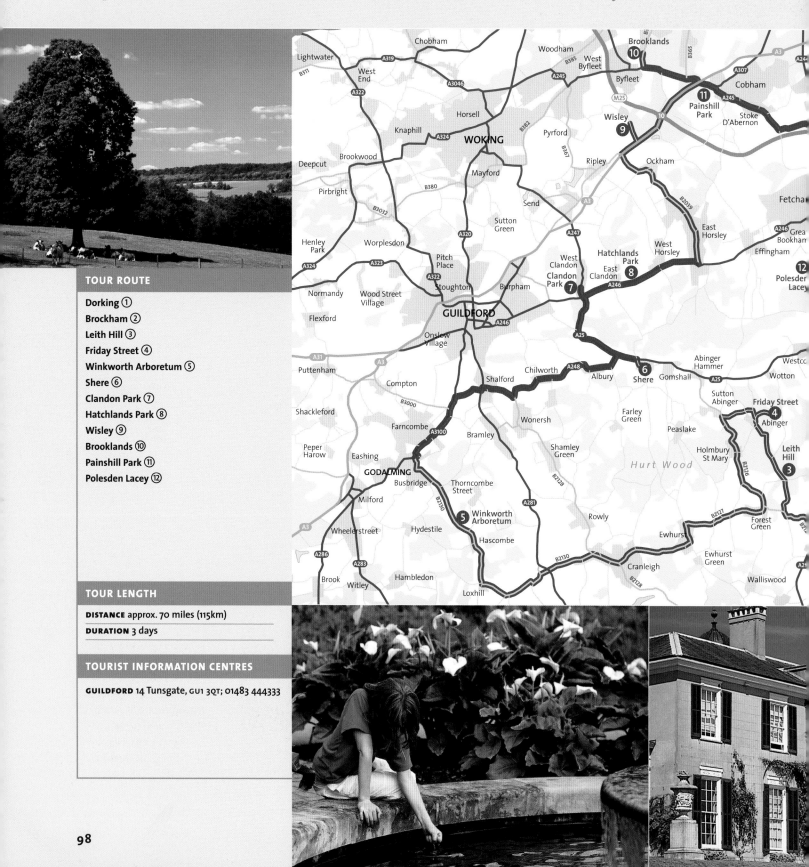

TOUR ROUTE

Dorking ①
Brockham ②
Leith Hill ③
Friday Street ④
Winkworth Arboretum ⑤
Shere ⑥
Clandon Park ⑦
Hatchlands Park ⑧
Wisley ⑨
Brooklands ⑩
Painshill Park ⑪
Polesden Lacey ⑫

TOUR LENGTH

DISTANCE approx. 70 miles (115km)

DURATION 3 days

TOURIST INFORMATION CENTRES

GUILDFORD 14 Tunsgate, GU1 3QT; 01483 444333

Clockwise from far left:
countryside, near Shere;
vineyards, Painshill Park;
cottage and church,
Brockham; Polesden Lacey;
RHS's gardens, Wisley

1 DORKING

Nestled in a gap in the North Downs, the historic market town of Dorking makes a pretty starting point for a tour of the surrounding, treasure-filled area. It is well worth strolling the high street with its higgledy-piggledy skyline of different architectural styles, ranging from timber-framed medieval inns to larger, grander Victorian and Edwardian buildings, all of them dwarfed by the mighty, 64m (210ft) spire of **St Martin's Parish Church**. Dorking was not always as quiet and civilised as it is today; horse races were periodically staged up and down the high street and a wild and often bloody version of football occasionally took place through the town. And on market days the town would really come alive.

There is still a market on Fridays, although it is a shadow of its former glory. Any day is a good day to browse the antique shops along West Street or follow the self-guided heritage trail, which explains the town's varied architecture and its many historical, literary and artistic links. Novelists Daniel Defoe and E M Forster lived in Dorking, Dickens drew inspiration from the town for the *Pickwick Papers* and composer Ralph Vaughan Williams grew up here and collected folk songs from the area.

*Head east out of Dorking on the A25 and after about 1 mile and a half turn right to **Brockham**.* ②

2 BROCKHAM

Brockham is a charming, photogenic village with a large green, a steepled Victorian church, two pubs and a bridge over the River Mole. It's a rewarding stop.

*Return to Dorking on the A25 and turn left onto the A24 heading south. At Beare Green turn right onto the A29, then right onto the B2126. Shortly after take the right turning following signs for **Leith Hill**.*

→ • • • • • • • • • • ③

Clockwise from above:
bluebell woods, Leith Hill;
White Horse pub, Shere;
Clandon Park; Winkworth
Arboretum

*Continue north on the
same road around the
south-western edge of
Leith Hill heading north
towards Abinger. Turn
right to **Friday Street** after
④ about half a mile.*

*Drive west to the B2126,
turn left heading south,
then turn right at Forest
Green onto the B2127.
Drive through Cranleigh
and join the B2130. Turn
right at the signs to
Winkworth Arboretum.*

⑤

BOX HILL

Box Hill has been a favoured spot for centuries,
since pilgrims on their way to Canterbury
stopped here. A measure of its popularity with
the leisured classes of Regency England is its
appearance in Jane Austen's novel *Emma*; a day
trip to Box Hill forms a pivotal, and painful,
moment of self-awareness for the heroine.

It is a mighty steep trudge up to Box Hill's
chalky summit, but it more than repays the effort
with breathtaking views *(below)* across a great
sweep of captivating Surrey and Sussex countryside. Several delightful nature trails meander
through woods and open downland, home to
rare flora including a dozen orchid species (May
to July) and the rare box tree. The colours in
autumn are stunning. A **visitors centre** at the
hill's summit offers some excellent background
on the locale and its rare plant species.

3 LEITH HILL

Commanding extraordinary views in every direction,
Leith Hill is a fantastic way to get to grips with a great
swathe of southern England. On a clear day, you can
see over the Surrey Hills as far as the Kent Hills and
even the Chilterns 50 miles away. Crowning the hill is
the 314m-high **Leith Hill Tower** (1,029ft), now sadly
closed due to centuries of vandalism. This gothic folly
was built in 1765 by the eccentric Richard Hull, who is
buried beneath it. Legend has it that Hull is buried
vertically and upside down (apparently due to his
belief that the world would turn on its axis on
Judgement Day, which he wanted to greet facing the
right way up). Several nature trails take in some lovely
hazel and oak woodland, home to rare fauna including
stonechats and woodlarks. It is a tranquil scene that's a
far cry from the events of AD851 when the Anglo
Saxons under Ethelwulf, father of Alfred the Great,
defeated the Danes here in a pitched battle of tens of
thousands of men, during which rivers of blood were
said to have flowed down the hill.

4 FRIDAY STREET

Nestled in a steep, wooded valley, this small, enhanting
hamlet has a decent gastropub and some excellent
walks nearby. Most of the buildings, hewn from local
stone, are more than 100 years old.

5 WINKWORTH ARBORETUM

Dr Wilfred Fox, an amateur horticulturalist, chose this unspoiled pastoral and wooded valley 'patterned with hedgerows and abounding with wild flowers' in which to establish this impressive arboretum in 1937. It is home to more than 1,000 plant species, including mountain ash and whitebeam, and is ablaze with colour in autumn and in spring and summer when the magnolias, bluebells and azalias are in bloom. A lovely raised walkway leads round the peaceful lake.

*Continue north on the B2130 into Godalming and join the northbound A3100. Turn right onto the A248, then right onto the A25 and right again into **Shere**.* ⑥

6 SHERE

White ducks glide across the River Tillingbourne, which runs wide and clear through heavenly Shere, quite simply the prettiest village in the area. Timber houses, some of them built by the architect Edwin Lutyens, look onto a pretty village green graced by a spreading oak. The **St James' Parish Church**, partly Norman but mainly medieval, is a magnificent edifice and contains some delightful treasures including 14th-century stained-glass windows. There is also a huge, 800-year-old crusader chest and a fine bronze Madonna and child statuette, probably lost by a Canterbury-bound pilgrim passing along the adjacent Pilgrim's Way, and unearthed nearby. It's worth stopping off at the 400-year-old White Horse pub for a drink.

7 CLANDON PARK

The fine 18th-century interiors of this Palladian mansion are the most compelling (but by no means the only) reason to visit Clandon Park. Huge marble-clad fireplaces compete for impact with lavish stuccos depicting classical Greek myths, but it is the vast, spectacularly decorated state rooms that most take the breath away. Amongst this splendour is an impressive collection of English furniture and exquisite Oriental and English porcelain. An unexpected discovery in the grounds is a Maori house with a rather curious history. Originally sited on New Zealand's North Island, the house became a refuge for Maori residents when the volcano Mount Tarawera erupted in the late 19th century, entombing the area in ash and soot. The residents, who survived, eventually abandoned the house, which was later dismantled by the then governor of New Zealand, Lord Onslow, and reassembled here at the family seat.

*Return to the A25 and turn left, briefly join the A247 and then turn left for **Clandon Park**.* ⑦

*Rejoin the A247 and turn right heading south, then turn left onto the A246, left into East Clandon and follow the signs to **Hatchlands Park**.* ⑧

Drive east on the A246,
turn left onto the B2039 at
East Horsley and then right
on the A3. Shortly after, turn
9 left following signs to **Wisley**.

Rejoin the northbound A3,
turning left at the Painshill
junction onto the A245.
Turn right onto the B374
and follow the signs
10 left to **Brooklands**.

8 HATCHLANDS PARK

Set in 175ha (430 acres) of graceful, landscaped wood and parkland, Hatchlands Park is a classic country mansion. The ornate formal gardens were the creation of Gertrude Jekyll, while much of the grand interior was designed by Robert Adam. The nautical motifs (friezes of Neptune, anchors and such) were commissioned by owner Admiral Edward Boscowen, a hero of the battle of Louisburg in Canada in 1758. Jostling for attention among the maritime knick-knacks are some fine Flemish, English and Dutch paintings. The world-class Cobbe Collection housed here offers a comprehensive history of keyboard instruments, many of them played by legendary composers including Bach, Chopin and Elgar.

9 WISLEY

The jewel in the Royal Horticultural Society's crown, Wisley is a 25-ha property (60 acres) of garden and woodland and charming Tudor half-timbered houses. The gardens re-create a wealth of environments, and were established to cultivate difficult-to-grow plants. There is plenty to see in the gardens proper including a glorious alpine meadow (covered by petticoat daffodils in spring and crocuses in autumn), yew-hedged monocot borders, a Mediterranean garden and an extensive plant centre. Wisley's Battleston Hill and Arboretum contain many wonderful specimens flowering from early in the year through to autumn, including fantastic magnolia, rhododendron and camellia plantings, heather beds and a varied mix of trees.

10 BROOKLANDS

This superbly presented museum site, richly redolent of the golden ages of the car and plane, makes a riveting half day. From 1907, when it was built, to the 1960s, Brooklands became synonymous with wealthy daredevils, such as world land speed record holders Malcolm Campbell and Kenneth Lee Guinness, who vied to be fastest round the purpose-built Grand Prix race track. Brooklands soon attracted aviation pioneers and British aeronautical excellence and innovation too, witnessing the first flight of a British-designed aircraft (by Thomas Sopwith), as well as the development of innovative and record-breaking planes. Aircraft on display include the Wellington Bomber and the VC10 airliner.

Return to the A245 and
turn left, then cross the A3
towards Cobham. The
turning to **Painshill Park** is
200m (650ft) east of the
A245/A307 roundabout.

11 PAINSHILL PARK

You almost expect to encounter a Jane Austen heroine strolling through the elaborately landscaped grounds of 18th-century Painshill Park, so reminiscent is it of the many country park scenes in Austen's novels. The park's creator, Charles Hamilton, found a inspiration in the lavish gardens he visited on a Grand Tour of Europe and in the wild, dramatic landscapes by Romantic painters such as Poussin. As you wander through the grounds, a series of carefully contrived vistas are revealed, peppered with fanciful romantic follies including a rustic hermitage, a Bacchanalian temple, a Gothic tower, a grotto and a ruined abbey. The story of this labour of love is a sad one: Hamilton, the younger (and so impecunious) son of an aristocrat, borrowed extensively to build the garden but had to sell it to repay his debtors, his only souvenir a series of paintings of his beloved gardens. His outstanding legacy remains, however, for all to enjoy.

12 POLESDEN LACEY

In a striking North Downs location, Regency-era Polesden Lacey is preserved largely as its last private owner, Mrs Ronald Greville, left it when she died in 1942. Greville was renowned for hosting fabulous house parties for the rich and famous of Edwardian society. Her collection of fine paintings, furniture, porcelain and silver is displayed in the reception rooms and galleries. There are extensive grounds and landscaped walks through the enormous estate. The garden – itself 12ha (30 acres) – is a splendid example of Edwardian orderliness and refinement with lawns and elegant grass terraces, a walled rose garden, summer border and winter displays. It is no wonder the future King George VI and Queen Elizabeth chose to spend part of their honeymoon here in 1923.

Clockwise from far left: gothic temple and lake, Painshill Park; painting, Polesden Lacey; vintage car, Brooklands

Follow the A245 south east to Leatherhead, then take the B2450 Dorking road south. Join the A24 continuing south and turn right via Westhumble to Polesden Lacey. 12

Head back to the A24 and turn right to return to Dorking.

WITH MORE TIME

Why the British Royal family doesn't occupy the magnificent **Hampton Court Palace** *(left)* rather than the cramped Windsor Castle is a wonder. It is one of the finest and most splendid historic houses in the country. There's the famous maze, the Real Tennis courts, the 230-year-old Great Vine, the vast kitchens (staffed by 200 servants during King Henry VIII's reign) and the extensive and lavish chambers and reception rooms replete with historical furnishings and Renaissance paintings. It is said that the ghosts of two of Henry's wives, Catherine Howard and Jane Seymour, still stalk the palace's rooms. Home to hundreds of fallow deer, the gardens and parkland alone offer more than enough to occupy an absorbing day.

East and West Sussex and Kent

In the footsteps of the Romans

Quite different in character from the open, rolling grass downs of East Sussex, this stretch of the South Downs is often thickly wooded and more imposing. Captivating at any time of year, the delightful expanse is at its blazing best in autumn. Palaces built by the nobility and wealthy elite have been dominant features of the landscape from the days when Romans prospered here through medieval times right up to the present day. It is a heavenly corner of Sussex, and one that also boasts unspoilt and uninterrupted stretches of coast and glorious lengths of fine, golden sand.

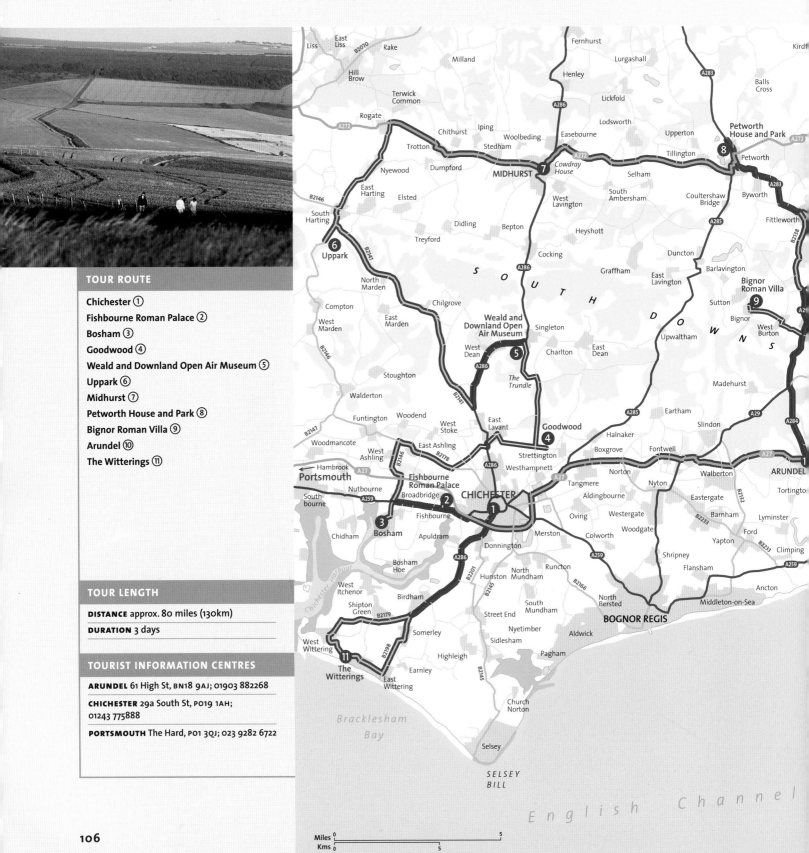

TOUR ROUTE

Chichester ①
Fishbourne Roman Palace ②
Bosham ③
Goodwood ④
Weald and Downland Open Air Museum ⑤
Uppark ⑥
Midhurst ⑦
Petworth House and Park ⑧
Bignor Roman Villa ⑨
Arundel ⑩
The Witterings ⑪

TOUR LENGTH

DISTANCE approx. 80 miles (130km)

DURATION 3 days

TOURIST INFORMATION CENTRES

ARUNDEL 61 High St, BN18 9AJ; 01903 882268

CHICHESTER 29a South St, PO19 1AH;
01243 775888

PORTSMOUTH The Hard, PO1 3QJ; 023 9282 6722

Miles 0   5
Kms 0   5

Clockwise from far left:
walkers, South Downs;
Petworth House and Park;
Chichester Cathedral;
mosaics, Fishbourne
Roman Palace

1 CHICHESTER

The best way to take in the many architectural gems, parks and gardens of this one-time Roman coastal settlement is to follow the circular walk around the city walls. Crowning the grand cityscape is Chichester's Gothic **cathedral**, its soaring spire so tall it is visible from the sea. The interior harbours several modern works of art including a stained-glass window by Marc Chagall and tapestries by John Piper. Also within the city walls, you'll find the **Tudor Market Cross**, marking the intersection of the city's four main Georgian thoroughfares, now lined with shops. Art enthusiasts should make time for the **Pallant House Gallery**, which exhibits a strong collection of modern art featuring artists such as Cézanne, Moore and Sutherland. Housed in a new extension, the gallery's Wilson Collection comprises more than 500 works of British pop and figurative art, including work by Lucian Freud.

Take the westbound A27 out of Chichester on to the A259 and then turn right after about 1 mile at the signs for Fishbourne Roman Palace. ②

2 FISHBOURNE ROMAN PALACE

The ruins of this spectacular Roman villa were accidentally uncovered by workmen in 1960, and so extensive is the site that archaeologists have only recently finished excavations. Vivid audio-visual displays around the museum offer plenty of insight into the lavish levels of comfort enjoyed at the palace, and an artist's impression of the original house suggests wealth of oil-tycoon proportions. Exquisite floor mosaics – the most spectacular of which depicts Cupid astride a dolphin – reveal the extraordinary talent of the artists involved, while evidence of a sophisticated under-floor central heating system highlights the technological ability of the artisans employed by the villa's owners.

Return to the A259, turn right heading west until the roundabout at Broadbridge, then turn left and follow the signs into Bosham. ③

*Return to the A259, cross it onto the B2146, then turn right onto the B2178. Head through East Ashling and turn left after about a mile onto the unclassified road to meet the A286. Turn left and then almost immediately right into East Lavant. Take the road heading south east from here past Goodwood Aerodrome Motor Racing Circuit and follow the signs left for **Goodwood**.*

3 BOSHAM

It is not the only delightful little waterside village in Chichester harbour, but as the first recorded place of Christian worship in Sussex, Bosham is without doubt the most historically interesting. In the 7th century, long before St Wilfred or St Augustine began converting the heathen Britons, an Irish monk named Dicul began to preach here. He slept in a small cell that still exists below the Saxon **church**. The church is thought to be one of the oldest in the country, although the structure standing today dates back to the reign of King Canute, who lived at Bosham for a time in the 11th century. The skeleton of an eight-year-old girl found beneath a stone slab bearing the Danish emblem of a raven is said to be that of Canute's daughter. Like many places Canute stayed, Bosham claims to be the place where he attempted to order the sea's retreat. Fanciful perhaps, but somewhat apt since the high tide laps to the edge of the village's shore-side cottages.

4 GOODWOOD

Situated in a breathtaking spot on a grandly wooded section of the South Downs, Lord March's Sussex pile occupies the loveliest of settings. Magnificent Regency interiors provide the backdrop for a fine collection of furniture, porcelain (including an extensive Sèvres collection) and paintings with works by Canaletto, Stubbs, Van Dyck and Reynolds. The typically Sussex-style flint walls of the house blend harmoniously with both the surrounding land and the nearby turf-roofed Rolls Royce factory, which turns out the £250,000 Phantom luxury cars (visits by arrangement). Cars are a popular theme in the area: each summer the Festival of Speed is held here *(see right)*, while the nearby **Goodwood Aerodrome Motor Racing Circuit** is a venue for regular classic car club gatherings and races.

It is worth making time for an enjoyable, slightly surreal stroll through the wooded glades and rolling parkland of the 10-ha **Sculpture Park** (26 acres) where you will chance every now and then upon one of the diverse sculptures; a 9-m orchid (30-ft) maybe or even a squat, rusting, industrial installation.

*Head back to Goodwood Aerodrome Motor Racing Circuit and turn right driving north on the unclassified road. Bear left just north of the Trundle and continue to the **Weald and Downland Open Air Museum** just before Singleton.*

5 WEALD AND DOWNLAND OPEN AIR MUSEUM

An architectural history lesson and a heartening example of restoration and preservation at its best, this museum recreates some 50 houses, gardens, farmyards and workshops through the ages from the 13th to the 19th centuries. There is a strong emphasis on recreating the livelihoods, crafts and tasks of those who would have lived and worked in these places. Many buildings have been restored to working order, including the flour-grinding watermill and the Tudor kitchen, which turns out period dishes such as sweetmeats.

*Continue to Singleton and turn left on the A286, then turn right onto the B2141. Turn left onto the B2146 and look out for the sign for **Uppark** on the left.*

SEASONAL SIGHTS AND FESTIVALS

Different times of year have their own distinct appeal in this diverse area of Sussex. In spring, bluebells and primroses carpet the wooded hillsides as the beech trees unfurl early leaves; while in autumn, the beech-, oak- and chestnut-covered downs are ablaze with stunning ochres, yellows and gold.

June and July are the months to visit for an exceptional calendar of events, three of which are hosted at Goodwood. **Glorious Goodwood** (late July) is the main horseracing meet; the **Festival of Speed** (June or July) is a spectacular jamboree of races, hill climbs and celebration of classic cars; and the **Goodwood Revival** (September) celebrates the golden era of Goodwood race track. Another starry gathering and polo's main annual event is the **Gold Cup**, contested at Cowdray House (June or July), while nearby Petworth House plays host to the **Petworth Festival** (July), a jazz and classical music extravaganza. Last but not least the **Chichester Arts Festival** (July) is a vibrant arts and culture festival.

Clockwise from above:
Midhurst; cottage, Midhurst;
stained-glass window,
Uppark; interior,
Goodwood House

6 UPPARK

Perfectly proportioned and occupying grounds of storybook beauty, National Trust-owned Uppark is like an ornate scaled up doll's house. It is an idyllic setting for an unlikely romance and an inspiring tale of triumph over adversity. The romance comes in the form of its 19th-century owner Sir Harry Featherstone-Hough, a 70-year-old bachelor who married his 20-year-old dairy maid. They lived together in the house for 20 years, during which time they made no changes to the interior. Subsequent owners preserved this wonderful time capsule maintaining the best-kept 18th-century house in Britain. Disaster struck in 1989 when a raging fire partially destroyed the shell of the building. Miraculously, however, the bulk of the paintings, furniture and other furnishings were salvaged, enabling an amazingly complete restoration. The grounds, laid out in 19th-century Picturesque style, overlook a great sweep of downland and coast, making an excellent picnic venue.

Head north on the B2146
to South Harting and
take unclassified roads
via Nyewood to the A272.
Turn right on the A272
to *Midhurst*. ⑦

7 MIDHURST

Escape from Midhurst's busy high street and you'll discover a delightful medieval town centre with an attractive muddle of period houses, including the 15th-century Spread Eagle (one of the oldest hotels in England) and a cluster of well-cared-for cottages. The pleasing streets and passageways – with equally pleasing names such as Knockhundred Row – include several tempting pubs and hostelries. At the edge of town stands the imposing ruin of the once magnificent **Cowdray House**, destroyed by fire in 1790.

Take the A272 east out
of town and follow it into
the centre of Petworth.
Petworth House and Park is
signposted to the left.

→ • • • • • • • • • • • ⑧

⊻ *Take the A283 south and
turn right on to the B2138
at Fittleworth. Turn right
onto the A29 and then
right again on unclassified
roads through West Burton*
⑨ *to **Bignor Roman Villa**.*

8 PETWORTH HOUSE AND PARK

High, forbidding walls (with a 10-mile circumference)
were built to screen this huge, stately 17th-century
mansion and its extensive grounds from the prying
eyes of locals. Within this boundary, the estate reveals
many treasures including the huge deer park,
landscaped by 'Capability' Brown and painted by Turner.
The most compelling reason to visit, however, is the
collection of paintings inside the house. It is the National
Trust's largest and most significant art collection with
works by Blake, Reynolds, Van Dyke and, of course,
Turner. Among the rich furnishings are extraordinarily
lavish, ornate carvings by Grinling Gibbons.

9 BIGNOR ROMAN VILLA

It may not be quite on the grand scale of Fishbourne
Roman Palace *(see p39)*, but Bignor Roman Villa is
nonetheless well worth a visit for its large, well-
preserved and stunning mosaics. The one that graces
the villa's north corridor is, at 24m (80ft), the largest
surviving Roman mosaic in Britain. Look out for several
beautifully rendered classical scenes including
gladiatorial battles, Venus and Cupid and the elegant
Medusa in what was once the bathhouse.

*Return to the A29 at Bury
and turn right heading
southbound. Turn left on
the A284 to **Arundel**.*

→ • • • • • • • • • • ⑩

Clockwise from far left:
Arundel Castle; townhouse,
Arundel; coastline, the
Witterings; gardens,
Petworth House and Park

10 ARUNDEL

The unmistakeable attraction in the pretty town of Arundel is the towering, stout-walled **castle**, which dominates the landscape for miles around. The seat of the powerful and well-connected Dukes of Norfolk for 850 years and counting, it has a long and illustrious history pre-dating Norman times. (The first castle is said to have been built by King Alfred.) The massive stone halls display a valuable and eclectic range of the dukes' riches including tapestries, stained glass, china, heraldic antiquities and armour. Look out for Morglay, said to be the mighty sword of Bevis, a giant who guarded the castle in exchange for a weekly payment of an ox and two hogsheads of beer. Legend has it Bevis threw the 1.75m (5ft 9in) blade (now kept in the armoury) from the battlements to mark the place where he was to be buried.

Arundel town itself is worth a stroll for the elegant townhouses, the pretty cottages that tumble down the hilly lanes and for its towering **cathedral**. The tombs of medieval knights inside are somewhat misleading since this is infact a Victorian Gothic fantasy designed by Joseph Hansom (inventor of the Hansom taxi cab) and completed in 1873.

11 THE WITTERINGS

Just a short drive from the bustle of Chichester, the Witterings offer the most magnificent stretch of coast in Sussex. The long golden strand extends along an unbroken line from the apostrophe-shaped west head to the wave-lapped tip of **Selsey Bill** to the east. Sailing, surfing, fishing and windsurfing are all popular pursuits, but simply strolling along these flat open spaces is a delight. Equally enjoyable is a visit to the the relaxed villages of **West** and **East Wittering**, where you can wander around the small chandleries, arts-and-crafts boutiques, cafes, pubs and windmills.

Take the A27 to the Stock-
bridge roundabout south of
Chichester. Turn left onto the
A286 heading south and
then right onto the B2179
to West Wittering. From
here continue east to
East Wittering. ⑪

Head north on the B2198
back to the A286 to
return to Chichester.

WITH MORE TIME

A short drive west from Chichester lies **Portsmouth** with its dozen museums and a rich maritime heritage. The star attraction is the Historic Dockyard and its museum dedicated to Henry VIII's ill-fated flagship the *Mary Rose*, painstakingly raised from the sea. Nearby, the *HMS Victory (left)* is the ship from which Nelson secured a stunning defeat of continental Europe's most powerful navies and aboard which he died in the same battle. As such, it is a wonderful piece of maritime history. For unrivalled views of the harbour ascend the new 170-m Spinnaker Tower (560ft).

Hidden treasures of the South Downs

An area of gentle and enchanting beauty, this stretch of Downs and Weald is environmentally and aesthetically rich. Nestling in undulating grass-clad hills are stately beech woods, horticulturally splendid gardens, rivers flowing lazily to wave-lapped estuaries, pebble beaches and the natural ramparts of chalk sea cliffs. There is also plenty to see of historical and cultural interest in the region's mighty castles, venerable houses, downland villages and historic towns. The vibrant metropolis of Brighton, meanwhile, has been a hedonist's home-from-home since Regency days.

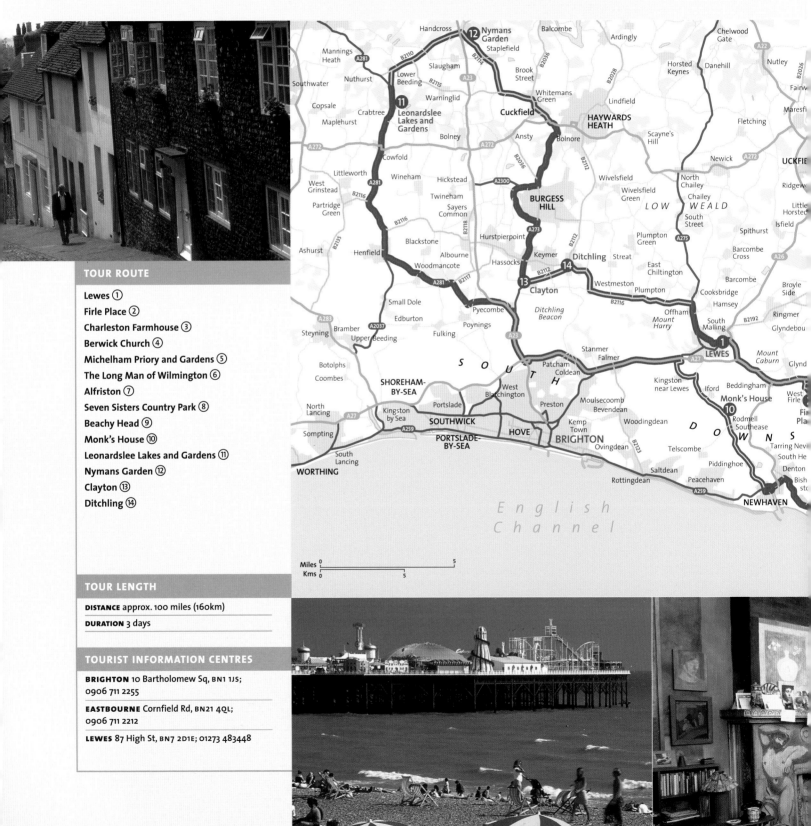

TOUR ROUTE

Lewes ①

Firle Place ②

Charleston Farmhouse ③

Berwick Church ④

Michelham Priory and Gardens ⑤

The Long Man of Wilmington ⑥

Alfriston ⑦

Seven Sisters Country Park ⑧

Beachy Head ⑨

Monk's House ⑩

Leonardslee Lakes and Gardens ⑪

Nymans Garden ⑫

Clayton ⑬

Ditchling ⑭

TOUR LENGTH

DISTANCE approx. 100 miles (160km)

DURATION 3 days

TOURIST INFORMATION CENTRES

BRIGHTON 10 Bartholomew Sq, BN1 1JS; 0906 711 2255

EASTBOURNE Cornfield Rd, BN21 4QL; 0906 711 2212

LEWES 87 High St, BN7 2D1E; 01273 483448

Clockwise from far left:
cottages, Lewes; Beachy Head;
studio items, Firle Place;
studio, Charleston Farmhouse;
Palace Pier, Brighton

1 LEWES

Compact and rich in history, Lewes offers much to the visitor along its steep, rambling lanes, many lined with black-timbered Tudor houses. Some are of historical significance, including **Bull House** (on the corner of Bull Lane) where the American revolutionary Tom Paine lived and worked as an excise agent before making his name in the American fight for independence. The town centre is an ideal place to potter among the quirky antique shops, second-hand booksellers and cosy tearooms that occupy the ancient timbered buildings.

Dominating the town is the imposing Norman **Lewes Castle**, which once defended this important pass through the South Downs. It is a wonderful place to take in the town's lovely setting among hills, river and meadows. Lewes is also famous for its annual bonfire parade when the townsfolk parade in costume, burn Papist effigies (along with other unpopular characters of the moment) and roll flaming tar barrels through the streets.

Head south out of Lewes on the A26, turn left onto the A27 and look out for the right-hand turning to Firle Place.

2 FIRLE PLACE

Set at the foot of the South Downs within its own parkland, Firle Place (limited opening hours in summer only) has been home to the Gage family for more than 500 years and contains a magnificent collection of Old Master paintings, porcelain and fine English and European furniture. **Firle Beacon** is within walking distance to the south east of the house and offers some grand views across the Sussex Weald.

Return to the A27 and continue east, then take the right-hand turning to Charleston Farmhouse.

⊕ Drive back to the A27 and
continue east, then take
the right-hand turning to
④ **Berwick Church**.

⊕ Head back onto the A27,
continue east for a few
hundred yards to the
roundabout, take the
exit left for Upper Dicker
and follow the signs on
unclassified roads via
Arlington to **Michelham**
⑤ **Priory and Gardens**.

Drive south on unclassified
roads to the A27. Cross over
the A27 and continue to
Wilmington village, then
head south through the
village following the
signs for **The Long Man
of Wilmington**.

→ • • • • • • • • • • • ⑥

3 CHARLESTON FARMHOUSE

There is something of the Marie Celeste about
Charleston, a secluded, delightful farmhouse that was
the home of the influential Bloomsbury Group *(see
right)* for almost half a century. This loosely connected
group of writers, artists and thinkers in Edwardian
England included writer Virginia Woolf. Virginia's sister,
Vanessa, an artist, and her art critic husband Clive Bell
set up home in 1916 with the artist Duncan Grant at
Charleston, and the house been maintained much as
they left it. Inside the pretty, creeper-clad house, the
painted walls, doors and furniture inspired by Italian
fresco and Post-Impressionist painting are a vibrant
testament to their talents. The impressive art collection
includes work by Renoir, Picasso, Derain, Matthew
Smith, Sickert, Tomlin and Delacroix. Outside, there is a
distinct Italian flavour to the walled garden with its
mosaics, box hedges and gravel pathways.

THE BLOOMSBURY GROUP

More of a loose affiliation of like-minded,
forward-thinking individuals than a coherent
artisitic, intellectual or literary movement, the
Bloomsbury Group nonetheless comprised an
influential set of people, who congregated in this
part of Sussex. They included the economist J M
Keynes, whose theories have become a central
part of economic theory, and Clive Bell, an
influential art critic and early champion of
Cézanne, Van Gogh and Picasso. The novelist
Virginia Woolf was arguably the most celebrated member of the group, known for her
advanced feminist ideas and the power and
originality of her writing. The group's members
rejected the era's strict religious, artistic, social
and sexual mores. Many were gay or bisexual
and most had liaisons with more than one
partner. By the end of World War II, Virginia
Woolf had committed suicide and the group
had disbanded, although the Bloomsbury way
of life continued at Charleston Farmhouse
(below) for several decades afterwards.

4 BERWICK CHURCH

The fabric of this historically and artistically rich church
is mainly Norman, but it was pre-dated by a wooden
Saxon building. In medieval times, local archers
gathered here for practice and sharpened their arrow
heads on the tower by the font (the marks remain)
before fighting in many of the important French
campaigns of the era. Another compelling draw is the
vivid series of religious murals painted by Bloomsbury
artists Duncan Grant, Vanessa Bell and her children.

5 MICHELHAM PRIORY AND GARDENS

This beautiful, historic moated house in Upper Dicker
dates back to 1229. Originally a priory, today it offers a
range of attractions including antique furniture and
tapestry, gardens with abundant wildlife, art exhibitions
and a working water mill. The annual Garden Sculpture
Trail each summer features works by local artists.

Clockwise from far left: self-portrait by Vanessa Bell, Charleston Farmhouse; Alfriston; The Long Man of Wilmington; façade, Charleston Farmhouse

6 THE LONG MAN OF WILMINGTON

Who is he, who created him and what does he represent? There are many theories about what this giant outline of a man on the northern flank of the South Downs signifies and how old it is, but no-one knows for sure. It certainly dates back to the 18th century, but could be the work of a medieval monk, ancient Britons or even earlier prehistoric people. It is an intriguing mystery in a lovely downland setting.

*Wind your way on unclassified roads south through Lullington, then north and west to **Alfriston**.* 7

7 ALFRISTON

It is easy to while away a rewarding half day in and around captivatingly pretty Alfriston. The busy high street of this quintessential downland village offers a number of antique shops along with several attractive teahouses and pubs. The **Alfriston Clergy House**, the first property owned by the National Trust, is a fine thatched medieval building with a delightful cottage garden. Just north of Alfriston, the **English Wine Centre** sells a selection of local white wines and gourmet goodies.

*Continue south on unclassified roads to the A259. Turn left and look for the signs to the **Seven Sisters Country Park** car parks on either side of the road.* 8

Rejoin the A259 and head east until East Dean village and then turn right to **9** **Beachy Head**.

Return to the A259 and turn left, heading west through Seaford and Newhaven. Just after Newhaven turn right onto unclassified roads through Piddinghoe to Rodmell, then follow the signs right **10** *to the* **Monk's House**.

Continue north on unclassified roads through Ilford and join the west-bound A27. Turn right onto the A23 and then left on the A281. Travel north past Cowfold to Crabtree and follow signs to **Leonardslee** **11** **Lakes and Gardens**.

Head north along the A281 and turn right onto the B2110. At Handcross turn right onto the B2114 and follow the signs to **Nymans Garden**.

→ • • • • • • • • • • • **12**

8 SEVEN SISTERS COUNTRY PARK

Several important natural habitats and some beautiful, but incredibly diverse, scenery occupy this 280-ha corner (700 acres) of Sussex. Extensive beech woods lie immediately to the north, while along the snaking River Cuckmere there are meadows rich in birdlife. At the river mouth the pretty Birling Gap estuary overlooks the towering white chalk cliffs. Seven cliffs are visible from here, hence the name Seven Sisters.

9 BEACHY HEAD

The bracing coastal pathway along the white cliffs of Beachy Head are a suitably dramatic opening for the 106-mile South Downs way. At 175m (575ft), the height of the cliffs is dizzying, particularly when you gaze down at the waves crashing on to the pebble beach far below.

10 MONK'S HOUSE

This modest weatherboard house with a large garden was the country retreat of novelist Virginia Woolf and her husband Leonard. Here, they entertained an elite group of writers and thinkers including E M Forster, Maynard Keynes and T S Eliot. There are a few remnants and mementos of Virginia Woolf's presence (including her ashes, which are buried in the garden) plus paintings, furniture and china by Vanessa Bell and Duncan Grant, who lived at nearby Charleston Farmhouse *(see p114)*. The house offers a beautiful view across the River Ouse to the South Downs, as well as an attractive flint-walled formal garden and an orchard planted with spring daffodils and autumn crocuses.

WALKS IN THE SOUTH DOWNS

For a scenic and reasonably challenging four-mile circular walk, park your car in Clayton *(see right)* and head east from the Jack and Jill pub (across the playing field from Clayton church). Walk along the road hugging the base of the downs and follow the gentle, wooded path up along the ridge to the top of Wolstonbury Hill (an old Iron age fortification). Then return down the steeper section on the north western flank of the hill and back along the road to the pub. A short but steep alternative walk begins along the path beside the church and leads to the **Jack** and **Jill windmills**. The views at the top are well worth the effort and Jill, which still grinds corn on occasion, is open to the public.

11 LEONARDSLEE LAKES AND GARDENS

This glorious 100-ha wooded valley (240 acres) is famous for its ornamental trees and shrubs, including a spectacularly colourful riot of rhododendrons, azaleas, camellias and magnolias. Autumn is a good time to visit, as is spring when the bluebells are out and the rock garden is in full blaze. Leonardslee also has important collections of bonsai and Alpine plants and exotic fauna such as Sika, Fallow and Axis deer, and there is even a tribe of wallabies.

Clockwise from bottom left:
rhododendrons, Leonardslee
Lakes and Gardens; the cliffs,
Seven Sisters; Nymans Garden

12 NYMANS GARDEN

More than 100 years in the making, National Trust-owned Nymans is one of Sussex's great gardens, internationally recognised for its collection of rare plants. The landscaping style of the 240-ha grounds (600 acres) ranges wildly from rustic meadow to carefully manicured ornamentation. Around the ruined old house, elegant topiary and borders come alive with summer colour. Beyond lie lakes, woods and the wild meadow, where you'll find many of the garden's historic collection of plants and trees from around the world.

13 CLAYTON

This tiny, but delightful, one-pub hamlet lies at the foot of the downs in the shadow of the **Jack** and **Jill windmills**. The star attraction here is the ancient Saxon **church**, built circa 1100, and enclosed by a small, serene churchyard. In the nave, there is an incredibly rare 12th-century fresco artwork depicting the Last Judgement.

14 DITCHLING

Ditchling is a lovely Sussex village with a couple of appealing pubs, antique shops, a pretty churchyard and the odd historic building, such as the **Anne of Cleves House**. This was part of Anne's divorce settlement from Henry VIII (although it is thought she never visited the house). Ditchling has something of a reputation for being a hub for artists, thanks largely to the controversial genius Eric Gill, a celebrated sculptor, typographer and engraver who lived here in the early 20th century.

Due south of Ditchling up a steep, narrow road lies **Ditchling Beacon**. One of the highest points on the South Downs, it offers magnificent views across the Weald and is an ideal base for rambling. Several paths radiate from here but an especially good two- to three-hour walk heads west along the well-signposted ridge to the Jack and Jill windmills *(see left)* and back again.

Head south on the B2114 and continue to the A273. Turn right and head south to **Clayton**. ⑬

Head east on the B2112 to **Ditchling**. ⑭

Take the B2116 and turn right onto the A275 to return to **Lewes**. ⓵

WITH MORE TIME

The charms of arty, hedonistic **Brighton** are numerous, but the city's historic and architectural show stopper is the Royal Pavilion *(left)*, an 1822 Indian-inspired fantasy brimming with over-the-top oriental opulence. The revamped, pebble-beached seafront is best experienced between the tacky but entertaining Palace Pier and the derelict West Pier. North west of the Palace Pier, the narrow, cobbled alleyways known as the Lanes offer a rich hunting ground for antique, art and curio hunters, as well as countless trendy cafes, bars and restaurants.

Great houses and gardens on top of the Downs

Rolling hills, wooded valleys, orchards, wild heathland and ancient villages form the fabric of the Weald of Kent and Sussex. Turn off the main roads to discover tunnel-like lanes beneath verdant arches of beech and larch, which open up suddenly onto broad crests with fabulous vistas. Thanks to its proximity to the capital, this area is blessed with a wealth of grand mansions and gardens, most created on top of the downs, with superb views.

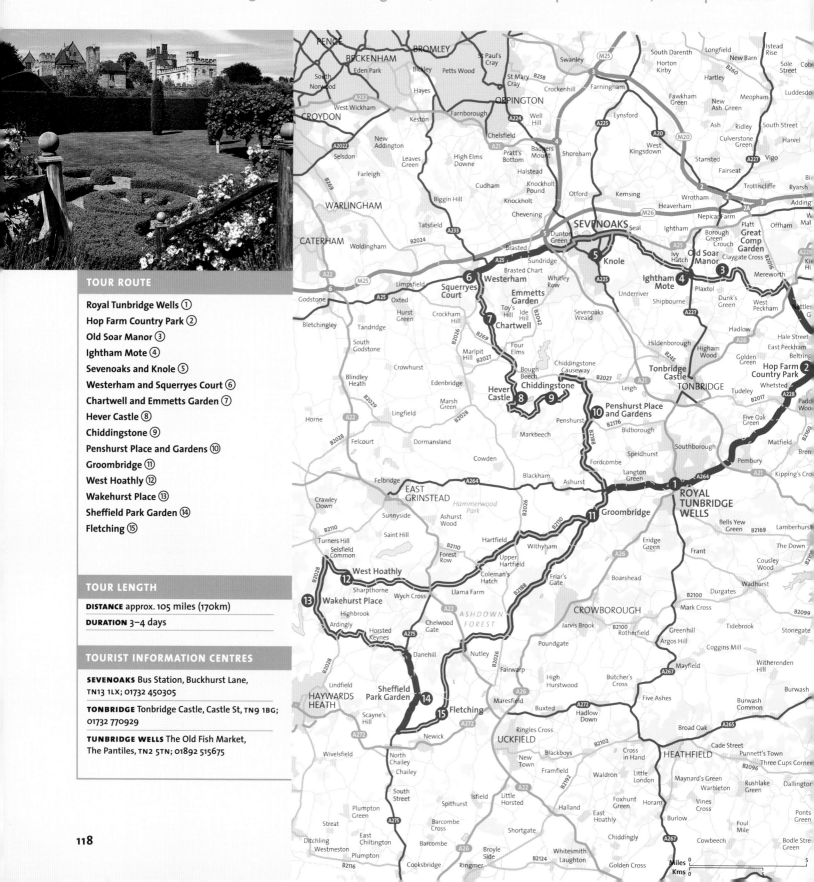

TOUR ROUTE

Royal Tunbridge Wells ①
Hop Farm Country Park ②
Old Soar Manor ③
Ightham Mote ④
Sevenoaks and Knole ⑤
Westerham and Squerryes Court ⑥
Chartwell and Emmetts Garden ⑦
Hever Castle ⑧
Chiddingstone ⑨
Penshurst Place and Gardens ⑩
Groombridge ⑪
West Hoathly ⑫
Wakehurst Place ⑬
Sheffield Park Garden ⑭
Fletching ⑮

TOUR LENGTH

DISTANCE approx. 105 miles (170km)

DURATION 3–4 days

TOURIST INFORMATION CENTRES

SEVENOAKS Bus Station, Buckhurst Lane, TN13 1LX; 01732 450305

TONBRIDGE Tonbridge Castle, Castle St, TN9 1BG; 01732 770929

TUNBRIDGE WELLS The Old Fish Market, The Pantiles, TN2 5TN; 01892 515675

Clockwise from far left:
Penshurst Place and
Gardens; Sheffield Park
Garden; oast houses, Hop
Farm Country Park; Italian
Garden, Hever Castle; maze,
Hever Castle; interior, Knole

1 ROYAL TUNBRIDGE WELLS

In spite of its stuffy and conservative reputation,
Tunbridge Wells is a charming town to explore and
an ideal base for visiting the area. At the heart of
the old town is the Pantiles, a delightful 18th-century
colonnaded walkway, harbouring an attractive mix of
restaurants, antiques dealers and stylish boutiques.
At its northern end lies the Chalybeate Spring, where
Lord North discovered 'healing waters' in 1606, thus
establishing Tunbridge as one of England's most
fashionable spas. Nearby, the **Church of King Charles
the Martyr** is one of very few English churches dedicated
to a monarch. After the restoration of the monarchy in
1660 some of the returned Cavaliers were so devoted
to the memory of King Charles I, and so eager to
take revenge on the ousted Cromwellians, that they
commissioned this beautifully serene church in the
king's name. It has a magnificent ceiling by Henry
Doogood, chief plasterer to Sir Christopher Wren.

*Take the A264 out of
Royal Tunbridge Wells to
Pembury. From there follow
the A228 north east to the
**Hop Farm Country
Park** in Beltring.* 2

2 HOP FARM COUNTRY PARK

This immaculate old farm has Kent's largest surviving
concentration of traditional oast houses, the brick
'pinnacles' used for drying hops. Several now host the
Hop Story Museum, which vividly recreates the days –
which continued right up until the 1950s – when the
crop was the county's foremost product and thousands
of East Enders flocked to work in the harvest every year.
The 'Decades Experience', on the rest of local life since
1900, a World War II exhibit, shire horses and many child-
friendly attractions add to the farm's varied programme.

*Continue north on the A228
to the A26 junction and
take the B2016 north. Soon
afterwards turn left on
unclassified roads to West
Peckham. Fork right in West
Peckham and continue
until the turning for **Old
Soar Manor**.* 3

↧
*Continue west on
unclassified roads via
Plaxtol to the A227. Turn
right, then take the
first turning left to Ivy
Hatch, then left again*
④ *to Ightham Mote.*

3 OLD SOAR MANOR

An extraordinary relic of the Middle Ages, Old Soar Manor has survived almost unchanged since it was constructed in 1290 through being incorporated into different farms that were built and rebuilt around it. This little stone manor house was originally the home of a local knight, and its spiral staircase and plain, vaulted chambers still give a strong sense of what life was like here. Old Soar itself is a placid village offering great walks just south in **Gower's Hill** woods, plus a three-mile footpath to Ightham Mote.

4 IGHTHAM MOTE

Enclosed by a moat and surrounded by stables, woods and magnificent gardens in a snug valley, this wonderfully atmospheric stone and half-timbered manor house seems almost too pretty to be real. Begun around 1330, it is associated with Sir Robert Clement, a courtier of Henry VIII, who added fine Tudor woodwork and other decorative flourishes to the original medieval courtyard. For 300 years it was home to the Selby family, but its last owner was American businessman Charles Robinson, who left it to the National Trust in 1985. Following a painstaking restoration programme, the house and its gardens can now be appreciated in their full glory. Wander through the chambers and up the creaking staircases to discover the marks left by Ightham's many occupants – stone chambers with shoes buried in the walls for good luck, the Tudor chapel with a painted ceiling, rare 18th-century wallpaper and an elegant Victorian billiard room with exquisite Jacobean wood panelling. Outside, explore the walled gardens, or enjoy the longer lakeside woodland walk. Nearby, **Ivy Hatch** is a charming old village with a very enjoyable pub, while **Stone Street**, another village to the north, has several fine oast houses.

*Return to Ivy Hatch and
turn left for Seal. In Seal
turn left onto the A25 to
Sevenoaks. **Knole** is
just south of the town
off the A225.*

→ • • • • • • • • • • • ⑤

Clockwise from far left:
grand staircase, Knole;
timber-framed house,
Westerham; Ightham Mote;
Squerryes Court

5 SEVENOAKS AND KNOLE

Sevenoaks is a pleasant town with a charming old centre of narrow lanes, 17th- to 18th-century buildings and shops with plenty to interest the antique-, art- and book-browser. The east side of the town is filled by the expansive deer park that surrounds **Knole**, the largest private house in England. This very grand Elizabethan mansion – with an alleged 365 rooms – has been home to the Sackville family since 1603. Knole's first Sackville owner, the Earl of Dorset, was a favourite courtier of Elizabeth I, who, as a sign of his status, lavishly extended the original 15th-century mansion. Centuries later, the house was the birthplace of Vita Sackville-West, and the setting for Virginia Woolf's novel *Orlando*, revealing Woolf's fascination with Vita and her family. The many treasures on display reflect the Sackvilles' eventful history and their royal connections, with paintings by Reynolds, Gainsborough and Van Dyck, and superb collections of rare 17th-century furniture, carpets and silverware. These items include many pieces that once belonged to King James I, as well as the 'Knole Settee', the original of a design that has been copied by furniture-makers ever since it was first made around 1610. The glorious Knole park, with its herd of graceful sitka deer, makes for an idyllic and tranquil picnic spot.

THE GHOST OF IGHTHAM MOTE

Ightham Mote's ghost story originates from the Gunpowder Plot of 1605. At the time, the house was owned by the Catholic Selby family, several of whom were involved in the conspiracy to blow up the king and parliament on the 5th of November. Dame Dorothy Selby sent a letter to her cousin Lord Mounteagle warning him to stay away from parliament on that day. The letter was intercepted, alerting the authorities, and Guy Fawkes was subsequently discovered in the parliamentary cellars with 36 barrels of gunpowder. Some of the plotters were so enraged with Dame Dorothy that they allegedly sealed her up in Ightham's tower. Her chilly presence has supposedly been felt there ever since. In 1872 a woman's skeleton was discovered in the tower, adding fuel to the tale, although there is no proof as to its identity.

*From Sevenoaks, drive west on the A25 to **Westerham**. **Squerryes Court** is half a mile west of the town on the A25.* 6

6 WESTERHAM AND SQUERRYES COURT

Spread along a lofty downland ridge, the engaging little country town of **Westerham** is known for its associations with two men: Sir Winston Churchill (through his home at Chartwell; *see p122*) and General James Wolfe, who died in the Battle of Quebec in 1759. Both are commemorated by monuments on Westerham's broad hilltop green. The general's childhood home, **Quebec House**, is a modest 18th-century house, where several of the rooms retain their original appearance, with portraits and other memorabilia. Just outside Westerham is **Squerryes Court**, an elegant 1680s country house that has been home to the Warde family since 1731. It has fine paintings, furniture and porcelain, but still feels like a real home, with an engaging mix of grandeur and warmth. The formal gardens are delightful.

*From Westerham, take the B2026 south and look for a sharp turn left to **Chartwell**. Walk to **Emmett's Garden** from Chartwell.* 7

Clockwise from above:
house and gardens,
Chartwell; Sir Winston
Churchill's hats, Chartwell;
Penshurst Place and
Gardens; statue,
Groombridge Place Gardens;
Hever Castle

7 CHARTWELL AND EMMETTS GARDEN

The much-treasured home of Sir Winston Churchill for more than 40 years, **Chartwell** still exudes his presence. The rooms remain virtually unchanged and are packed with books, letters and memorabilia that portray a vivid picture of the great statesman and his family. Churchill bought Chartwell as a country home in 1922, and it benefited greatly from his long periods out of office in the 1920s and 30s, when he lived here full-time and focused his energies on laying out the superb gardens, including the brick wall he famously built himself. Another of his passions, painting, is well reflected in the studio, which is lined with vigorous landscapes painted on his travels. The house occupies one of the finest downland settings, with truly fabulous views.

A footpath leads (about 2 miles) east from Chartwell to **Emmetts Garden**, a lovely woodland garden with many rare trees, occupying one of the highest points in Kent.

*Head south to the B269
and turn left; drive through
Four Elms, then look out
for a lane on the right to*
⑧ *Hever Castle.*

8 HEVER CASTLE

Another of Kent's grand mansions, this 13th-century moated castle is best known as the home of Henry VIII's second wife, the unfortunate Anne Boleyn, mother of Elizabeth I. Among the house's greatest treasures are two prayer books signed by Anne and a remarkable collection of Tudor portraits, including paintings of Anne and Henry's other wives. In the early 1900s, Hever was acquired by the wealthy American Astor family, who turned the damp old castle into a luxurious Edwardian residence and laid out the exuberant gardens. In addition to the grand chambers and historic exhibits, the huge estate offers plenty to see. Lose yourself in the famous yew tree maze or the more recently created water maze. Visit the model houses exhibition or wander through the rose and blue gardens to the lake, with blazing contrasts of colour. Look out too for the many special exhibitions and events hosted at Hever, from medieval jousts to garden festivals.

*Continue south on the
same lane to a T-junction,
and then turn left
to Chiddingstone.*

→ • • • • • • • • • • • ⑨

ASHDOWN FOREST

Covering more than 500ha (6,000 acres), including long stretches that are still wild and empty, Ashdown Forest is the largest area of ancient heathland in southern England. Amid the open heath, however, there are still patches of real wooded 'forest'. The forest is closely associated with A A Milne, who lived at Hartfield in the 1920s while writing the *Winnie the Pooh* books. Virtually all 'enchanted places' from the stories, such as Pooh Bridge *(below)* and the Hundred-Acre Wood, can be easily identified with places nearby. The **Pooh Corner shop** in Hartfield, stocking books, information and souvenirs, is a Pooh fan magnet.

The helpful **Ashdown Forest Centre** (between Hartfield and Wych Cross) has leaflets on an enticing range of walks. The most popular one is around the 'Pooh sites' near Gills Lap. This area and the west side of the forest are wooded and leafy; on the east side, the hills are steeper, the heath more open and the views more spectacular.

9 CHIDDINGSTONE

Half-lost in a maze of tiny lanes, National Trust-owned Chiddingstone is perhaps the loveliest of the Weald's villages. The main street is made up entirely of 15th- to 17th-century buildings, including the wonderful Castle Inn, part-dating from 1420. Just outside the village, **Chiddingstone Castle** is an unconventional 19th-century neogothic stately home. It is crammed with the amazing legacy of its last owner, Denys Bower, whose eclectic acquisitions included fine paintings, Egyptian antiquities, Japanese suits of armour and many other surprises.

10 PENSHURST PLACE AND GARDENS

Home to the Sidney family since 1552 – and most famously to the Elizabethan poet Sir Philip Sidney – Penshurst is a masterpiece of English manor house architecture. At its heart is the remarkable Gothic Barons' Hall from 1341, a magnificent hall that still retains its original 18m-high chestnut ceiling (60ft). Many more rooms and wings were added in later centuries, creating a sprawling, rambling mansion. Just as exceptional as the Barons' Hall is a rare Elizabethan walled garden. The rest of the grounds are equally sumptuous and there's an enchanting woodland trail.

11 GROOMBRIDGE

One of the Weald's most picturesque and historic pubs, the 1585 Crown Inn, presides over Groombridge. The pub was celebrated as the base of the 'Groombridge Gang', a band of smugglers who operated throughout Kent in the 1730s. Just outside the village at **Groombridge Place Gardens** is a magical series of walled gardens, first laid out around a manor house in the 1670s by the diarist John Evelyn. Designed as 'outside rooms' with different themes and colours, the gardens have been extended and developed by many later gardeners incorporating an unusual mix of historic and contemporary styles. They have featured in several films, including Peter Greenway's *The Draughtsman's Contract* and the BBC TV production of *Pride and Prejudice*. There is also now a vineyard – home-grown wines can sometimes be sampled – and, in the woods alongside, the Enchanted Forest is a mystery tour that's great fun for families.

*Follow the lane east out of the village to meet the B2027. Turn right and then turn right again onto the B2176 to **Penshurst Place and Gardens**.* ⑩

*Continue on the B2176 to Penshurst village, then right onto the B2188. When this meets the A264, cross straight over it onto the B2110 to **Groombridge**.* ⑪

*From Groombridge, take the B2110 south west via Hartfield until it meets the A22. Continue straight across the A22 and look out for a left turn to Sharpthorne and **West Hoathly**.* ⑫

Clockwise from above:
Wakehurst Place; Sheffield
Park Garden

⊕
⋮
⋮
⋮
Drive through West Hoathly
to the B2028, then turn left
⑬ *to Wakehurst Place.*

12 WEST HOATHLY

This delightful village sits atop one of the steepest of the downland hills. Alongside its venerable old church is the **Priest House**, a scarcely altered 15th-century timber-frame cottage housing a fascinating collection of rustic furniture, kitchen equipment and other relics of village life. Outside there's a fragrant herb garden.

13 WAKEHURST PLACE

The country outpost of Kew Gardens, Wakehurst Place is the largest and most spectacular of the Weald's many gardens. It surrounds an Elizabethan mansion, which now houses a small display on the estate, as well as changing botanical-related exhibitions. The 175-ha estate (460 acres) invites hours of exploration along its endlessly varied, beautifully landscaped paths. Particular highlights include the Millennium Seed Bank – the world's largest conservation project, in which more than 24,000 plant species from around the world are preserved to ensure their survival – the Asian Heath Garden, the Himalayan Glade and the gorgeous lakes and water gardens.

Continue south on the
B2028 and just beyond
Ardingly turn left on to
unclassified roads to
Horsted Keynes and
Danehill to meet the
A275, then turn right to
Sheffield Park Garden.

→ • • • • • • • • • • ⑭

THE BLUEBELL RAILWAY

This much-loved steam railway has been run
by enthusiasts since the 1950s. Each of its three
stations houses a museum of a different railway
era: Victorian (Sheffield Park), the 1930s (Horsted
Keynes) and the 1950s (Kingscote, near East
Grinstead). As well as three to five trains running
along the 10-mile line each day in summer
(with more regular services at weekends) there
are frequent 'special' trains, using Sheffield Park
station's impressive collection of rare old
locomotives, including the historic Golden Arrow
with its luxurious 1920s Pullman coaches.

14 SHEFFIELD PARK GARDEN

Occupying more than 50ha (120 acres), this exquisite
park was landscaped in the 1770s by 'Capability' Brown,
who included four lakes – one for each season – linked
by cascades and cleverly presenting a wonderful range of
hilltop vistas. It changes dramatically through the seasons,
with an explosion of azaleas in summer and gold and
russet leaves in autumn. Enjoy the garden at its best in
the late afternoon, when the colours of its exotic plants
are heightened by the magnificent downland sunsets.

*Drive south on the A275
and turn left onto
unclassified roads to
Fletching.* 15

15 FLETCHING

A classically pretty Sussex village, with a snug main
street of old houses centred on a 400-year-old pub, the
Griffin Inn. The imposing 13th-century **church** is
celebrated as the place where Simon de Montfort and
his barons came to pray before defeating King Henry III
in the Battle of Lewes in 1264. Fletching is also an
excellent base for walks, offering a lovely stroll just
around the village itself, along streams, through stiles
and past the old cricket field, as well as longer walks
up the downs towards Sheffield Park Garden.

*Continue north to meet
the A22 at Nutley. Turn left,
then almost immediately
right, to cut across to meet
the B2188. Turn left and
continue back to the A264,
then turn right to return to
Royal Tunbridge Wells.*
← • • • • • • • • • • • 1

WITH MORE TIME

Just a few miles off the route lie two additional attractions. **Tonbridge Castle**
(left), west of the Hop Farm Country Park, is a dramatic, 13th-century fortress
beside the River Medway, with a massive turreted gatehouse. Inside, modern
displays and special effects re-create life inside a medieval stronghold. Further
north, not far from Old Soar Manor and near Borough Green, is **Great Comp
Garden**, an imaginative downland garden created over a period of 40 years as a
labour of love by Eric Cameron and his late wife Joy. The formal and informal
gardens include many rare shrubs and exotics and a huge collection of salvias.

Around Rye and the smuggler's coast

Sussex's downland and Kent's wooded Weald fade into a strange and captivating hinterland of marsh and misty meadow between Rye and Hythe, much of it tentatively reclaimed from the sea. Maritime influences prevail in this region, which centres on marshland and the once wealthy, semi-autonomous Cinque Ports. When these port towns declined in strategic military importance, heavily armed gangs of smugglers took over. There is an attractive brooding quality to the area, and it is easy to see why Joseph Conrad (just one noted literary visitor) was inspired to write some of his darker tales of seafaring treachery and folly here.

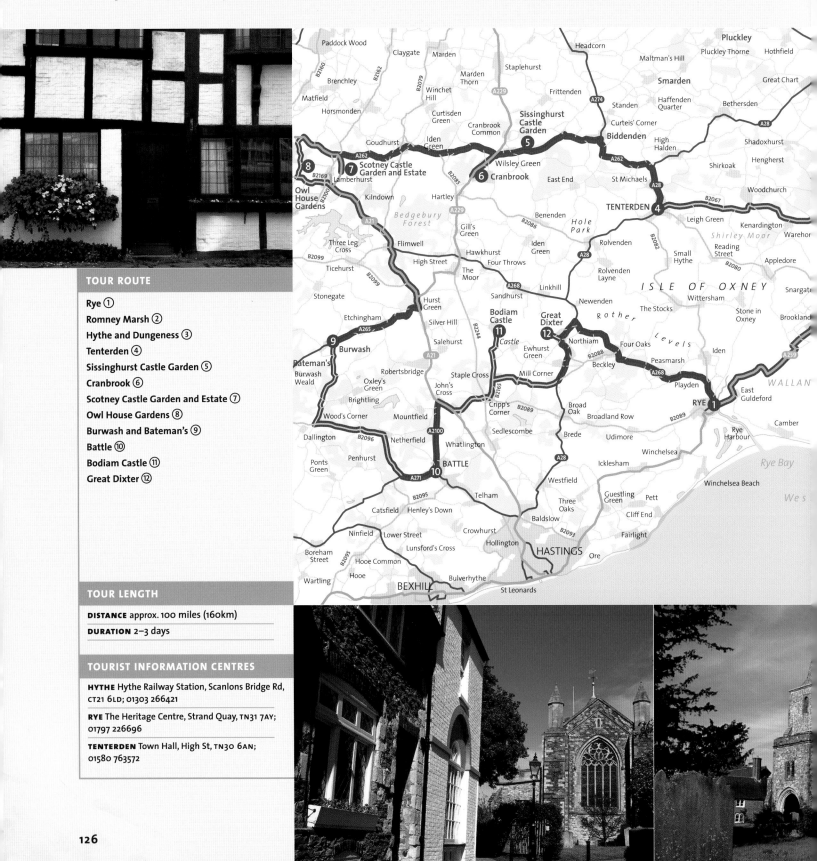

TOUR ROUTE

Rye ①
Romney Marsh ②
Hythe and Dungeness ③
Tenterden ④
Sissinghurst Castle Garden ⑤
Cranbrook ⑥
Scotney Castle Garden and Estate ⑦
Owl House Gardens ⑧
Burwash and Bateman's ⑨
Battle ⑩
Bodiam Castle ⑪
Great Dixter ⑫

TOUR LENGTH

DISTANCE approx. 100 miles (160km)
DURATION 2–3 days

TOURIST INFORMATION CENTRES

HYTHE Hythe Railway Station, Scanlons Bridge Rd, CT21 6LD; 01303 266421

RYE The Heritage Centre, Strand Quay, TN31 7AY; 01797 226696

TENTERDEN Town Hall, High St, TN30 6AN; 01580 763572

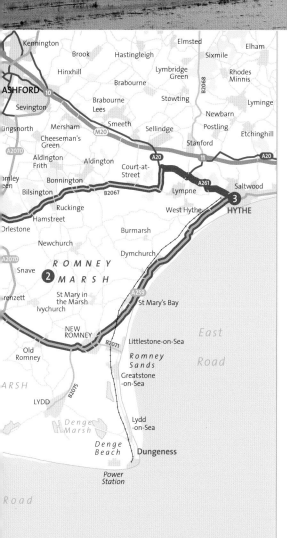

Clockwise from far left:
half-timbered house,
Biddenden; St Thomas à
Becket church, Romney Marsh;
church, Pluckley; cottages
and St Mary's church, Rye

1 RYE

Stand close to the old **Martello Tower** at Rye's delightful little harbour to look back up the once mighty channel carved by the River Rother and you'll see exactly how irreversibly silt has clogged this once great artery. Hundreds of years ago its tidal surge took ships, men and supplies right to Rye's fortified town walls. The water's retreat has left a charming, picturesque time capsule in Rye with a warren of historic, cobbled lanes and secret passageways, which host a plethora of bookshops and antique stores in which to browse.

Many authors and artists have lived and found inspiration here, including Henry James (who resided at the National Trust-owned **Lamb House**), Joseph Conrad and Ford Madox Ford. The town also provides the setting for E F Benson's Mapp and Lucia novels of the 1930s.

Neighbouring **Winchelsea** is officially the smallest town in England. This charming town was built in 1287 under the royal patronage of Edward I, and it remains a delightful and relaxing place from which to explore the beautiful surrounding countryside and coast.

*Take the A259 north east from Rye to Brookland and **Romney Marsh** beyond.* ②

2 ROMNEY MARSH

Wide open skies, ruler-straight horizons and, bisecting them, the distant outlines of church spires make the peaceful nature reserve of Romney Marsh a magical place to embrace a delicious solitude. The excellent bike and walking trails offer the best way to explore, including one that hugs the banks of the Royal Military Canal (dug as a defence against Napoleonic invasion). An excellent place for bird watching, the reserve has enough rare avian species to get any twitcher twitching. There are several interesting churches on the marsh, perhaps the most striking of which is **Brookland Church**, built with a separate bell tower to reduce the weight of the church on the soggy ground. This engineering ruse was only partially successful as the tower has been subsiding at the rate of one inch every century since it was built. Another church, the **St Thomas à Becket** at Fairfield near the pretty village of Appledore, is striking in its isolation amid the marsh.

*Continue on the A259 heading north east along the coast to **Hythe**. (To reach **Dungeness** by road en route to Hythe, turn right onto the B2071 at New Romney and follow the coast south.)* ③

Clockwise from above:
boats, Hythe; Scotney Castle
Garden and Estate;
Cranbrook; Sissinghurst
Castle Gardens

THE CINQUE PORTS AND SMUGGLING

Before Henry VIII's eye expanded the Royal Navy, the monarch of the day granted special licence to the ports along this coast to run their own trade and tax affairs in return for repelling coastal invasion. Initially, five ports earned this right (hence the name Cinque, from the French five), but eventually most of the coastal settlements between Dover and Hastings joined this free trade area.

It is perhaps no real surprise that in such an independently minded part of the world smuggling also flourished. Edward I had unwittingly kick-started the smuggling industry by introducing an export tax on wool around 1300, but it was after 1614 when a ban on wool exports was initiated that smuggling (or owling, as it was named after the owl-like noises the smugglers made to communicate) truly flourished. The lure of profits outweighed the threat of execution, and rather than give up, the smugglers merely armed themselves. This was no cottage industry either; local records show that almost the entire population in the area was involved with smuggling in the early 1700s, and it was only after organised coastal policing arrived in 1830 that smuggling ceased here.

⊕ *Head north west out of*
    Hythe on the A261, then
    turn left onto the B2067,
④ *heading west to* ***Tenterden***.

Drive north out of
Tenterden on the A28, turn
left onto the A262, then
continue west through
Biddenden and follow the
signs right for ***Sissinghurst***
Castle Garden.

→ • • • • • • • • • • ⑤

3 HYTHE AND DUNGENESS

One of the Cinque Ports *(see left)* that flourished during medieval and Elizabethan times, Hythe comprises a lovely jumble of streets lined with historic houses that wind gently up a hill crowned by **St Leonard's**, the 11th-century parish church. In its crypt there is an extraordinary and rather sobering array of human remains, with skulls stacked high in their thousands: they are thought to be from an ancient burial ground, possibly Saxon in origin. Hythe's long, usually empty beach offers bracing walks, and on a clear day France is sometimes visible.

Take a ride on the **Romney, Hythe and Dymchurch Railway**, which follows the atmospherically bleak coastline south to Dungeness. There are some interesting beach houses along the shingle at Dungeness, including **Prospect Cottage**, that of the late film-maker Derek Jarman, with its unusual and somewhat surreal garden.

4 TENTERDEN

Once a prosperous town of wool weavers and merchants, Tenterden both flourished and suffered with the Cinque Ports with which it was affiliated. Its slow decline has left a well-preserved historic town centre and a high street largely uncluttered by the bland signage of most. It is a town made for a morning's browsing among the antique shops and boutiques. The other compelling reason to visit Tenterden is for a ride aboard a steam train on the **Kent and East Sussex Railway**, which chugs its way to Bodiam. Just south of the town is **Smallhythe Place**, former home of the Victorian actress Dame Ellen Terry, where you can discover her theatrical memorabilia and costumes and explore the cottage grounds.

5 SISSINGHURST CASTLE GARDEN

We have the writer Vita Sackville-West and her husband Harold Nicolson to thank for the glory that is Sissinghurst, a romantic moated Tudor house girdled with roses, honeysuckle and spectacular grounds. During the 1930s, the couple turned it from a dilapidated ruin into a magnificently designed garden. Sackville-West had a modern sensibility; spurning regimented rows of flowers, she instead carefully grouped plants according to colour, texture and season. The roof of the four-storey Elizabethan prospect tower offers majestic vistas of the garden and the Weald, views that are said to have been enjoyed by Elizabeth I when she visited Sissinghurst's owner Sir Richard Baker in 1573.

Return to the A262 and turn right, then turn left onto the A229 heading south and left again following the signs to Cranbrook. 6

6 CRANBROOK

A pretty village with an ancient church and several pubs, Cranbrook makes a good refreshment stop. The white, weatherboarded smock **windmill**, dominating the centre of the village's charming conservation area, is the finest example of its kind. At a height of 21m (70ft), including its squat brick base, it is also the tallest mill in Kent.

Drive back to the A262 and turn left heading west. Exit left on the A21 and follow signs to Scotney Castle Garden and Estate. 7

7 SCOTNEY CASTLE GARDEN AND ESTATE

The romantic gardens at Scotney, built for full dramatic effect around the ruins of the 14th-century moated castle, offer wonderful woodland walks and, in summer, dazzling displays of rhododendrons, azaleas and roses. The grounds offer many fine vistas, viewpoints and plenty of idyllic picnic spots.

Return to the A21 and drive north west for about 3 miles, then turn left on unclassified roads to Owl House Gardens. 8

⤓ *Drive south and turn left
onto the B2169. Join the
A21 southbound to Hurst
Green, then turn right onto
the A265 to Burwash.
Bateman's is half a mile
⑨ south west of Burwash.*

⤓ *Head south out of Burwash
on the unclassified road to
Wood's Corner. Turn left
onto the B2096 and then
left again onto the A271
⑩ into Battle.*

⤓ *Drive north on the A2100
and right onto the A21.
Shortly after, turn left onto
the B2089 and left again
onto the B2165 to Staple
Cross and follow the signs
⑪ left to Bodiam Castle.*

*Clockwise from above:
Great Dixter; Bodiam Castle;
Battle Abbey; Bateman's*

8 OWL HOUSE GARDENS

The cottage is picture pretty, the gardens are a delight and even the name, Owl House – so called after the smugglers' hooting-calls used to warn of tax inspectors – is romantic. Lady Dufferin bought the cottage and grounds in the 1950s and set about creating the expansive lawns, woodland walks and water gardens, which are at their best in spring when daffodils, bluebells and primroses carpet the grounds. It is an idyllic place for a contemplative walk.

9 BURWASH AND BATEMAN'S

An attractive town with some of the most arresting views to be found in Sussex, Burwash features a historic high street that has retained its character despite its A-road location. The 11th-century **Church of St Bartholomew** is packed with historical interest, including the earliest known Sussex grave slab, cast in iron in the 14th century. In the churchyard, look out for graves marked with the skull and crossbones, the last resting place of the privateers and smugglers that once flourished in the area. The star attraction in town is **Bateman's**, the old Jacobean manor house bought by Rudyard Kipling in 1902. Its interior is still stuffed with Kipling's possessions, including his book-lined study, Oriental rugs and artefacts from his travels in India and Asia. The large, peaceful gardens run down to the small River Dudwell and the old mill, in which Kipling installed one of the first water turbine electric generators.

10 BATTLE

They say the first knight to fall at the Battle of Hastings still rides the ridge at Battle, his horse's hooves thundering, his battle colours flying. Even if you don't see or hear the knight at the **battlefield**, a guided audio tour recalls in vivid detail the defining moment in British history when William of Normandy defeated Harold to become King of England in 1066. **Battle Abbey**, constructed in 1070 on the site of the battle, was built by William on the pope's orders as an act of atonement for the bloody loss of life here. Only fragments of the abbey remain, but in the grounds you'll find a plaque marking the very spot where Harold was said to have fallen. There's an excellent **visitors' centre** offering clear, insightful background on the battle and the era.

11   BODIAM CASTLE

Situated in a lovely landscaped setting, Bodiam is the archetypal castle with its regular square shape, a stout crenellated tower on each corner, and a circular spring-fed moat crossed by a narrow drawbridge. Built by an ambitious knight in 1385, as both redoubt and home, it was twice besieged, once during the War of the Roses and once during the Civil War. The exterior is virtually complete, and the ramparts rise dramatically above the moat. The interior is not so well preserved, but it gives an idea of the original layout and allows visitors to climb its spiral staircases and battlements and take in the enchanting views of the Rother Valley beneath.

12   GREAT DIXTER

Exotic topiary, boldly designed gardens and constant experimentation with planting make Great Dixter a compelling destination for any garden lover. A quintessential Wealden idyll created by gardening writer and owner Christopher Lloyd, the garden features meadow gardens, colourful borders, ponds, a formal pool and an enchanting sunken garden, as well as a handsome complex of buildings, parts dating back to the Middle Ages, which include an oast house, a barn and a large, rare timber-framed hall.

Return to Staple Cross and turn left onto the B2165. Turn left onto the A28 to Northiam and left again onto the Dixter Road to Great Dixter. 12

Rejoin the A28 at Northiam, and turn left heading briefly north before turning right onto the southbound A268 to return to Rye.

WITH MORE TIME

Just north west of Ashford, you'll discover a delightful rural idyll where Kent truly earns its sobriquet, the 'garden of England'. This is the classic Kent countryside of oast houses and fruit trees, where the TV series the *Darling Buds of May* was filmed. Meander along the country lanes that connect the pretty villages of Pluckley *(left)*, Smarden and Biddenden (one of Kent's finest villages with a charming main street of half-timbered houses). All around, you'll find vineyards and orchards with adjacent farm shops offering wine and cider to taste and buy.

Kent: Christian and literary inspiration

This atmospheric slice of Kent is evoked time and again in the novels of Charles Dickens, who lived and wrote so many of his famous novels here. At the heart of Kent lies the county's greatest historical treasure, the glorious city of Canterbury with its stunning Norman cathedral. Dotted around the surrounding countryside are a wealth of quintessential Kent orchards, oast houses, historic villages and alluring castles, while along Kent's northern boundaries where coast, river and estuary hold sway, you'll discover an area defined by the tang of the sea and the haunting stillness of marsh and mud flat.

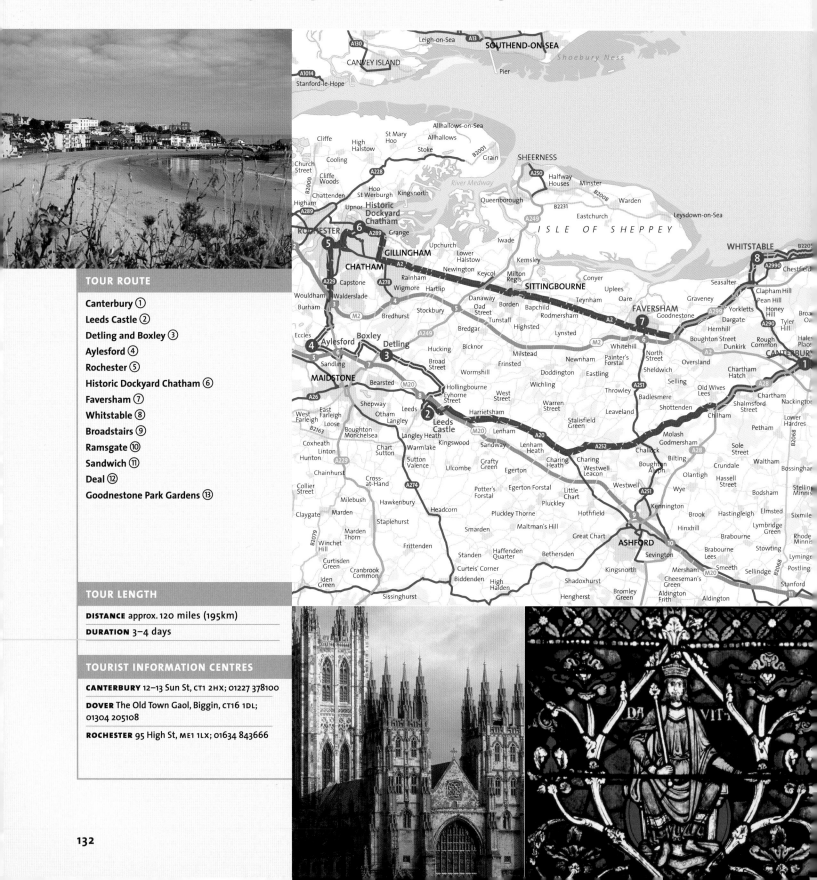

TOUR ROUTE

Canterbury ①
Leeds Castle ②
Detling and Boxley ③
Aylesford ④
Rochester ⑤
Historic Dockyard Chatham ⑥
Faversham ⑦
Whitstable ⑧
Broadstairs ⑨
Ramsgate ⑩
Sandwich ⑪
Deal ⑫
Goodnestone Park Gardens ⑬

TOUR LENGTH

DISTANCE approx. 120 miles (195km)
DURATION 3–4 days

TOURIST INFORMATION CENTRES

CANTERBURY 12–13 Sun St, CT1 2HX; 01227 378100

DOVER The Old Town Gaol, Biggin, CT16 1DL; 01304 205108

ROCHESTER 95 High St, ME1 1LX; 01634 843666

Clockwise from far left:
beach, Broadstairs; Leeds
Castle; Christchurch Gate,
Canterbury; St Augustine's
chair, Canterbury Cathedral;
stained-glass window,
Canterbury Cathedral; façade,
Canterbury Cathedral

1 CANTERBURY

The rambling medieval and Tudor city centre, crowned by a magnificent Early English Gothic **cathedral**, ensures Canterbury remains the compelling destination it has been to pious pilgrims for almost a millennium. The tradition of a pilgrimage to Canterbury – immortalised so memorably in Chaucer's *Canterbury Tales* – grew up around Archbishop Thomas à Becket, who was murdered here by knights of King Henry II in 1170. His life, bloody death and martyrdom inspired Britons and Europeans to flock to Canterbury in droves. King Henry VIII stopped the pilgrimages after he created the Church of England, and had Thomas à Becket's tomb destroyed. Today, a candle flickers where the tomb used to be. Canterbury's religious status is not solely related to Thomas à Becket, however, for this city has been the seat of early Christianity since AD597, when St Augustine set up an abbey here. Canterbury's UNESCO World Heritage-listed cathedral is brimming with historical interest illustrating the city's religious and social heritage. There are excellent guided tours and the enchanting evensong is well worth staying for.

There is plenty to see beyond the cathedral, including the ruins of **Canterbury Castle**, the fragments of the once mighty city walls at the **West Gate** with its pretty adjacent public gardens, the witches' ducking stool and the many well-preserved Tudor buildings. Boat trips along the River Stour are a leisurely way to take in some of the city sights.

*Head south west out of Canterbury on the A28, then turn right onto the A252 at Chilham. At Charing turn right onto the A20 and continue until the signs left to **Leeds Castle**.*

Clockwise from above:
Leeds Castle; Historic
Dockyard Chatham;
Rochester Castle;
Rochester Cathedral

2 LEEDS CASTLE

Arguably the most stunning castle on the British Isles,
medieval Leeds Castle is well worth half a day's
exploration. Its grand edifice is encircled by a huge
romantic moat (part of the River Len). The 200-ha
grounds (500 acres) include a vast expanse of park,
meadow, vineyard and woodland, as well as a
Mediterranean garden stocked with sub-tropical plants
and the English country cottage-style Culpeper Garden,
making it a magnet for gardening enthusiasts. There is
also an aviary and a yew maze. The slightly less
impressive interiors include an extensive complex of
rooms and halls graced with tapestries, paintings and
antiques that tell the story of this historic site from its
early days as the stately home of a Saxon royal family.

*Travel north out of Leeds
village, cross the A20
and the M20 and follow
unclassified roads west to
Detling. Continue about
one mile to the north
3 west to Boxley.*

3 DETLING AND BOXLEY

Sheltering in the shadow of the North Downs are the
delightfully unspoilt and peaceful villages of Detling
and Boxley. **Detling** makes a good base for rambling
along the nearby stretch of the North Downs Way,
while **Boxley** offers pretty, traditional weatherboarded
cottages and the 13th-century All Saint's Church. Look
out for the inscription of gratitude by Sir Henry Wyatt
to a cat he credits with having saved his life.

*Follow the unclassified
roads south west
from Boxley through
Sandling and then
west on to Aylesford.*

WALKING IN DICKENS COUNTRY

The legacy of great Victorian novelist Charles
Dickens *(below)* pervades this part of Kent. The
writer grew up, lived, wrote and holidayed in
many places in the area from Rochester to
Broadstairs, and he based many fictional
locations and characters on his experiences
here. If you've time, a walk around the
estuarine marshes near **Cliffe** (a short drive
north from Rochester) offers a wonderful way to
experience the atmosphere Dickens invokes in
the opening chapters of one of his finest novels,
Great Expectations. The peaceful shoreline
around **Cliffe Fort** and **Cliffe Creek** passes silent
old churchyards, bullrushes, drainage ditches
and mud flats rich in birdlife. The churchyard
of St James's church in **Cooling** contains the
'five stone lozenges' (the tombs of five children
from the same family) described by Pip in the
dramatic opening page of the novel.

4 AYLESFORD

Its appealing jumble of cottages nestled around an elegant 14th-century, five-arched bridge and its delightfully picturesque setting astride the River Medway are reason enough to visit Aylesford, but the town has plenty of historical as well as visual attractions. This strategic river crossing has been contested in pitched battles as far back as AD455. It was here that King Alfred saw off the Danes in the late 9th century and Edmond Ironside defeated Canute and his Vikings in the early 10th century. Don't miss **The Friars**, a Carmelite priory dating back more than 800 years with tranquil grounds that are open to the public. The chapel contains some striking modern religious artworks.

5 ROCHESTER

The jewel in the muddy mosaic of the Medway Estuary, charming Rochester has a rich historical and literary heritage. The foundations of the town's lofty **cathedral** date back to AD604, although the current building is a mere 900 years old. Two brass curves on the floor inside the West Door mark the site of the first Saxon cathedral. Beside it towers **Rochester Castle**, a huge and superbly preserved Norman fortress. Constructed in 1087 by Bishop Gundulf – chief architect of William the Conqueror – it has endured a turbulent history. It was besieged three times, but only one attempt (by King John in 1215) was successful. This was the first and possibly the last time that pig fat was used as a weapon of mass destruction; the fat from 40 hogs was smeared on pit props dug under the castle walls causing a ferocious fire. Climb the battlements for an unrivalled view over town, river and estuary.

The town has strong links to Charles Dickens, who spent much of his childhood here. The handsome Victorian high street, now lined with antique shops, cafés and pubs, provided the inspiration for three of his novels including *Great Expectations*, while the Dickens' galleries in the town's **Guildhall Museum** have plenty of Dickens memorabilia and provide a good introduction to the many places in Kent that feature in his novels. His extraordinary literary legacy is also commemorated by two annual festivals each Christmas and summer.

6 HISTORIC DOCKYARD CHATHAM

From the days when Nelson's *Victory* set sail from here in 1759, Chatham was a fulcrum of the British Empire, producing ships that enabled Britain to dominate the world's trade routes. This huge site does full justice to Chatham's historic role offering a feast of maritime lore, fascinating industrial architecture and plenty of hands-on exhibits, including the 'ropery' where craftsmen teach the tricks of the trade. There are also three historic warships to explore, including the Victorian Sloop *Gannet* and the tiny, claustrophobic submarine *Ocelot*. The museum's Road to Trafalgar exhibition on Nelson's campaigns is also well worth visiting. In summer, you can arrive in style from Rochester aboard the paddle steamer *Kingswear Castle*.

7 FAVERSHAM

A pleasing old market town lapped by the tidal River Swale and threaded with crooked streets, Faversham offers numerous homely pubs, its own brewery and a market square crowned by the handsome 16th-century Guildhall. The **Fleur de Lis Heritage Centre** tells the town's story over the last 1,000 years. At the **Brogdale Horticultural Trust** you can see more than 4,000 varieties of fruit trees and plants, including the National Fruit Collection, in 60ha (150 acres) of beautiful orchards.

Head north on unclassified roads to join the A229 and turn left to Rochester. **5**

Head south from Rochester town centre past Rochester railway station, turn left onto Globe Lane, left again onto Dock Road and follow the signs to Historic Dockyard Chatham. **6**

Take the A289 south east, then turn left onto the A2 in Gillingham and continue east to Faversham following the signs left into the town centre. **7**

Continue south east on the A2 and turn left onto the A299, then turn left onto the B2205 to Whitstable. **8**

Clockwise from above:
Walmer Castle, Deal;
stained-glass window in
the Guildhall, Sandwich;
Goodnestone Park Gardens;
weatherboard cottages,
Whitstable

Continue on the B2205 east
and turn left onto the A299
at Herne Bay. Turn left again
onto the A28 to Margate
and from there follow the
A255 south east through St
Peters to **Broadstairs**.

Head south on the B2052
to join the A255 south
to **Ramsgate**.

Drive south on the A255 to
join the A256. Turn left
heading south and then
take the signposted turning
left on the unclassified
road to **Sandwich**.

8 WHITSTABLE

Once a proud working port landing fish and loading
coal, post-industrial Whitstable sank for decades into a
sad decline. Its fishermen managed to survive, thanks
in part to the fine oysters grown here, which are now
synonymous with the town and its revival. Excellent
seafood restaurants are an obvious attraction,
particularly during the July Oyster Festival, a week-long
feeding, drinking and fish-slapping fiesta (fish slapping
being a nautical morris dance). Whitstable and its
coast is also a magnet for artists and artisans, and
you'll find the high street's arts and crafts boutiques
packed with the fruits of their labour.

9 BROADSTAIRS

'A good sea – fresh breezes – fine sands – and pleasant
walks – with all manner of fishing boats. Light houses,
piers, bathing machines and so forth are its only
attractions, but it's one of the fresh and free-est little
places in the world'. The bathing machines may have
gone, but Broadstairs retains much of the appeal that
inspired Charles Dickens to write these words (as well
as several of his novels) about Broadstairs. **Dickens
House Museum**, occupying a handsome historic
seafront townhouse near the enchanting esplanade, is
a captivating time capsule. On display is some
interesting Dickens memorabilia, including a fine series
of illustrations from his novels. Chalk cliffs and sandy
bays stretch along the coast on either side of the town,
and to the north, almost at the tip of Kent, lies
Kingsgate, a pretty little cove, once a smugglers'
landing ground, which is worth visiting for its picture-
postcard charm. It was at this gate, or gap in the cliffs, that
Charles II made a chance landing in 1683, hence the name.

10 RAMSGATE

Elegant Victorian architecture, a pretty harbour and the
modest but diverting **Ramsgate Maritime Museum** are
the main reasons to visit Ramsgate. The museum offers
an absorbing collection of maritime flotsam and jetsam,
as well as boat models, displays on the maritime
heritage of the coast and artefacts rescued from wrecks
along it. Adjacent to the museum is the restored 1791
Dry Dock and historic ship collection, which includes
the Steam Tug *Cervia* and two Dunkirk Little Ships,
which helped snatch the bulk of the British Army from
death or capture by Hitler's advancing forces.

11 SANDWICH

One of the original Cinque Ports (see p128), Sandwich is so packed with architectural gems that the entire town centre is a conservation area. Wander its maze of historic alleys and passages and it is easy to understand why. Houses of interest (both privately owned), include the 12th-century Long House and the 16th-century King's Lodging. The small **Guildhall Museum** inside the Elizabethan Guildhall offers some information about these as part of its displays detailing Sandwich's history.

12 DEAL

The fact that you can visit three castles in the modest town of Deal demonstrates the strategic importance it has had over the years since Julius Caesar landed here with his legions in 55 and 54BC. Henry VIII built two castles – Deal and Walmer – to repel invading Catholics from the Continent. Now run by English Heritage, **Deal Castle** is the largest: a massive complex of concentric defences that once housed entire garrisons. At the northern edge of town lie the ruins of **Sandwich Castle** (where there is little to see), while at the southern end stands **Walmer Castle** with its beautifully maintained grounds and lawns. It has an interesting history as home to the Prime Minister William Pitt and the military hero the Duke of Wellington, who died here in 1842.

Deal's **Maritime and Local History Museum** tells tales of smuggling, naval battles and of the nearby Goodwin Sands, a treacherous expanse of shifting channels and shallows responsible for claiming countless lives and ships over the centuries. The seafront, the shingle beach and the pier offer good strolling and promenading in this charming seaside backwater.

13 GOODNESTONE PARK GARDENS

Something of a hidden gem, Goodnestone offers 6ha (15 acres) of captivatingly beautiful English gardens, without quite the press of visitors found at other exemplary gardens, such as nearby Sissinghurst (see p129). The clematis- and jasmine-clad brick walls of the Walled Garden reveal show-stopping displays and a classic vista of a succession of brick arches framing the distant church tower.

Head south east out of Sandwich on the unclassified coastal toll road to Deal. 12

Take the A258, heading north west to the A256 and turn right. Turn left onto the A257 heading west until Wingham, then turn left again onto the B2046 and after about one mile follow the signs to the left for Goodnestone Park Gardens. 13

Return to the B2046 and turn right to Wingham, then left onto the A257 to return to Canterbury. 1

WITH MORE TIME

A homing beacon for seaborne returnees (among them the almost annihilated British forces evacuated from Dunkirk in World War II) and an artistic inspiration to writers, painters, poets and lyricists, the quintessentially English **White Cliffs of Dover** have a deep symbolic resonance. Additionally, they are a wonderful destination for walkers. The mighty medieval fortress of **Dover Castle** (left) is also worth visiting for terrific views across the channel as well as for a tour of the secret underground tunnels from World War II.

Gazetteer

Along the rugged Cornish coast

The Abbey Garden and Valhalla Collection
Tresco, Isles of Scilly TR24 OQQ
Tel: 01720 424105
www.tresco.co.uk

Barbara Hepworth Museum & Sculpture Garden
Barnoon Hill, St Ives TR26 1AD
Tel: 01736 796226
www.tate.org.uk

Geevor Tin Mine
Pendeen, Penzance TR19 7EW
Tel: 01736 788662
www.sennen-cove.com

Glendurgan Garden
Mawnan Smith, nr Falmouth TR11 5JZ
Tel: 01326 250906
www.nationaltrust.org.uk

The Leach Pottery
Higher Stennack, St Ives TR26 2HE
Tel: 01736 796398
www.leachpottery.com

Marazion Marsh Nature Reserve
nr Penzance
Tel: 01736 711682
www.rspb.org.uk

The Minack Theatre Visitor Centre
Porthcurno, Penzance TR19 6JU
Tel: 01736 810181
www.minack.com

National Maritime Museum Cornwall
Discovery Quay, Falmouth TR11 3QY
Tel: 01326 313 388
www.nmmc.co.uk

The National Seal Sanctuary
Gweek, nr Helston TR12 6UG
Tel: 01326 221361
www.sealsanctuary.co.uk

Newlyn Art Gallery
24 New Road, Newlyn TR18 5PZ
Tel: 01736 363715
www.newlynartgallery.co.uk

Pendennis Castle
Falmouth
Tel: 01326 316594
www.english-heritage.org

Penlee House Gallery and Museum
Morrab Road, Penzance TR18 4HE
Tel: 01736 363625
www.penleehouse.org.uk

Porthcurno Telegraph Museum
Eastern House, Porthcurno TR19 6JX
Tel: 01736 810966
www.porthcurno.org.uk

Royal Cornwall Museum
River Street, Truro TR1 2SJ
Tel: 01872 272205
www.royalcornwallmuseum.org.uk

St Mawes Castle
St Mawes
01326 270526
www.english-heritage.org.uk

St Ives Society of Artists
Norway Square, St Ives TR26 1NA
Tel: 01736 795582
www.stivessocietyofartists.com

St Michael's Mount
Marazion, Pensance TR17 OEF
Tel: 01736 710507
www.nationaltrust.org.uk

Tate St Ives
Porthmeor Beach, St Ives TR26 1TG
Tel: 01736 796226
www.tate.org.uk

Trebah Garden
Mawnan Smith, nr Falmouth TR11 5JZ
Tel: 01326 250448
www.trebahgarden.co.uk

Trelissick Garden
Feock, nr Truro TR3 6QL
Tel:01872 862090
www.nationaltrust.org.uk

Truro Cathedral
14 St Mary's Street, Truro TR1 2AF
Tel: 01872 276782
www.trurocathedral.org.uk

Wayside Folk Museum
Zennor TR26 3DA
Tel: 01736 796945
www.cornwall-online.co.uk

The wilds of Bodmin Moor

Bodmin Jail
Berrycoombe Road, Bodmin PL31 2NR
Tel: 01208 76292
www.cornwall-online.co.uk

Bodmin Town Museum
Mount Folly, Bodmin PL31 2HQ
Tel: 01208 77067
www.north-cornwall.com

The Courtroom Experience
Shire Hall, Mount Folly, Bodmin PL31 2DQ
Tel: 01208 76616
www.bodminmoor.co.uk

Daphne du Maurier's Smuggler's Museum at Jamaica Inn
Bolventor, Launceston PL15 7TS
Tel: 01566 86838
www.jamaicainn.co.uk**

Eden Project
Bodelva, St Austell PL24 2SG
Tel: 01726 811911
www.edenproject.com

The John Betjeman Centre
Southern Way, Wadebridge PL27 7BX
Tel: 01208 812392

Lanhydrock
nr Bodmin PL30 5AD
Tel: 01208 265950
www.nationaltrust.org.uk

The Lost Gardens of Heligan
Pentewan, St Austell PL26 6EN
Tel: 01726 845100
www.heligan.com

Military Museum
The Keep, Bodmin PL31 1EG
Tel: 01208 72810
www.cornwalltouristboard.co.uk

The Minions Heritage Centre
Minions, Liskeard PL14 5LJ
Tel: 01579 362350
www.caradon.gov.uk

The Museum of Witchcraft
The Harbour, Boscastle PL35 OHD
Tel: 01840 250111
www.museumofwitchcraft.com

National Lobster Hatchery
South Quay, Padstow PL28 8BL
Tel: 01841 533877
www.chycor.co.uk

Pencarrow House and Gardens
Bodmin PL30 3AG
Tel: 01208 841369
www.pencarrow.co.uk

Prideaux Place
Padstow PL28 8RP
Tel: 01841 532411
www.prideauxplace.co.uk

St Neot Pottery
The Old Chapel, St Neot, Liskeard PL14 6NL
Tel: 01579 320216
www.caradon.gov.uk

Tintagel Castle
Tintagel
Tel: 01840 770328
www.english-heritage.org.uk

Tintagel Old Post Office
Fore Street, Tintagel PL34 0DB
Tel: 01840 770024
www.nationaltrust.org.uk

Beneath Dartmoor's craggy heights

Buckland Abbey
Yelverton PL20 6EY
Tel: 01822 853607
www.nationaltrust.org.uk

The Cardew Teapottery
Newton Road, Bovey Tracey TQ13 9DX
Tel: 01626 832172
www.cardewdesign.com

Castle Drogo
Drewsteignton, nr Exeter EX6 6PB
Tel: 01647 433306
www.nationaltrust.org.uk

Cotehele
St Dominick, nr Saltash PL12 6TA
01579 352739
www.nationaltrust.org.uk

Cotehele Quay Museum
Cotehele Quay, St Dominick, Saltash PL12 6TA.
Tel: 01579 350830
www.tamarvalley.org.uk

The Garden House
Buckland Monachorum, Yelverton PL20 7LQ
Tel: 01822 854769
www.thegardenhouse.org.uk

House of Marbles
The Old Pottery, Pottery Road
Bovey Tracey TQ13 9DS
Tel: 01626 835358
www.houseofmarbles.com

Morwellham Quay
Nr Tavistock PL19 8JL
Tel: 01822 832766
www.morwhellam-quay.co.uk

Mount Edgcumbe House
Cremyll, Torpoint PL10 1HZ
Tel: 01752 822236
www.mountedgcumbe.gov.uk

Plymouth Dome
Hoe Road, Plymouth PL1 2NZ
Tel: 01752 603300
www.plymouthdome.info

Riverside Mill
Bovey Tracey TQ13 9AF
Tel: 01626 832223
www.boveytracey.gov.uk

The English Riviera and the sleepy South Hams

Berry Pomeroy Castle
nr Totnes
Tel: 01803 866 618
www.english-heritage.org.uk

Brixham Heritage Museum
Bolton Cross, Brixham TQ5 8LZ
Tel: 01803 856267
www.devonmuseums.net

Cockington Court Craft Centre
Cockington, Torquay TQ2 6XA
Tel: 01803 606035
www.theenglishriviera.co.uk

Coleton Fishacre
Coleton, Kingswear, Dartmouth TQ6 0EQ
Tel: 01803 752466
www.nationaltrust.org.uk

Cookworthy Museum
The Old Grammar School
108 Fore Street, Kingsbridge TQ7 1AW
Tel: 01548 853235
www.devonmuseums.net

Dart Valley Light Railway
Queens Park Station, Torbay Road,
Paignton TQ4 6AF
Tel: 01803 555872
www.torbay.gov.uk

Dartmouth Castle
Dartmouth
Tel: 01803 833588
www.english-heritage.org.uk

Elizabethan Museum
70 Fore Street, Totnes TQ9 5RU
Tel: 01803 863821
www.devonmuseums.net

Exeter Cathedral
Exeter EX1 1HS
Tel: 01392 285983
www.exeter-cathedral.org.uk

Golden Hind
Brixham Harbour, Brixham
Tel: 01803 856223
www.goldenhind.co.uk

Greenway
Greenway Road, Galmpton, nr Brixham TQ5 0ES
Tel: 01803 842382
www.nationaltrust.org.uk

The Guildhall
Ramparts Walk, Totnes TQ9 5QH
Tel: 01803 862147
www.devon-online.com

Kents Cavern
Cavern House, Ilsham Road, Torquay TQ1 2JF
Tel: 01803 215136
www.kents-cavern.co.uk

Living Coasts
Torquay Harbourside, Beacon Quay
Torquay TQ1 2BG
Tel: 01803 202499
www.livingcoasts.org.uk

Overbeck's Museum & Garden
Sharpitor, Salcombe TQ8 8LW
Tel: 01548 842893
www.nationaltrust.org.uk

Royal Albert Memorial Museum and Art Gallery
Queen Street, Exeter EX4 3RX
Tel: 01392 665858
www.exeter.gov.uk

Slapton Ley National Nature Reserve
Slapton, Kingsbridge TQ7 2QP
Tel: 01548 580685
www.slnnr.org.uk

Torquay Museum
529 Babbacombe Road
Torquay TQ1 1HG
Tel: 01803 293275
www.torquaymuseum.org

Torre Abbey Historic House and Gallery
The King's Drive, Torquay TQ2 5JE
Tel: 01803 293593
www.torre-abbey.org.uk

Rural backwaters of North Devon

Arlington Court
Arlington, nr Barnstaple EX31 4LP
Tel: 01271 850296
www.nationaltrust.org.uk

Barnstaple Heritage Centre
Queen Anne's Walk, The Strand
Barnstaple EX31 1EU
Tel: 01271 373003
www.devonmuseums.net

The Burton Art Gallery and Museum
Kingsley Road, Bideford EX39 2QQ
Tel: 01237 471455
www.burtonartgallery.co.uk

Cobbaton Combat Collection
Chittlehampton, Umberleigh EX37 9RZ
Tel: 01769 540740
www.cobbatoncombat.co.uk

Dartington Crystal Visitor Centre
Torrington EX38 7AN
Tel: 01805 626242
www.dartington.co.uk

Hartland Abbey
Hartland, Bideford EX39 6DT
Tel: 01237 441264/234
www.hartlandabbey.com

Hartland Quay Museum
Hartland, nr Bideford EX39 6DU
Tel: 01288 331353
www.devonheritage.com

Kingsley Museum
Clovelly, Bideford EX39 5SY
Tel: 01237 431781
www.north-cornwall.com

Marwood Hill Gardens
Barnstaple EX31 4EB
Tel: 01271 342528
www.marwoodhillgarden.co.uk

Museum of Barnstaple and North Devon
The Square, Barnstaple EX32 8LN
Tel: 01271 346747
www.devonmuseums.net

North Devon Maritime Museum
Odun Road, Appledore, Bideford EX39 1PT
Tel: 01237 422064
www.devonmuseums.net

Rosemoor
Great Torrington EX38 8PH
Tel: 01805 624067
www.rhs.org.uk

Tapeley Park
Instow, Bideford EX39 4NT
Tel: 01271 342558
www.tapeleypark.com

Torrington 1646
Castle Hill, South Street,
Great Torrington EX38 8AA
Tel: 01805 626146
www.torrington-1646.co.uk

Watermouth Castle
Berrynarbor, Ilfracombe EX34 9SL
Tel: 01271 864474
www.watermouthcastle.com

The magic of Exmoor

Cothay Manor and Gardens
Greenham, Nr Wellington TA21 0JR
Tel: 01823 672283
www.somerset.gov.uk

Dunster Castle
Dunster, nr Minehead TA24 6SL
Tel: 01643 823004
www.nationaltrust.org.uk

Dunster Working Watermill
Mill Lane, Dunster, nr Minehead TA24 6SW
Tel: 01643 821759
www.nationaltrust.org.uk

Exmoor National Park Authority
Exmoor House, Dulverton TA22 9HL
Tel: 01398 323665
www.exmoor-nationalpark.gov.uk

Hestercombe Gardens
Cheddon Fitzpaine, Taunton TA2 8LG
Tel: 01823 413923
www.hestercombegardens.com

Knightshayes Court
Bolham, Tiverton EX16 7RQ
Tel: 01884 254665
www.nationaltrust.org.uk

Lyn and Exmoor Museum
St Vincent's Cottage, Market St, Lynton EX35 6HJ
Tel: 01598 752317
www.devonmuseums.net

Lynton and Lynmouth Cliff Railway
Bottom Station, The Esplanade, Lynmouth
Tel: 01598 753486
www.cliffrailwaylynton.co.uk

The West Somerset Railway
The Railway Station, Minehead TA24 5BG
Tel: 01643 704996
www.west-somerset-railway.co.uk

Inland form the Jurassic Coast

Barrington Court
Barrington, nr Ilminster TA19 0NQ
Tel: 01460 242614
www.nationaltrust.org.uk

Beer Quarry Caves
Quarry Lane, Beer, nr Seaton
Tel: 01297 680282
www.eastdevon.net

Branscombe
Branscombe, Seaton EX12 3DB
Tel: 01297 680333 (Old Bakery); 01392 881691
(Manor Mill); 01297 680481 (Forge)
www.nationaltrust.org.uk

Bridport Museum
South Street, Bridport DT6 3NR
Tel: 01308 422116
www.bridportmuseum.co.uk

Brown and Forrest
Bowdens Farm, Hambridge TA10 0BP
Tel: 01458 250875
www.smokedeel.co.uk

Charmouth Heritage Coast Centre
Lower Sea Lane, Charmouth DT6 6LL
Tel: 01297 560772
www.charmouth.org

Dinosaurland
Coombe Street, Lyme Regis DT7 3PY
Tel: 01297 443541
www.dinosaurland.co.uk

East Lambrook Manor Gardens
South Petherton TA13 5HH
Tel: 01460 240328
www.eastlambrook.co.uk

Forde Abbey
Chard TA20 4LU
Tel: 01460 220231
www.fordeabbey.co.uk

Forde Abbey Fruit Farm
Chard TA20 4LU
Tel: 01460 30460
www.somerset.gov.uk

The Heritage Centre
Market Square, Crewkerne TA18 7JU
Tel: 01460 77079
www.somerset.gov.uk

Lyme Regis Philpot Museum
Bridge Street, Lyme Regis DT7 3QA
Tel: 01297 443370
www.jurassiccoast.com

Norman Lockyer Observatory
Salcombe Hill, Sidmouth EX10 0NY
www.projects.ex.ac.uk

Perry's Cider
Dowlish Wake, Ilminster TA19 0NY
Tel: 01460 55195
www.perryscider.co.uk

Seaton Tramway
Riverside Depot, Harbour Road, Seaton EX12 2NQ
Tel: 01297 20375
www.tram.co.uk**

**The Somerset Cider Brandy Company Ltd &
Burrow Hill Cider**
Pass Vale Farm, Burrow Hill, Kingsbury Episcopi
Martock TA12 5BU
Tel: 01460 240782
www.ciderbrandy.co.uk

Thomas Hardy's Dorset

Abbotsbury Sub-Tropical Gardens
Bullers Way, Abbotsbury DT3 4LA
Tel: 01305 871387
www.abbotsbury-tourism.co.uk

Abbotsbury Swannery
New Barn Road, Abbotsbury DT3 4JG
Tel: 01305 871858
www.abbotsbury-tourism.co.uk

Abbotsbury Tithe Barn
New Barn Road, Abbotsbury DT3 4JG
Tel: 01305 871817
www.abbotsbury-tourism.co.uk

Athelhampton House & Garden
Athelhampton, Dorchester DT2 7LG
Tel: 01305 848363
www.athelhampton.co.uk

The Blue Pool
Furzebrook, nr Wareham BH20 5AT
Tel: 01929 551408
www.blue.pool.users.btopenworld.com

Clouds Hill
Wareham, BH20 7NQ
Tel: 01929 405616
www.nationaltrust.org.uk

Corfe Castle
The Square, Corfe Castle BH20 5EZ
Tel: 01929 481294
www.nationaltrust.org.uk

Dorset County Museum
High West Street, Dorchester DT1 1XA
Tel: 01305 262735
www.dorsetcountymuseum.org

Durlston Country Park
Lighthouse Road, Swanage BH19 2JL
Tel: 01929 424443
www.durlston.co.uk

Hardy's Cottage
Higher Bockhampton, nr Dorchester DT2 8QJ
Tel: 01305 262366
www.nationaltrust.org.uk

Kingston Lacy
Wimborne Minster BH21 4EA
Tel: 01202 880413
www.nationaltrust.org.uk

Lulworth Heritage Centre
Main Road, Lulworth BH20 5QS
Tel: 01929 400587
www.lulworth.com

Max Gate
Alington Avenue, Dorchester DT1 2AA
Tel: 01305 262538
www.nationaltrust.org.uk

Old Crown Court and Cells
Stratton House, High West Street
Dorchester DT1 1UZ
Tel: 01305 252241
www.westdorset.com

The Roman Town House
Colliton Park, Dorchester
Tel: 01305 228507
www.visit-dorchester.co.uk

Swanage Railway
Station House, Swanage BH19 1HB
Tel: 01929 425800
www.swanagerailway.co.uk

Tolpuddle Martyrs Museum
Tolpuddle, Dorchester DT2 7EH
Tel: 01305 848 237
www.tolpuddlemartyrs.org.uk

Wimborne Minster
High Street, Wimborne BH21 1HT
Tel: 01202 884753
www.wimborneminster.org.uk

On the trail of King Arthur

Bishops' Palace
Wells BA5 2PD
Tel: 01749 678691
www.bishopspalacewells.co.uk

Cadbury Castle
South Cadbury BA22 7HA

Chalice Well
Chilkwell Street, Glastonbury BA6 8DD
Tel: 01458 831154
www.chalicewell.org.uk

Cheddar Caves and Gorge
Cheddar BS27 3QF
Tel: 01934 742343
www.cheddarcaves.co.uk

Clarks Village
Farm Road, Street BA16 0BB
Tel: 01458 840064
www.clarksvillage.co.uk

Fleet Air Arm Museum
Yeovilton, nr Ilchester BA22 8HT
Tel: 01935 840565
www.fleetairarm.com

Glastonbury Abbey
Magdalene Street, Glastonbury BA6 9EL
Tel: 01458 832267
www.glastonburyabbey.com

Glastonbury Tor
nr Glastonbury
Tel: 01985 843600
www.nationaltrust.org.uk

Montacute House
Montacute TA15 6XP
Tel: 01935 823289
www.nationaltrust.org.uk

Sherborne Abbey
Sherborne DT9 3LQ
Tel: 01935 812452
www.sherborneabbey.com

Sherborne Castle
Cheap Street, Sherborne DT9 3PY
Tel: 01935 813182
www.sherbornecastle.com

Sherborne House
Newland, Sherborne DT9 3JG
Tel: 01935 816426
www.sherbornehouse.org.uk

Sherborne Old Castle
Sherborne
Tel: 01935 812730
www.english-heritage.org.uk

Sherborne Museum
Abbey Gate House, Sherborne DT9 3BP
Tel: 01935 812252
www.westdorset.com

Wells Cathedral
Wells BA5 2UE
Tel: 01749 674433
www.wellscathedral.org.uk

Wookey Hole Caves
Wells BA5 1BB
Tel: 01749 672243
www.wookey.co.uk

In and around Bath: elegant legacy of times past

Alexander Keiller Museum
High Street, Avebury, nr Marlborough SN8 1RF
Tel: 01672 539250
www.nationaltrust.org.uk

Avebury Manor & Garden
nr Marlborough SN8 1RF
Tel: 01672 539250
www.nationaltrust.org.uk

Bath Abbey
Bath BA1 1LT
Tel: 01225 422462
www.bathabbey.org

Bath Assembly Rooms
Bennett Street, Bath BA1 2QH
Tel: 01225 477752
www.nationaltrust.org.uk

Bowood House & Garden
Calne SN11 0LZ
Tel: 01249 812102
www.bowood-house.co.uk

Bradford-on-Avon Museum
19 Bridge Street, Bradford-on-Avon BA15 1BY
Tel: 01225 863280
www.visitwiltshire.co.uk

Corsham Court
Corsham SN13 0BZ
Tel: 01249 701610
www.corsham-court.co.uk

The Courts Garden
Holt, nr Bradford-on-Avon BA14 6RR
Tel: 01225 782875
www.nationaltrust.org.uk

Dyrham Park
Dyrham, nr Chippenham SN14 8ER
Tel: 0117 9372501
www.nationaltrust.org.uk

Farleigh Hungerford Castle,
Farleigh Hungerford BA2 7RS
Tel: 01225 754026
www.english-heritage.org.uk

Holburne Museum of Art
Great Pulteney Street, Bath BA2 4DB
Tel: 01225 466669
www.bath.ac.uk

Jane Austen Centre
40 Gay Street, Queens Square, Bath BA1 2NT
Tel: 01225 443000
www.janeausten.co.uk

Lacock Abbey, Fox Talbot Museum & Village
Lacock, nr Chippenham SN15 2LG
Tel: 01249 730459
www.nationaltrust.org.uk

No 1 Royal Crescent
Bath BA1 2LR
Tel: 01225 428126
www.bath-preservation-trust.org.uk

The Peto Garden at Iford Manor
Bradford-on-Avon
Tel: 01225 863146
www.ifordmanor.co.uk

Pump Room
Stall Street, Bath BA1 1LZ
Tel: 01225 477785
www.bath-preservation-trust.org

Roman Baths
Bath BA1 1LZ
Tel: 01225 477785
www.romanbaths.co.uk

Tithe Barn
Barton Farm, Pound Lane,
Bradford-on-Avon BA15 1LF
Tel: 01225 865797
www.visitwiltshire.co.uk

Wiltshire Heritage Museum
41 Long Street, Devizes SN10 1NS
Tel: 01380 727369
www.wiltshireheritage.org.uk

Around Salisbury Plain: megaliths and mansions

Heale Gardens
Middle Woodford, Salisbury SP4 6NT
Tel: 01722 782504
www.visitwiltshire.co.uk

Longleat
Warminster BA12 7NW
Tel: 01985 844400
www.longleat.co.uk

The Medieval Hall
Sarum St Michael, West Walk
Cathedral Close, Salisbury SP1 2EY
Tel: 01722 412472
www.medieval-hall.co.uk

Mompesson House
The Close, Salisbury SP1 2EL
Tel: 01722 420980
www.nationaltrust.org.uk

Old Sarum
Castle Road, Salisbury SP1 3SD
Tel: 01722 335398
www.english-heritage.org.uk

Old Wardour Castle
nr Tisbury SP3 6RR
Tel: 01747 870487
www.english-heritage.org.uk

Salisbury Cathedral
Salisbury SP1 2EF
Tel: 01722 555 121
www.salisburycathedral.org.uk

Shaftesbury Abbey Museum & Garden
Park Walk, Shaftesbury SP7 8JR
Tel: 01747 852910
www.shaftesburyabbey.co.uk

Shaftesbury Town Museum
1 Gold Hill, Shaftesbury SP7 8JW
Tel: 01747 852157
www.shaftesburydorset.com

Stonehenge
nr Amesbury
Tel: 0870 333 118
www.english-heritage.org.uk

Stourhead
Stourton, Warminster BA12 6QD
Tel: 01747 841152
www.nationaltrust.org.uk

Wilton House
Wilton, Salisbury SP2 0BJ
Tel: 01722 746714
www.wiltonhouse.co.uk

'The Island' and its idyllic pleasures

Calbourne Water Mill and Museum
Newport Road, Calbourne PO30 4JN
Tel: 01983 531227
www.calbournewatermill.co.uk

Carisbrooke Castle Museum
Newport PO30 1XY
Tel: 01983 523112
www.carisbrookecastlemuseum.org.uk

Dinosaur Farm Museum
Military Road, Brighstone PO30 4PG
Tel: 01983 740844
www.dinosaur-farm.co.uk

Place Mill
The Quay, Christchurch BH23 1BY
Tel: 01202 487626
www.bournemouth.uk.com

The Model Village,
Godshill, Isle of Wight PO38 3HH
Tel: 01983 840270
www.iowight.com

Mottistone Manor Garden
Hoxall Lane, Mottistone PO30 4ED
Tel: 1983 741302
www.nationaltrust.org.uk

The Needles Old Battery
West Highdown, Totland PO39 0JH
Tel: 01983 754772
www.nationaltrust.org.uk

Osborne House
East Cowes PO32 6JY
Tel: 01983 200022
www.english-heritage.org.uk

Yarmouth Castle
Yarmouth
Tel: 01983 760678
www.english-heritage.org.uk

The New Forest's atmospheric woods and heathland

Beaulieu Abbey, Palace House and National Motor Museum
Brockenhurst SO42 7ZN
Tel: 01590 612345
www.beaulieu.co.uk

Buckler's Hard Story
The Maritime Museu, Buckler's Hard, Beaulieu
Brockenhurst SO42 7XB
Tel: 01590 616203
www.bucklershard.co.uk

Exbury Gardens
Exbury, Southampton SO45 1AZ
Tel: 02380 899422
www.exbury.co.uk

Furzey Gardens
Minstead SO43 7GL
Tel: 02380 812464
www.hants.gov.uk

Hurst Castle
Milford-on-Sea
Tel: 01590 642500
www.hurst-castle.co.uk

Oceanarium
Pier Approach, West Beach,
Bournemouth BH2 5AA
Tel: 01202 311 993
www.oceanarium.co.uk

Red House Museum
Quay Road, Christchurch BH23 1BU
Tel: 01202 482860
www.hants.gov.uk

The Russell-Cotes Art Gallery and Museum
East Cliff, Bournemouth BH1 3AA
Tel: 01202 451858
www.russell-cotes.bournemouth.gov.uk

St Barbe Museum and Art Gallery
New Street, Lymington SO41 9BH
Tel: 01590 676969
www.stbarbe-museum.org.uk

Around England's ancient capital

Bishop's Waltham Palace
Bishop's Waltham, Southampton
Tel: 01489 892460
www.hants.gov.uk

Broadlands
Romsey SO51 9ZD
Tel: 01794 505010
www.broadlands.net

King John's House & Heritage Centre,
Church Street, Romsey SO51 8BT
Tel: 01794 512200
www.kingjohnshouse.org.uk

Mottisfont Abbey Garden, House & Estate
Mottisfont, nr Romsey, SO51 0LP
Tel: 01794 341220
www.nationaltrust.org.uk

The Museum of Army Flying
Middle Wallop, Stockbridge SO20 8DY
Tel: 01264 784421
www.flying-museum.org.uk

Gilbert White's House
Selborne, Alton GU34 3JH
Tel: 01420 511275
www.hants.gov.uk

The Great Hall
The Castle, Winchester
Tel: 01962 846476
www.hants.gov.uk

Jane Austen's House
Chawton, Alton GU34 1SD
Tel: 01420 83262
www.jane-austens-house-museum.org.uk

Queen Elizabeth Country Park
Gravel Hill, Horndean
Tel: 023 9259 5040
www.hants.gov.uk

Romsey Abbey
Romsey
Tel: 01794 513125
www.romseyabbey.org.uk

Romsey Tourist Information and Heritage Centre
13 Church Street, Romsey SO51 8DF
Tel: 01794 512987
www.romseynet.org.uk

St Cross Hospital
St Cross Road, Winchester SO23 9SD
Tel: 01962 878218
www.hants.gov.uk

The Watercress Line
The Railway Station, Alresford SO24 9JG
Tel: 01962 733810
www.watercressline.co.uk

Winchester Cathedral
Winchester SO23 9LS
Tel: 01962 857200
www.winchester-cathedral.org.uk

Wolvesey Castle (Old Bishop's Palace)
Winchester
Tel. 01424 775705
www.english-heritage.org.uk

Stately mansions and picture-perfect villages of the Surrey Hills

Box Hill Visitor Centre
The Old Fort, Box Hill Road
Box Hill, Tadworth KT20 7LB
Tel: 01306 888793
www.nationaltrust.org.uk

Brooklands
Brooklands Road, Weybridge KT13 0QN
Tel: 01932 857381
www.brooklandsmuseum.com

Clandon Park
West Clandon, Guildford GU4 7RQ
Tel: 01483 225971
www.nationaltrust.org.uk

Hampton Court Palace
East Molesey KT8 9AU
Tel: 0870 752 7777
www.hrp.org.uk

Hatchlands Park
East Clandon, Guildford GU4 7RT
Tel: 01483 225971
www.nationaltrust.org.uk

Painshill Park
Portsmouth Road, Cobham KT11 1JE
Tel: 01932 868113
www.painshill.co.uk

Polesden Lacey
Great Bookham, nr Dorking RH5 6BD
Tel: 01372 458203
www.nationaltrust.org.uk

Winkworth Arboretum
Hascombe Road, Godalming GU8 4AD
Tel: 01483 208477
www.nationaltrust.org.uk

Wisley
Woking GU23 6QB
Tel: 01483 224234
www.rhs.org.uk

In the footsteps of the Romans

Arundel Castle
Arundel BN18 9AB
Tel: 01903 882173
www.arundelcastle.org

Arundel Cathedral
London Road, Arundel
Tel: 01903 882297
www.arundelcathedral.org

Bignor Roman Villa
Bignor, nr Pulborough RH20 1PH
Tel: 01798 869259
www.allaboutsussex.co.uk

Chichester Cathedral
Chichester PO19 1PX
Tel: 01243 782595
www.chichestercathedral.org.uk

Fishbourne Roman Palace
Salthill Road, Fishbourne PO19 3QS
Tel: 01243 785859
www.sussexpast.co.uk

Goodwood House and Motor Racing Circuit
Goodwood PO18 0PX
Tel: 01243 755040
www.goodwood.co.uk

Pallant House Gallery
9 North Pallant, Chichester PO19 1TJ
Tel: 01243 774557
www.pallant.org.uk

Petworth House and Park
Petworth GU28 0AE
Tel: 01798 343929
www.nationaltrust.org.uk

Portsmouth Historic Dockyard
Portsmouth PO1 3LJ
Tel: 02392 861512
www.flagship.org.uk

Sculpture Park
Goodwood PO18 0QP
Tel: 01243 531853
www.sculpture.org.uk

Spinnaker Tower
Gunwharf Quays, Portsmouth PO1 3TT
Tel: 02392 85 7520
www.spinnakertower.co.uk

Uppark
South Harting, nr Petersfield GU31 5QR
Tel: 01730 825857
www.nationaltrust.org.uk

Weald and Downland Open Air Museum
Singleton, Chichester PO18 0EU
Tel: 01243 811363
www.wealddown.co.uk

Hidden treasures of the South Downs

Alfriston Clergy House
The Tye, Alfriston, Polegate BN26 5TL
Tel: 01323 870001
www.nationaltrust.org.uk

Ann of Cleaves House
52 Southover High Street, Lewes BN7 1JA
Tel: 01273 474610
www.sussexpast.co.uk

Brighton Pavilion
Brighton BN1 1EE
Tel: 01273 292820/2
www.royalpavilion.org.uk

Charleston Farmhouse
Charleston Firle, Lewes BN8 6LL
Tel: 01323 811265
www.charleston.co.uk

The English Wine Centre
Alfriston BN26 5QS
Tel: 01323 870164
www.englishwine.co.uk

Firle Place
Firle, Lewes BN8 6LP
Tel: 01273 858307
www.firleplace.co.uk

Jill Windmill
Clayton, West Sussex
www.jillwindmill.org.uk

Leonardslee Lakes & Gardens
Lower Beeding, Horsham RH13 6PP
Tel: 01403 891212
www.leonardsleegardens.com

Lewes Castle & Barbican House Museum
169 High Street, Lewes BN7 1YE
Tel: 01273 486290
www.sussexpast.co.uk

Michelham Priory & Gardens
Upper Dicker, nr Hailsham BN27 3QS
Tel: 01323 844224
www.sussexpast.co.uk

Monk's House
Rodmell, Lewes BN7 3HF
Tel: 01372 453401
www.nationaltrust.org.uk

Nymans Garden
Handcross, nr Haywards Heath RH17 6EB
Tel: 01444 400321
www.nationaltrust.org.uk

Seven Sisters Country Park
Exceat, Seaford BN25 4AD
Tel: 01323 870280
www.sevensisters.org.uk

Great houses and gardens on top of the Downs

Ashdown Forest Centre
Wych Cross, Forest Row RH18 5JP
Tel: 01342 823583
www.ashdownforest.org

The Bluebell Railway
Sheffield Park Station TN22 3QL
Tel: 01825 720825
www.bluebell-railway.co.uk

Chartwell
Mapleton Road, Westerham TN16 1PS
Tel: 01732 866368
www.nationaltrust.org.uk

Chiddingstone Castle
Near Edenbridge TN8 7AD
Tel: 01892 870347
www.chiddingstone-castle.org.uk

Emmetts Garden
Ide Hill, TN14 6AY
Tel: 01732 868381
www.nationaltrust.org.uk

Great Comp Garden
Platt, nr Borough Green TN15 8QS
Tel: 01732 886154
www.greatcomp.co.uk

Groombridge Place Gardens
Tunbridge Wells TN3 9QG
Tel: 01892 861444
www.groombridge.co.uk

Hever Castle
Hever, nr Edenbridge TN8 7NG
Tel: 01732 865224
www.hever-castle.co.uk

Hop Farm Country Park
Paddock Wood TN12 6PY
Tel: 01622 872068
www.thehopfarm.co.uk

Ightham Mote
Ivy Hatch, Sevenoaks TN15 0NT
Tel: 01732 811145
www.nationaltrust.org.uk

Knole
Sevenoaks TN15 0RP
Tel: 01732 450608
www.nationaltrust.org.uk

Old Soar Manor
Plaxtol, Borough Green N15 0QX
Tel: 01732 811145
www.nationaltrust.org.uk

Penshurst Place & Gardens
Penshurst TN11 8DG
Tel: 01892 870307
www.penshurstplace.com

The Priest House
North Lane, West Hoathly RH19 4PP
Tel: 01342 810479
www.allaboutsussex.co.uk

Quebec House
Quebec Square, Westerham TN16 1TD
Tel: 01732 868381
www.nationaltrust.org.uk

Sheffield Park Garden
Sheffield Park TN22 3QX
Tel: 01825 790231
www.nationaltrust.org.uk

Squerryes Court & Gardens
Westerham TN16 1SJ
Tel: 01959 562345
www.squerryes.co.uk

Tonbridge Castle
Castle Street, Tonbridge TN9 1BG
Tel: 01732 770929
www.tonbridgecastle.org

Wakehurst Place
Ardingly, nr Haywards Heath RH17 6TN
Tel: 01444 894066
www.nationaltrust.org.uk

Around Rye and the smuggler's coast

Bateman's
Burwash, Etchingham TN19 7DS
Tel: 01435 882302
www.nationaltrust.org.uk

Battle Abbey and Battlefield
Battle TN33 0AD
Tel: 01424 773792
www.english-heritage.org.uk

Bodiam Castle
Bodiam, nr Robertsbridge TN32 5UA
Tel: 01580 830436
www.nationaltrust.org.uk

Great Dixter
Northiam, Rye TN31 6PH
Tel: 01797 252878
www.greatdixter.co.uk

Kent and East Sussex Railway
Tenterden Town Station, Tenterden TN30 6HE
Tel: 01580 762943
www.kesr.org.uk

Lamb House
West Street, Rye TN31 7ES
Tel: 01372 453401
www.nationaltrust.org.uk

Owl House Gardens
Lamberhurst, Tunbridge Wells TN3 8LY
Tel: 01435 865904
www.owlhouse.com

Romney, Hythe & Dymchurch Railway
New Romney Station, New Romney TN28 8P
Tel: 01797 362353
www.rhdr.org.uk

Scotney Castle Garden & Estate
Lamberhurst, Tunbridge Wells TN3 8JN
Tel: 01892 893820
www.nationaltrust.org.uk

Sissinghurst Castle Garden
Sissinghurst, nr Cranbrook TN17 2AB
Tel: 01580 710701
www.nationaltrust.org.uk

Smallhythe Place
Smallhythe, Tenterden TN30 7NG
Tel: 01580 762334
www.nationaltrust.org.uk

Kent: Christian and literary inspiration

Brogdale Horticultural Trust
Brogdale Road, Faversham ME13 8XZ
Tel: 01795 535286
www.brogdale.org

Canterbury Cathedral
Canterbury CT1 2EH
Tel: 01227 762 862
www.canterbury-cathedral.org

Deal Castle
Victoria Road, Deal
Tel: 01304 372762
www.english-heritage.org.uk

Dickens House Museum
2 Victoria Parade, Broadstairs CT10 1QS
Tel: 01843 861232
www.dickenshouse.co.uk

Dover Castle
Kent CT16 1HU
Tel: 01304 211067
www.english-heritage.org.uk

Fleur de Lis Heritage Centre
13 Preston Street, Faversham ME13 8NS
Tel: 01795 534542
www.kenttourism.co.uk

The Friars
Aylesford Priory, Aylesford ME20 7BX
Tel: 01622 717272
www.thefriars.org.uk

Goodnestone Park Gardens
nr Wingham
Tel: 01304 840107
www.goodnestoneparkgardens.co.uk

Guildhall Museum
High Street, Rochester ME1 1PY
Tel: 01634 848717
www.medway.gov.uk

Guildhall Museum
Cattle Market, Sandwich CT13 9AH
Tel: 01304 617197
www.sandwichtowncouncil.co.uk

The Historic Dockyard Chatham
Chatham ME4 4TZ
Tel: 01634 823800
www.chdt.org.uk

Leeds Castle
Leeds, Maidstone ME17 1PL
Tel: 01622 765400
www.leeds-castle.com

Maritime and Local History Museum
22 St Georges Road, Deal CT14 6BA
Tel: 01304 381344
www.kenttourism.co.uk

Ramsgate Maritime Museum,
Clock House, Pier Yard, Royal Harbour, Ramsgate CT11 8LS
Tel: 01843 587765
www.ekmt.fsnet.co.uk

Rochester Castle
Rochester
Tel: 01634 402276
www.english-heritage.org.uk

Rochester Cathedral
Rochester ME1 1SX
Tel: 01634 401301
www.rochestercathedral.org

Walmer Castle
Deal CT14 7LJ
Tel: 01304 364288
www.english-heritage.org.uk

Index

Credits

t = top; tl= top left; top centre = tc; top right = tr; centre = c; bottom = b; bottom left = bl; bottom centre = bc; bottom right = br

VisitBritain would like to thank the following for their assistance with photographic material for this publication: Skyscan/Corbis jacket

Beaulieu Motor Museum 91tr; permission British Library c4190-04 96c; Jane Collinson 132t; Devon Tourism 26b, 27b, 38t, 38b, 40b, 41; Copyright of the Julia Margaret Cameron Trust, Dimbola Lodge Museum 86b; Fleet Air Museum 67c; Isle of Wight Tourism 84br, 85bl, 87c; Hampshire County Council 96b, 97t; New Forest District Council 91tr; Queen Elizabeth Country Park 97b; Somerset Tourism 48–9c, 50b, 55t; Tourism South East 125b; Winkworth Arboretum 101bl

All remaining photographs have been sourced from VisitBritain's online picture library (www.britainonview.com) with credits to:
Jean Brooks 110t; Roger Covey 10–11; Helen Harrison 42b, 127t; Nigel Hicks 44–5, 35, 37t, 51t; Gail Kellshall 90t; Ady Kerry 126b; Doug McKinley 6–7; John Miller 82–83; Howard Morrow 136t; David Sellmann 69t; Howard Taylor 104–5, 109t; Roger Westlake 33t; Robert Westwood 43t, 76bl

Design: Clare Thorpe, Janis Utton
Index: Hilary Bird
Picture research: Rebecca Shoben
Proof reader: Gary Werner